Professional Charcuterie

Sausage Making, Curing, Terrines, and Pâtés

Chef John Kinsella, C.M.C., A.A.C.

A.C.F.E.I. Certified, American Culinary Federation
American Academy of Chefs
Cincinnati State Technical & Community College
Cincinnati, Ohio

Chef David T. Harvey, C.C.

A.C.F.E.I. Certified
American Culinary Federation

WILEY

John Wiley & Sons, Inc.

Publisher: Margaret K. Burns
Senior editor: Claire Thompson
Production coordinator: Ira Brodsky
Developmental editor: Carol Brown
Illustrations: Stephen James Miller
Text design: Figaro, Inc.
Text composition: The Composing Room of Michigan, Inc.
Printed and bound by Hamilton Printing

This text is printed on acid-free paper.

This publication is designed to provide accurate and
authoritative information in regard to the subject
matter covered. It is sold with the understanding that
the publisher is not engaged in rendering legal, accounting,
or other professional services. If legal advice or other
expert assistance is required, the services of a competent
professional person should be sought.

Library of Congress Cataloging-in-Publication Data:

Kinesella, John.
     Professional charcuterie : sausage making, curing, terrines, and
  pâtés / John Kinsella, David T. Harvey.
      p. cm.
    ISBN-13 978-0-471-12237-1 (alk. paper)
    ISBN-10 0-471-12237-8 (alk. paper)
    1. Cookery (Pork). 2. Cookery (Meat). 3. Cookery (Fish).
  I. Harvey, David T. II. Title.
  TX749.5.P67K56   1996
  641.6—dc20   95-43662

Printed in the United States of America

19 18 17 16

With heartfelt thanks, we dedicate Professional Charcuterie *to the Chef Technology students at Cincinnati State Technical & Community College. Only through such educational programs can we expand the splendid arts of classic charcuterie and fine sausage making. We earnestly hope that charcutiers continue to hand down their knowledge and experience. The students of today are the promise and the future of our profession.*

Contents

Preface

Recognizing that there were few textbooks devoted to charcuterie, we set out to create one that would be genuinely useful. We wanted to address the professional chef, student, and the dedicated amateur—anyone, in fact, who wants to explore the art and practice of fine charcuterie.

The Chef Technology Program at Cincinnati Technical College offered us the ideal environment for such an endeavor. The students in Chef Kinsella's kitchen classroom used our recipes many, many times. As we worked, listened, tested, and tasted, we were able to modify and improve the recipes. The generous evaluations of both faculty and students enhanced our writing experience, and we learned a great deal while producing this book. After working with these wonderful advantages, we proudly present this set of well-honed recipes. We hope to relate not just the knowledge we gained, but also the pleasure and satisfaction we felt. Making such high-quality charcuterie was certainly rewarding, and it was also very enjoyable.

During the five years we worked on this book, we spent many hours researching textbooks, industry reports, and historical information. We also interviewed master sausage makers and fellow chefs; without them our project would not have been possible, and we thank them for their guidance. We especially thank Mr. Rytec Kutas, whose book, *Great Sausage Recipes and Meat Curing,* piqued our interest and inspired us.

We thank Dean Dan Cayse at Cincinnati Technical College for his encouragement and support.

We are very grateful to our wives and children for their generosity and patience.

Here's to Your Health— and That of Your Appreciative Customers as Well!

Our book would be incomplete should we not be ready with a reasonable response to frequent queries regarding *nutritional aspects* of our fine products. Students, along with all others who will effectively utilize this text and its recipes, need to recognize some specific and remarkable facts regarding the true composition of their sausages. They will then be fully able to provide sound and convincing answers as well.

Many of the best classical and contemporary sausage recipes do indeed call for large quantities of meats, fish, fowl, or game. Some specify "fatty meat," or "not too lean." One very common ingredient is *fatback*. Cholesterol and salt (sodium) are not strangers to traditional and contemporary recipes. Do we, or should we, cringe at these recipe calls? Perhaps we might routinely modify them with a heavy hand—all in a sincere effort to satisfy our quest for ever leaner cuisine. The very question will raise many eyebrows—and ring in the ears of any person who is motivated and concerned with their own and their family's health. This concern demands our best, most truthful response. We will supply the means for your response to the many—for they will ask! We offer for your use both our successful technique and our philosophy. It is based on considerable gratifying personal experiences, along with accurate facts.

As you work with this text, you will soon come to realize and appreciate several important reasons for the significant quantities of fats, along with several other "restricted ingredients," in many excellent charcuterie products. By working with and presenting your own charcuterie products, you will also acquire considerable skill and knowledge in proper presentation and cooking of the products. You will then be able to make specific, well-informed recommendations to anyone. You will easily give strong support to a personal passion for the making, eating, and promoting of charcuterie products!

Two approaches are reasonable for applying expertise and providing accurate information regarding the ingredients that may be in question. First, consider the complete processing of any sausage product, and the method of cooking prior to consumption. *It is at this point—after the product is cooked—that accurate analysis of available fats, cholesterol content, and sodium is possible.* But wait just a minute! We are sausage makers and we are chefs! We do defer accurate and meaningful analysis to the capabilities of today's lab technicians and registered dietitians. They are the ones to perform this analysis and chart the information for our benefit. We may not ignore this fact. A large portion of fat in the recipe ingredients is not found in the finished product. It is routinely cooked out in normal processing. So, why are fats there in the first place? The major role of the fats is to secure necessary flavor distribution, full intensity, and desirable texture. Fats are quite essential for excellence of the product. Salt as a seasoning is adjustable, but with due care. Salt invites careful reduction from levels once prevalent in many older recipes. Herbs and spices today are used for fine flavor. They can replace excessive salt in many recipes. These considerations address the *mechanics of sausage* regarding certain ingredients, ones that we may want to monitor more carefully.

Let's consider the second approach. *Here, the good chef, and you, as the person who actually made the product, can really be effective.* Keep firmly in mind the role of fats and reliable information sources such as the recently revised USDA Food Pyramid. Use it for your guide in daily food selection. Combine reasonable balance and this knowledge of the role and the true amount of fats in our products to firmly enforce your position. Be well versed, always ready to explain, or recommend appealing, healthful ways to prepare and serve all your products. This includes ways to remove excess fats in preparation. Practice variation in menu combinations for taste and sight appeal with nutritive balance. This fits very well with the sound philosophy, "All things in moderation."

More than ever before, abundant, highly beneficial dietary information is readily available to all. Today's research, with excellent distribution through so many media sources, continues to provide much soundly based dietary advice. With this in mind, we recommend using these two interconnected and simple approaches to answering queries. Join us please, in a well-informed, rational consumption of all the unique and delicious charcuterie products. There is *nothing* quite like them.

À votre santé!

Introduction

The modern world of professional charcuterie rests on generations of tradition and knowledge. It offers a vast range of culinary invention, from the everyday fare of hearty sausages to the great delicacies of haute cuisine. The word itself is French, derived from *chair* and *cuit*—"cooked meat." For a long time, *charcuterie* referred only to pork preparations, but today we use it to describe products that are made with all kinds of meat, fish, and game.

The origins of the art of charcuterie lie in remote antiquity. History shows us that people have been salting, curing, and smoking food for many centuries. The pig was the animal most favored by the Greeks for religious sacrifices to their gods. References to sausages are made in Homer's *Odyssey* and later Greek literature. The Romans shared this fondness for pork cookery, and they developed and refined it. Our word sausage comes from the Latin *salsus*—"salted." We know of one ancient Roman sausage made with chopped pork, pine nuts, cumin seed, bay leaf, and black pepper. The Italians continued this development, and today they are renowned for the quality of their hams, sausages, and bacon.

The history of charcuterie followed a parallel course in other countries. We know that the Irish were curing salmon and hams around the seventh century, probably earlier. St. Kevin, who died around A.D. 618, described the salting and smoking of fish. Even though modern curing methods are different, we still make and enjoy these same foods.

Sausagemaking is one of the most ancient and fundamental elements of charcuterie. It blossomed as a real art during the Middle Ages when sausages began to take their names from their places of origin. Today we still know and savor frankfurters (Frankfurt am Main, Germany); bologna (Bologna, Italy); berliners (Berlin, Germany); goteborgs (Göteborg, Sweden); and many others.

In medieval France, royal decrees divided various activities among rival guilds. For a long time, the charcutiers were allowed to make and sell only cooked pork products. The right to slaughter and dress the hogs was jealously guarded by *les bouchers*, the butchers. As the rigid guild system broke down, the charcutiers were freer to develop and practice their craft.

Unhappily, the history of sausage making offers some examples of abuse. During our research, we found sausages referred to as "little bags of mystery." The process of making sausages—chopping, mixing, seasoning, stuffing—offered many opportunities for adulteration with inferior and undesirable ingredients. Over the centuries, it seems that people had reason to be suspicious of some sausages. Fortunately, today's consumer is protected by well-written standards and meaningful labeling laws. The "mystery" has been removed, and we can enjoy sausages with confidence in their wholesomeness.

Through the ages, countless artisans have contributed to charcuterie as we know it today. By improving the methods of salting and preserving food, they have fed the hungry. By learning and passing on the skills of earlier generations, they have been faithful to a long and proud tradition. By employing their artistic imaginations, they have created dishes that delight our senses and enrich our lives. This blend of skill, tradition, and imagination has earned charcuterie its revered place in the world of gastronomy.

PART ONE

Basic Information

CHAPTER

1

Equipment

Proper equipment is fundamental to the success of any charcuterie kitchen; it must be chosen carefully to perform the required tasks. Always keep in mind durability, serviceability, efficiency, and affordability.

As you assess the design of equipment, you must consider two other critical factors—sanitation and safety. To ensure proper sanitation, the equipment design must permit easy cleaning; commercial equipment that meets high professional standards will carry the seal of the National Sanitation Federation (NSF). Well-designed equipment will be easy to maintain and safer to use.

SAFETY RECOMMENDATIONS

Safeguards are important for the protection of all kitchen staff. Take a minute to read these safety recommendations and bear them in mind as you work.

- Understand how to assemble and operate all equipment correctly. Take care not to overload or obstruct the machinery.

- Regularly lubricate the moving parts of your machine according to the manufacturer's instructions.

- Always turn off the power before assembling, cleaning, or servicing equipment.

- Use the pusher tool, never your hands, to feed food into a grinder.

- Permit only fully trained personnel to operate cutters, grinders, saws, and similar equipment. Pay special attention to guards, interlocks, and other safety devices. "HANDS CLEAR" whenever the power is on.

• Be alert to any potentially unsafe conditions. The best way to deal with accidents is to prevent them.

TOOLS AND OTHER EQUIPMENT

Below we describe some of the most important equipment in a charcuterie kitchen.

Brine Pump: Also called a spray pump, this device comes in many sizes. An 8-fluid-ounce injector should be sufficient for most jobs. If you produce more than 50 pounds of ham per day, you will need something larger, such as a 1-quart multiple-prong injector.

Brine Tubs: These large plastic tubs come in various sizes. To eliminate any possibility of cross contamination or chemical food poisoning, use them only for brining and salting.

Buffalo Chopper: This versatile meat chopper, universally known as a buffalo chopper, has a rotating dish which carries the food under very efficient knives. It is an excellent bulk chopper and mixer which is widely used because of its relatively modest cost.

It has two particular safety features: (1) you cannot overload this chopper because it will throw off any excess, and (2) the motor cannot be started until all blades and other parts are in place. Although it is one of the most frequently used pieces of equipment, it can also be one of the most dangerous. Always understand safety instructions for this kind of equipment. It should be operated only by fully trained personnel.

Cutting Boards: Wooden cutting boards were banned long ago; commercial kitchens must use boards made of nonporous material. Those that bear the NSF seal are recommended. Buy at least two sizes, and buy enough so that nobody has to wait for a board.

Wash and sanitize boards after each use. To prevent them from souring, stack them on racks so that air will circulate easily around them. Never put cooked food on a board where you have prepared raw food; avoid cross contamination by washing and sanitizing the board between uses.

Grinder: Grinders vary in capacity from 1 pound to 300 pounds. Sausage manufacturers commonly use the very large machines. The most popular grinder is an easily assembled attachment for the mixer or chopping machine. As with other equipment, choose a grinder that is easy to set up and to clean. Pay particular attention when using a grinder. Next to knives, grinders are the leading cause of finger injuries. Never stuff the feed tube with your hand; always use the pusher tool provided with the machine.

Grinding Plates and Knives: These are the most important parts of a grinding machine. Always choose the plate called for in the recipe because it will determine the texture of the finished product. Because plates and knives are easy to misplace and are prone to rust, they require some extra care. Clean and dry them well, then coat with food-grade oil; store them in a separate locked compartment. It is practical to have a few spare plates, knives, and springs on hand. To prevent dry seizing, always apply a light

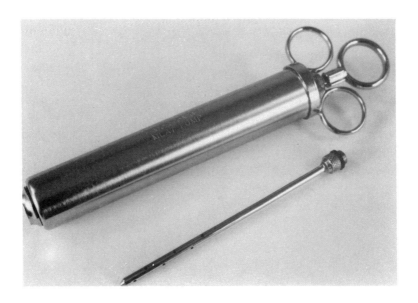

A hand-held brine pump. (Photo courtesy of The Sausage Maker, Buffalo, NY)

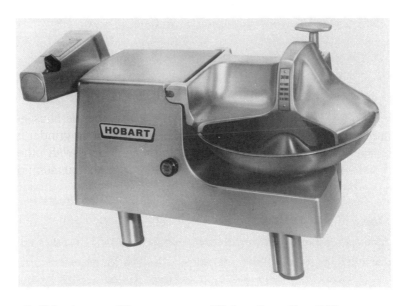

Buffalo chopper. (Photo courtesy of Hobart Corp., Troy, OH)

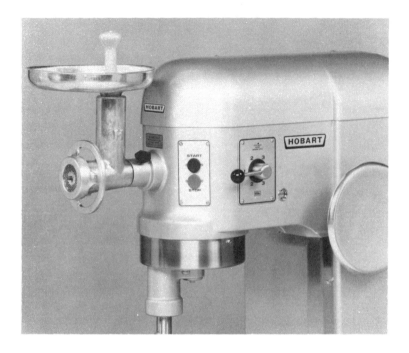

Grinder mixer attachment. (Photo courtesy of Hobart Corp., Troy, OH)

coat of vegetable oil to the working surfaces of the plate and knife before turning on the grinder. Be sure to unplug the grinder before changing knives and plates. Grinder plates can be ordered in the following standard U.S. and metric sizes:

U.S. Size Inches (in.)	Metric Size (cm)
³⁄₁₆	0.47
¼	0.63
⅜	0.95
½	1.27
¾ in.	1.90 cm

Number 10: 2¾ in. diameter, ⅜ in. center hole. Knife has ⁷⁄₁₆ in. square hole.

Number 22: 3¼ in. diameter, ⁷⁄₁₆ in. center hole. Knife has ½ in. square hole.

Number 32: 3¹⁵⁄₁₆ in. diameter, ⁹⁄₁₆ in. center hole. Knife has ⁹⁄₁₆ in. square hole.

Hanging Sticks: These stainless metal sticks are used for smoking and drying. Most commercial smokers come with these accessories. An extra set is desirable for maximum efficiency; one set can be used for drying in the cooler while the other set is being used in the smoker.

Food processor. (Photo courtesy of Hobart Corp., Troy, OH)

Stainless steel bacon hangers are available, as well as special hangers for extra heavy or irregularly shaped items. Natural or synthetic mesh bags are useful for hanging fish. Hanging devices can also be fashioned from racks and custom-made grids. Always choose an inert material such as stainless steel. Consider the weight the device must carry, and allow for adequate circulation of heat and smoke.

Hobart Food Processor: This is the most versatile of the cutting machines, and it can be used for many recipes. It has several blades that cut, blend, and mix. Its low cost and portability make it very desirable for the small kitchen.

Hog Rings and Casing Clips: Two kinds of closures are available for crimp-sealing the ends of large sausages. Hog rings are used on the fill end of a casing at the stuffer. A casing clip is applied to one end of a casing as it is being prepared for stuffing. Hand

Heavy duty butcher shop grinder. (Photo courtesy of Hobart Corp., Troy, OH)

tools are necessary to apply these closures. These rings, which are versatile and attractive, come in packages of one hundred and are sized for various casings. Use either of these for a professional finish on your products.

Hydrometer and Hydrometer Jar (Salimeter): This delicate glass instrument measures either the percentage of salt (or other component) in a solution or the specific gravity of a solution. You should have a hydrometer and jar if you do much work with brines; it will give you consistent results every time. This precision instrument will break easily, so store it carefully.

Knives: Invest in good knives and care for them. They will serve you well throughout your career. Learn how to sharpen and store them properly. Remember, a dull knife is more likely to cause injury than a sharp one.

Meat Lugs: Even in a small operation, separate meat lugs should be used for mixing and storing various meats and fish; do not store anything else in these tubs. This will lessen the threat of cross contamination. The lugs can be marked or identified by color to distinguish them from other equipment.

Mixer: An electric mixer is very practical; the 5-quart model is ideal for a small operation. To prevent damaging the meat, always use #1 speed when mixing forcemeat; we recommend using a dough hook instead of the paddle. Mixing by hand is fine, but use disposable gloves to be hygienic. Meat grinder and stuffing horn attachments can be purchased for the 5-quart mixer.

Refrigeration: The decisions you make about refrigeration may be the most important of all. We often take for granted the silent service of refrigerators, but it would be impossible to make sausages today without adequate refrigeration to preserve quality and prevent spoilage.

Vertical cutting machine. (VCM) (Photo courtesy of Hobart Corp., Troy, OH)

Estimate your refrigerator and freezer needs carefully; anticipate your production and the volume of storage you will need. Be generous; we recommend adding 50 percent to your estimate to allow for future growth. A separate shelf for each product is practical and desirable. Don't forget to consider service and maintenance costs.

Most health departments now require that sausages be dried under refrigeration; this controlled and uniform environment reduces the threat of bacterial contamination and achieves good results. It is best to have a separate refrigerator for drying sausages; this will prevent cross contamination and the exchange of flavors and aromas.

Sausage Stuffer: The capacity of sausage stuffers ranges from 5 pounds to 300 pounds. The large commercial units use electro-hydraulic power. A 100-pound water-powered stuffer is ideal for a small commercial sausage producer.

10-pound sausage stuffer. (Photo courtesy of The Sausage Maker, Buffalo, NY)

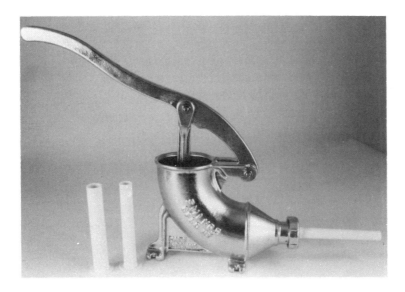

A small family sausage stuffer. (Photo courtesy of The Sausage Maker, Buffalo, NY)

The smaller sizes, often manually powered, are the most commonly used. Because most sausage today is made in small batches, the 10-pound stuffer is most suitable for the small operation.

Scales: Weighing ingredients accurately is essential, not only for safety but also for profitability. Ease of use, accuracy, cleanability, and durability are things to consider when selecting a scale.

Skin Buckets: These are used to store and transport sausage casings. Sort the casings by size and type, and keep them ready for use in clearly labeled, covered buckets. Do not use these buckets for any other purpose.

Smokehouse: Occasionally someone suggests saving money by converting an old refrigerator into a smoker. This may sound like a good idea, but we find it unrealistic. Health departments consistently frown on these "do-it-yourself" smokehouses; they are an invitation to inferior and even unsafe products and can be hazardous to children.

Monitoring smoking temperatures is easiest with modern electronically controlled smokehouses. The comprehensive convection models are exceptionally well designed, and they consistently produce a perfect finish. Buy a smoker from a trustworthy vendor. Inquire about starter kits; they are practical and economical. Professional smokers range from $120 to $21,000.

Spray Head and Hose: Some sausages require a cool shower of water as they come out of the smoker; others need a warm-water shower during processing. A hose that reaches a convenient water faucet is recommended. For maximum control, have an on–off switch on the spray head.

Stainless Steel Ware: High-quality stainless steel items are universally available for the commercial kitchen. They are ideal in the charcuterie kitchen where salt and other ingredients can react adversely with some metals, especially aluminum. Any equipment used in sausage production—meat lugs, brine pans, bowls, spoons, forks—should be made of an inert material such as stainless steel, glass, or NSF-certified plastics.

Stuffing Table: The stuffing table provides work space where the stuffed casings can be gathered and linked. It should be made of nonporous, easily cleaned materials. It should have drilled or slotted holes where the stuffer can be mounted. The stuffer is often cranked by hand, and a smooth turn will prevent air bubbles from getting into the sausage. The table must be heavy enough to remain firmly in place during the stuffing process.

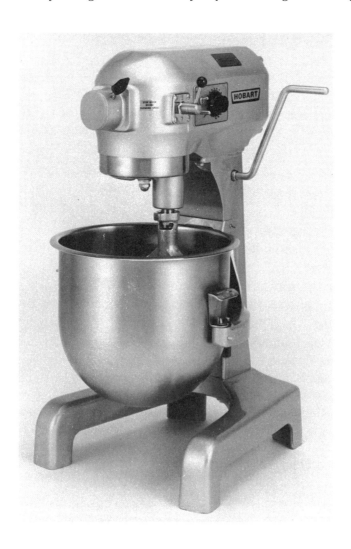

40-quart mixer. (Photo courtesy of Hobart Corp., Troy, OH)

Thermometers: Thermometers are essential for monitoring the temperatures of coolers, freezers, ovens, and smokers; most commercial units feature an external thermometer for easy checking. In addition, you should always have a certified quick-read thermometer at hand to read the internal temperatures of food products. Insert the probe deeply into the approximate center of the item. To ensure accuracy, avoid readings close to bone or in fatty areas. It is good practice to take more than one reading on large cuts. With large batches of smoking sausages, check the temperature of sausages in several zones of the smoker. This will not only confirm the proper temperature of the sausages, it will also monitor the smoker's efficiency and your method of loading the sausages into the smoker.

You must keep your quick-read thermometer reliable with periodic recalibration. Check the accuracy of the high readings by holding the thermometer in boiling water. Do the same for the low temperature readings in a glass of crushed ice and water. Adjust with a slight turn of the nut at the top of the probe. Have your maintenance service check the calibration of your refrigerator and freezer thermometers on a regular basis.

Vertical Cutting Machine (VCM): We consider this the "big brother" to the buffalo chopper and the blender. It will purée and blend; it can be used to make pâtés, terrines, sausages, doughs, and sauces. The models with variable speeds are especially efficient. This machine can save you time and labor.

CHAPTER

2

Sanitation

In the eighth century B.C., ancient Greeks worshiped their goddess of health, Hygea, from which the word "hygiene" was derived. Then as now, people valued good health. The rules of hygiene tell us to keep food clean and safe. This sounds simple enough, but the history of foodborne illness through the ages shows us that it is not so easy after all. Present-day statistics suggest there is still room for improvement.

When we ask what is required for success in a foodservice establishment, large or small, many things come to mind—culinary skill, business acumen, a well-equipped kitchen. But we often fail to consider the importance of sanitation. Imagine how long someone with a reputation for serving unsafe food would stay in business. Because none of us wants our work to cause illness or death, correct sanitation practices are imperative.

This is even more important in the charcuterie kitchen because sausage products are especially susceptible to contamination. Sausages are relatively complicated to make because they require a lot of handling—grinding, mixing, marinating, stuffing, drying, smoking, aging, and more. The synergism of this complex process makes wonderful sausages, but there are many opportunities for health hazards. We must be vigilant to create the most wholesome foods possible.

This starts long before we open the door for business. A foodservice enterprise can legally trade with the public only after all the necessary health permits, licenses, and tax documents have been obtained. It can seem like an endless procession of forms, fees, and inspections, so be sure to allow enough time for this in your business plan. Call your local health department to find out how to start. They will guide you to the necessary state and federal agencies. Seek the advice of others who are already doing business.

Foodborne illness is caused by three groups of agents: microbiological organisms such as bacteria, parasites, and viruses; chemicals that are accidentally introduced into foods; and physical objects. We will concentrate on the causes of illness that are most likely to originate in the sausage kitchen.

MICROBIOLOGICAL HAZARDS

Because the microbiological agents are by far the leading causes of food poisoning, they pose the greatest problems for the foodservice worker. We should know how they grow and how to control the harm they do.

Bacteria

Of all the microorganisms, bacteria play the largest role in food poisoning. They exist almost everywhere in our environment. Because they are truly microscopic (2,500 can easily fit across the head of a pin), they can be found in the millions on unwashed hands and dirty utensils. Although they cannot get around on their own very well, they can easily hitch a ride; for example, they travel very efficiently on moisture from a sneeze or a cough.

To survive and multiply, bacteria require food, moisture, time, and a favorable temperature. The temperature range that is most hospitable for bacterial growth is 40–145°F (4–63°C); this is called the *danger zone*. We must bring food out of this range as quickly as possible at every step of preparation. Bacteria are very adaptable and can thrive even at extreme temperatures. Some can change into spores when threatened by unfavorable conditions; these tough spores resist even boiling temperatures and revive to grow again when conditions improve.

SALMONELLA

Salmonella bacteria cause the infection salmonellosis. They live in the intestinal tracts of humans and animals. They pass in the excreta of an infected host and are then spread by untreated water, unwashed hands, flies, or other vermin. Once inside the intestines of a new host, they multiply rapidly. Within 6–48 hours, salmonellosis will produce such symptoms as abdominal pain, headache, nausea, vomiting, fever, and diarrhea. The illness will last for two or three days, but death can occur in severe cases. A carrier of *Salmonella* may have no symptoms and thus spread bacteria unknowingly.

The foods most likely to be infected are poultry, eggs, and meats of all kinds. Thoroughly cooking these foods to at least 165°F (74°C) will destroy the *Salmonella* bacteria.

STAPHYLOCOCCUS AUREUS

Whereas *Salmonella* causes infection, *Staphylococcus aureus* poisons through intoxication. This means that the bacteria produce toxins, and the toxins, in turn, produce the symptoms of illness. The symptoms of a "Staph" intoxication will appear several hours after eating and may include nausea, vomiting, diarrhea, and abdominal cramps. These bacteria are often found on sores and around the nose and throat. They travel from these areas on hands. Most frequently contaminated with *Staphylococcus* are moist, high-protein foods such as meats (ham in particular), cheese, stews, gravies, potato salads, custards, and pastry fillings. There is no way to know if a food is contaminated with *Staphylococcus;* taste, aroma, and appearance all seem normal. Temperature plays a very important part in the development of a "Staph" culture. Cooked foods that are not cooled rapidly enough or that are allowed to stand at room temperature, even for short periods, are susceptible to infection.

CLOSTRIDIUM PERFRINGENS

The symptoms of *Clostridium perfringens* poisoning show characteristics of both infection and intoxication. Symptoms appear 8–12 hours after a meal and are generally milder than those of a *Staphylococcus* episode; sufferers usually recover within 24 hours. Like *Salmonella,* these bacteria are present in the intestines of humans and animals. They form spores which survive well in the soil, so vegetables can carry the organisms. Many raw foods, meats, and poultry (frequently turkey) are common sources. Because this pathogen naturally occurs on so many kinds of food, complete exclusion from the kitchen is all but impossible. Although the spores of this bacterium can withstand both freezing and boiling, we can accomplish much with good temperature management.

Following is a list of procedures we recommend to help to control the spread of bacteria:

- Never put cooked food on a cutting board that you have used for raw food without adequately cleaning and sanitizing it first. This will control cross contamination, the most common means of spreading *Salmonella.*

- Use disposable gloves frequently. To minimize cross contamination, wash your hands and take a fresh pair of gloves for each production step when working with food that is susceptible to *Salmonella.*

- Wash up properly after using the toilet; train all staff to do the same.

- Do not allow workers with respiratory infections, boils, pimples, burns, or infected cuts to handle food.

- Maintain proper vermin and fly control.

- Thaw frozen foods in the refrigerator or with potable running water. Cook at once or hold at a safe temperature.

- Refrigerate foods promptly; take to 40°F (4°C) or lower as quickly as possible. Shallow containers aid quick cooling.

- Chill batch pans and all sausage ingredients. Keep ambient room temperature as low as practical.

- Break down large batches into smaller ones to speed chilling.

- Monitor steam table temperatures. Reheat foods quickly, stirring often.

- Discard or chill leftovers. To reheat later, stir often while bringing rapidly to a temperature above 165°F (74°C).

- Avoid day-ahead preparations. Serve hot and cold dishes as soon as they are cooked or chilled.

- Examine procedures for preparing susceptible foods; the more stages in the recipe, the more chance for a dish to spend time in the danger zone.

- Properly wash, peel, and prepare all raw fruits and vegetables.

CLOSTRIDIUM BOTULINUM

Due to the media attention it gets, botulism is probably the best-known foodborne illness. The sensationalism that accompanies outbreaks results from the relatively high mortality rate (20–35 percent in the United States) associated with it. Botulism attacks the nervous system and is caused by the toxin of the bacterium *Clostridium botulinum,* a spore-forming organism. Symptoms appear 12–36 hours after eating; they include abdominal pain, diarrhea, headache, nausea, and double vision. Progressive respiratory paralysis sets in and may result in death. Recovery usually involves a long convalescence.

This bacterium is different from the others we have described because it grows only in the absence of oxygen; such *anaerobic* bacteria can thrive in sealed cans and jars. Principal sources are improperly processed containers of meat (like ham and sausage) and canned smoked fish and tuna. In addition, all nonacid vegetables such as beans, corn, beets, and spinach are vulnerable. The toxin is rendered harmless when exposed to 176°F (80°C) for 30 minutes or to 212°F (100°C) for 10 minutes; the food must be evenly exposed to the heat. Recognizing possible contagion is the first line of defense. Follow these procedures:

- Never use home-canned foods of any kind in a commercial foodservice establishment. This would violate most health department codes.
- Examine all commercially canned goods. Never use any with signs of internal pressure such as bulging or leaking. Foul-smelling, foamy, or slimy foods should be discarded at once. Because even a very small taste can kill, **never taste suspect foods.**
- Obtain prompt medical attention if there is any suspicion of botulism. There is an antitoxin available from state or local health departments. Assistance is also available from the Foodborne Disease office at the Centers for Disease Control in Atlanta, Georgia (404-639-2206).

Parasites

Trichinella spiralis is a parasitic worm whose larval form may be present in the flesh of pork or wild game; it can cause trichinosis, a painful but seldom fatal disease. Symptoms can develop up to a month after ingestion. These symptoms include pain, nausea, vomiting, and diarrhea; in 1–2 weeks, muscular symptoms occur such as swelling, unusual firmness, and extreme pain. Sweating, facial edema, high fever, and difficult breathing are also present. In 3–6 weeks, the symptoms will resemble those of encephalitis and meningitis, with hearing and vision problems. This range of symptoms indicates that trichinosis is a disease to take seriously; fortunately, modern practices have all but eradicated it. Hogs are no longer fed a swill of uncooked garbage that may contain infected meat scraps. However, we stress the importance of faithfully following the recommended procedures.

The main line of defense against the trichina larva is cooking the pork or game completely, although curing and freezing are also effective. Always follow the recipe instructions for the equipment temperature settings and the internal finishing temperature of a product. Fresh pork must be cooked to an internal temperature of at least 150°F (65.5°C). All hot-smoked sausages should be cooked to 155°F (68°C). Cold-smoked or air-dried sausages, whose formulas contain Prague powder #2, should be cooked to 120–135°F (49–57°C). The temperature requirement for microwave cooking is 170°F (77°C). Do not judge the degree of doneness by the color of the meat; some well-cooked meat will show pink, and not all gray meat has reached a safe temperature. Use an accurate meat thermometer.

CHEMICAL HAZARDS

Chemical food poisoning occurs when chemicals of one kind or another are introduced into food. One type of chemical contamination occurs when pesticides, fungicides, fumigants, or cleaning products are accidentally spilled. These agents must be handled with great care; they should be locked in separate storage, properly labeled, and used only by fully trained personnel. Even when outside licensed operators are hired to fumigate, it is the responsibility of the foodservice management to remove all food from the treatment area.

Food additives may pose another problem. Because excessive amounts can cause illness, additives in foods should not exceed the levels recommended by the Food and Drug Administration (FDA) and the U.S. Department of Agriculture (USDA). Strictly follow the guidelines for using approved additives such as emulsifiers, potassium nitrate, MSG, and colorants.

Poisonous metals form a third group of potential contaminants. Metals occur naturally in food, often in harmless trace quantities. They become a health hazard when present in excessive amounts. Copper, cadmium, and lead are three examples of toxic metals that are sometimes used in kitchen utensils. These metals can leach out when acidic foods are cooked in chipped or cracked enamelware. Stainless steel has reduced this hazard. The prohibition of lead in plumbing and cookware has eliminated another source of toxic metal. Although the likelihood of such contamination has diminished in today's kitchen, we must be alert to potential sources of harmful or deadly metals. We highly recommend using NSF-approved cookware, utensils, and work surfaces.

PHYSICAL HAZARDS

This group includes harmful objects such as glass fragments, metal shards, and other inedible materials that get into food accidentally or through carelessness. The best example of inexcusable carelessness is using a drinking glass as a scoop in an ice machine. Metal from a worn, poorly functioning can opener may contaminate food; equipment breakdowns sometimes introduce foreign matter into food.

Health codes try to eliminate many of these hazards by requiring adequate kitchen lighting and limiting personal jewelry. Alert staff provide the most effective defense against the embarrassment of such incidents. A well-run kitchen with a good equipment maintenance program helps morale and provides the necessary supervision.

To summarize, four main factors contribute to poor sanitation practices:

- **Ignorance** of the rules of hygiene. "Ignorance is no excuse." Prevention of these various hazards is unquestionably the responsibility of the kitchen staff. We strongly recommend taking advantage of the foodservice sanitation classes offered at technical schools. Certification courses are available; someone who has been certified can offer valuable in-house training for all kitchen personnel.

- **Carelessness** or disregard of established practice. This, of course, is worse than ignorance. Once proper food preparation procedures have been learned, they should always be practiced.

- **Poorly designed equipment or facilities,** or lack of necessary maintenance. The foodworker must be alert to equipment design faults and compensate for them. If a piece of equipment is hard to clean due to poor design, it still must be cleaned thoroughly, even if it means extra time and effort.

- **Accidents.** Although some accidents just happen, most are preventable. Always report accidents and get help when needed. Communicate with others so that quick and effective action is possible. This will remedy the immediate situation and reduce the chances for similar accidents in the future.

Because foodservice mistakes can have such serious consequences, we must work "smart" and do our best to prevent them. Below we list 13 ways to prevent food poisoning; happily, this is many more than the four causes above. Your vigilance and attention to detail will reward you with satisfaction and your customers with wholesome food products.

1. Keep well and physically fit.
2. Maintain high standards of personal hygiene.
3. Know and follow personal wash-up procedures.
4. Provide easy access to wash stations.
5. Establish and maintain good working conditions.
6. Maintain equipment properly and keep it clean.
7. Store food in proper containers at correct temperatures.
8. Reheat foods correctly and hold at safe temperatures on the serving line.
9. Cool foods quickly for storage.
10. Protect food from vermin and insects.
11. Train all staff to prevent contamination of foods.
12. Supervise all operations to ensure that procedures are being followed. Without this attention, bad habits can develop.
13. Encourage open communication among personnel. Problems can be more readily solved, and morale will be good.

CHAPTER

3

Ingredients for the Charcuterie Kitchen

Every successful charcuterie preparation begins with suitable ingredients of the highest quality. The chef must make decisions about many diverse components such as meat, fish, vegetables, casings, curing agents, seasonings—even woods for smoking. The guidelines and advice in this chapter will prepare you for making those decisions.

MEATS

The first thing to consider is the meat. All meat intended for human consumption must be inspected in accordance with established programs. Many people believe that only scraps and inferior cuts are used to make sausages, but this is untrue. For quality and wholesomeness, very good grades and cuts of meat should always be used. Normally, meat and fish constitute about one third of the total food cost in a commercial kitchen. But in the charcuterie kitchen, meat is two thirds of the total food cost. We recommend using meats that are graded Select or Choice, Yield Grade 3; this provides the optimum fat-to-lean ratio for sausage. High-quality meat will pay for itself and contribute to the success and profitability of the whole operation.

Below are our buying recommendations for suitable meat cuts. Study the cutting diagrams to become familiar with each animal. Many cuts are interchangeable; as you make your own refinements to recipes, an intimate knowledge of these meat cuts will be valuable. Know your supplier and buy from reliable sources.

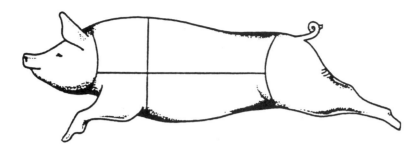

Pork cutting diagram

Pork

Weight:	Available by the carcass.
	Range A—120–150 lb
	Range B—150–180 lb
	Range C—180–210 lb
Yield Grade:	Grade 3 or 4
Quality Grade:	Grades U.S. No. 1, 2, 3, 4
Cuts:	Everything but the squeal! The entire animal has use in charcuterie. Use head, cheek, neck, belly, loin, shoulder, leg, liver, blood, kidney, intestines, heart, caul fat, feet, ears, tail, fatback, and carcass fat.

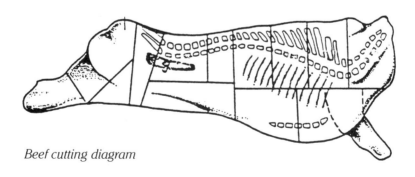

Beef cutting diagram

Beef

Weight:	Approximate weight of side is 360 lb (180 kg).
Yield Grade:	Grade 3 or 4
Quality Grade:	Grade Good or better
Mark of Federal Inspection:	From the 1986 *Meat Buyer's Guide*, "The mark of Federal Inspection is a round stamp identifying the slaughterhouse of origin for car-

casses and the meat-fabricating house for further cuts. The stamped federal inspection logo on each carcass is the federal government's guarantee that the meat has been identified, inspected, passed and found to be pure and wholesome and is in accordance with the standards established by members of The National Association of Meat Purveyors."

Cuts: Brisket, top round, shin, shank, short ribs, chuck, liver, cheek, heart, kidney, brains, sweetbreads, silverside (top round), bottom round, plate, tongue, and suet fat.

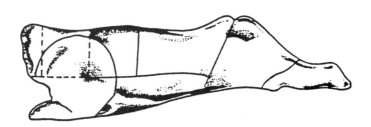

Veal cutting diagram

Veal

Weight: Weight of side is 88–113 lb (Range D).

Yield Grade: Grade 3

Quality Grade: Standard or Good

Mark of Federal
  Inspection: As for beef; carcass will bear stamp.

Cuts: Shoulder, breast, neck, kidney, brains, heart, rack trimmings, loin trimmings, shank off the leg, flap and knuckle meat, bottom of the silverside, and suet fat.

Lamb, Mutton, Goat

Weight: Lamb is available by the carcass, saddle, and various cuts. A Range-D carcass weighs 65–75 lb. Mutton carcass weight range is 115–130 lb. Goat will fall into the lower weight ranges.

Yield Grade: Grade 3

Quality Grade: Choice grade lamb; Good grade mutton

Mark of Federal
  Inspection: As for beef; carcass will bear stamp.

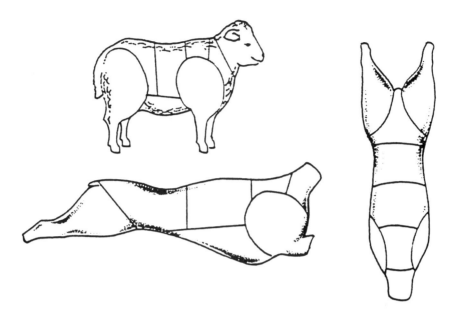

Lamb cutting diagram

Cuts: Leg, neck, shoulder, breast, scrag end (neck end), kidney, heart,
                         tongue, head, liver, and lamb fat. Reserve costly Choice lamb for
                         grilling, roasting, and sautéing; use trimmings for pâtés and terrines.
                         Use mutton for Greek sausages.

GAME MEATS AND FOWL

To protect your reputation and the health of your patrons, always use caution when working with any wild game or fowl. As with other meats, be aware of the legal requirements that apply. We recommend buying game that has state or federal inspection and certification. Exotic animals such as lion, zebra, buffalo, crocodile, and antelope are being served more often today. Remember that novelty can be short-lived; we recommend caution.

Venison

Venison may be used for pâtés, terrines, and sausages. This brand of meat needs no tenderizing and is ideal for all sausage making tasks. The leg and rack (haunch) are ideal for roasting as well. Venison bones make a great stock and game aspic. Cervena cuts: all loin cuts of the deer, and primary leg muscles. Excludes shoulder, as the cut is not consistently tender.

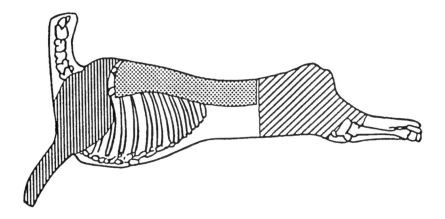

Venison cutting diagram (Courtesy of the Cervena Company Ltd., New York)

Uses of Game Meats

Type of Game	Marinade*	Best Uses
Alligator (highly recommended)	No	Grill, ravioli, sausage, sauté
Boar	Optional; Carbonnade recommended.	Braise, grill, pâté, roast, sausage, stew, terrine
Buffalo	Yes; Carbonnade recommended.	Braise, grill, pâté, roast, sausage, stew, terrine
Elk	Yes	Braise, grill, pâté, roast, sausage, stew, terrine
Hare	Yes	Braise, jug, pâté, sausage, sauté, terrine
Moose	Yes	Braise, grill, pâté, roast, sausage, stew, terrine
Opossum	Yes	Bake, braise, sausage
Rabbit	Optional	Bake, braise, pâté, sausage, sauté, terrine
Squirrel	Yes	Bake, braise, sausage
Venison	Yes	Braise, grill, pâté, roast, sausage, stew, terrine

* Refer to the various marinades described in Chapter 4, "Wet and Dry Curing."

Uses of Feathered Game

Type of Game	Marinade*	Best Uses
Duck (Wild)	Yes	Braise, pâté, roast, sausage, terrine
Grouse	Yes	Braise, pâté, roast, terrine
Partridge	Yes	Braise, pâté, roast, terrine
Pheasant	Yes	Braise, pâté, roast, sausage, terrine
Snipe	Yes	Braise, pâté, roast, terrine
Teal	Yes	Braise, pâté, roast, sausage, terrine
Turkey	No	Pastrami, pâté, roast, salami, sausage, sauté

* Refer to the various marinades described in Chapter 4, "Wet and Dry Curing."

POULTRY

All poultry for the charcuterie kitchen should be high quality and very fresh. As always, it is good policy to find and rely on a dependable supplier. Fresh poultry should be well-iced and delivered on refrigerated trucks. Frozen poultry must be held at 0°F (17.8 °C) or lower, then thawed for use.

Young birds can be recognized by white skin that has a faint bluish cast; the flesh should be firm, the breast plump, and the breastbone pliable. Older and larger birds will have a coarser appearance with a layer of yellow fat under the skin. The feet are an excellent indicator of age; young fowl have not developed the large spurs or scales that are seen on the feet and legs of older birds.

Popular Median Weights

Chicken breast, skin on	8 oz
Chicken breast, skinless	8 oz
Cornish game hens	16–24 oz
Roasting chicken	2½–3 lb
Capon for sausage	5 lb
Long Island duckling	5 lb
Gosling	8 lb
Boiling hen for sausage and pâté	8 lb
Goose	12 lb
Tom turkey	18–41 lb

FISH AND SEAFOOD

Fish and seafood enjoy considerable popularity today, and we believe the demand for well-made fish products will increase in the future. Although not widely used in sausage making, fish does have a place in the charcuterie kitchen. A knowledge of fish cookery is a prerequisite for success and will enhance the skills of both the accomplished chef and the aspiring student.

Visiting his native Ireland, Chef Kinsella learned that the famed Dublin Bay prawns had been contaminated by atomic waste from British power stations in the 1950s. A catastrophe like this might be prevented with effective safeguards. Good seafood inspection programs should contribute to the preservation of irreplaceable species and to the health and enjoyment of consumers. Government inspection programs are presently under review; some are being expanded, and some are being implemented for the first time. This should benefit producers and consumers alike.

The success of any seafood preparation depends completely on the freshness of the fish; any trace of unpleasant flavor will be apparent immediately. Because fresh fish is so perishable, order only what you need for two days of production and store it on ice. When delivered, the fish should be well wrapped with the shipping package intact. Fish must be frozen or well-iced, never soaking in water. Inspect the fish carefully; it should have a pleasant odor and firm flesh with no gaps in the tissue. In a whole fish, look for clear, full (not sunken) eyes and bright red gills. Scales should be adhering and abundant.

Fish are divided into two groups—white fish and oily fish. Understanding the different flavors and textures will help you choose the best fish for a given recipe. Often a mixture of two or more kinds of fish is successful. With practice and careful sampling, you will soon establish guidelines for selecting top-quality fish.

White Fish

Some of the best-known saltwater white fish are sole, whiting, turbot, cod, haddock, scrod, plaice, and halibut. The most popular freshwater fish include trout, bass, pike, and bluegill. Carp is a desirable freshwater fish if it comes from clean waters.

Most of these white nonoily fish are not good candidates for smoking. Famous and delicious Finnan Haddie, made from haddock, is a successful exception. The fish in this group make very fine sausages, mousses, pâtés, and terrines.

Oily Fish

Well-known oily fish are salmon, tuna, herring, mackerel, striped bass, trout, grouper, snapper, mullet, redfish, eel, and tile. These versatile fish may have dark or light flesh, and they are known for their fine texture. Although well-suited for mousses, pâtés, and terrines, they can also be cured and smoked. Smoked eels are usually sold without heads or tails as "eel centers."

Mollusks

This large group of invertebrates includes univalves, bivalves, squid, octopuses, and periwinkles. Oysters, clams, and scallops are the mollusks most likely to be used in the charcuterie kitchen. They are normally used as garnish, not as the main ingredient in a recipe. They can add artistic contrast in mousses, pâtés, and terrines. Although squid are good candidates for smoking, the structure and high water content of other mollusks limit their use for smoking. Exceptions are the very fine smoked oysters and clams exported by the Japanese.

Crustaceans

These marine and freshwater shellfish feature an exoskeleton, jointed legs and antennae, and a body composed of a head, thorax, and tail. This popular but relatively expensive group includes shrimp, prawns, crabs, crayfish, lobsters, and spiny lobsters. Shellfish are superb for gourmet eating and specialty products. Great value is placed on the claw and tail meat, but the outer shell and some inner parts can also be used to add flavor to a dish. The fine-grained flesh is firm but tender; it has a rich flavor that is often nutty or sweet.

Supply always lags demand. Although air shipments have opened up new production areas, these delectable shellfish can command premium prices. Because price can be a factor, the meat is often combined with other fish for delicious pâtés and mousses. All shellfish are excellent for smoking; a fine dish can become an outstanding one with smoked lobster, prawn, or shrimp as garnish. Grilling smoked shellfish can give memorable results.

Shellfish spoil easily if not handled properly from harvest to table; in addition, they can cause severe illness if they come from contaminated waters. To get quality and wholesomeness for the premium price you pay, choose your supplier with care. Work with the supplier to make the most of seasonal price advantages.

SAUSAGE CASINGS

Sausage was developed for one primary reason—to preserve meat. Flavors and textures were refined in various ways through the ages, but extending the life of the meat was the most important motivation. From the earliest times, people discovered that parts of the slaughtered animal such as the intestines, stomach, caul, and bladder made practical stuffing bags for the seasoned meat; these casings are at the very heart of the sausage making process.

A sausage starts with chopped or ground fresh meat which is mixed with flavoring ingredients and curing agents such as salt and nitrite compounds. After the seasoned meat is stuffed into the casings, it dries for a specified time in an environment of controlled temperature and humidity. As the casing holds the ingredients in close proximity, complex chemical reactions take place and transform the meat into sausage. Flavors mature, enzymes modify the texture, and the meat is preserved; like the ripening of cheese, this activity continues for days, weeks, even months. This curing period may be followed by smoking; the permeability of the casings allows the smoke to penetrate and create a distinctive flavor, color, and an outer protective layer.

The casing gives each sausage its identifying size, shape, and color. Using high-quality casing helps ensure an excellent product. Because the demand for casing material is so high, man-made casings supplement the inadequate supply of natural ones.

Natural Casings

Natural casings are secured at the time of slaughter; their size depends on the animal. The casings are cleaned, scraped, and graded by size; they are then cut into uniform lengths.

Large and small intestines of all slaughter animals are highly prized for casings. Hog stomachs are traditionally used for headcheese, souse, and blood sausages; haggis, a Scottish sausage, must go into a sheep's stomach. Hog and beef bladders are in demand for headcheese, mortadella, and minced specialties.

The small and large intestines provide a size range of 16–127 mm. Larger casings are made by cutting and sewing together small casings; they start at 5 inches in diameter and are called Sewed Beef Middles and Sewed Hog Bungs. Some casings are made in a "double wall style" and are used for liver, genoa, and braunschweiger sausages. Special sizes and shapes are custom-made for the large sausage making firms.

Casings are packed in dry salt or brine solution and shipped in 5-gallon containers. The dry-salt casings require no refrigeration; they may be stored for years prior to use. Also available is a deluxe wet-pack casing which is ready to be stuffed with no advance preparation.

Manufactured Casings

Some man-made casings are made from animal products such as collagen, while others are manufactured from approved plastic materials. These are economical and practical, and improve on the natural casings in many ways: they require very little preparation before use, they come on easy-to-handle rolls in various colors and lengths, and their uniform dimensions make accurate portion control easier. Casings may be reinforced with natural fibers or nylon; some can shrink onto the sausage to create a pleasing appearance. Both plastic and collagen casings offer the same control of smoking as the natural ones.

Collagen casings can be made very thin; they are delicate enough to be completely edible. The collagen is made from the inside, or corium layer, of cattle hides (the hair side becomes leather). The casings are available in a size range of 14–45 mm. They hold up especially well on today's high-speed stuffing and linking machines. They can be linked quite short without unraveling, a feature lacking in many other casings. Shrinkage loss is less with collagen casings because the uptake of color is very rapid, resulting in faster processing. These casings arrive both sanitary and clean, thus saving time and labor. They are also available in a curved style.

Collagen casings require refrigerated storage at 50°F (10°C) or lower. They do not need, nor will they tolerate, prolonged soaking. A colored collagen casing can be used for an unsmoked product which needs an inviting darkened exterior; the deep brown casing colors the sausage without smoking.

The Hukki Knitted Collagen Casing® is formed around a nylon web which creates a very strong casing. It is highly recommended for dry and semi-dry sausages that will not be exposed to high smoking temperatures; the upper limit for this casing is 170°F (76.6°C). It is available in several popular sizes, and stores indefinitely at room temperature. A 10-minute soak is required before use.

Plastic or cellulose casings can be tailor-made in almost any size, and they are very strong when necessary. They do not need refrigeration; cleaning them before use is not necessary. They can be colored and imprinted with labels and logos. This helps a customer quickly single out a brand and variety of sausage; red suggests bologna, white indicates liverwurst, and clear or brown will identify other sausages.

Plastic casings are widely used in the manufacture of skinless hot dogs and frankfurters. The meat mixture is machine-stuffed into thin plastic casings and linked; the sausage is then heated until it is cooked and a thin layer of coagulated protein forms just under the plastic coating. Because plastic casings are inedible, they are removed by efficient high-speed machines which leave a fine cut line on the wieners.

Collagen and plastic casings provide a practical answer to the ongoing shortage of natural casings. They play a role in the production of fine sausages and have won full acceptance by both the manufacturer and customer.

Tables 3.1 and 3.2 list natural and man-made casings which are readily available to the trade. Order casings well ahead of production; the availability of certain casings may be limited. When necessary, substitutions among several sizes or types of casings can often be made without sacrificing authenticity or quality.

Table 3.1. Natural Casings

Name and Sizes	Storage Tips	Typical Uses
Hog 29–32 mm	Salt or brine. Rinse in cold water before use.	Breakfast, Italian, frankfurters, brats
Hog 32–35 mm	Salt or brine. Rinse in cold water before use.	Brats, bocks, and Italian
Hog 35–38 mm	Salt or brine. Rinse in cold water before use.	Kielbasa, knockwurst
Hog 38–42 mm	Salt or brine. Rinse in cold water before use.	Polish, summer sausage, bangers
Hog middles, large intestine	Salt or brine. Rinse in cold water before use.	Blood, sausage, salami
Stomachs (sizes vary from one animal to another)	Salt or brine. Rinse in cold water before use.	Souse, head cheese
Sheep or lamb 22–24 mm (a very tender casing)	Salt or brine. Rinse in cold water before use.	Breakfast sausage, seafood sausage
Sheep or lamb 24–26 mm (a very tender casing)	Salt or brine. Rinse in cold water before use.	Hotdogs, wieners, chicken and tarragon sausage
Natural Beef 4–4½ in.	Salt or brine. Rinse in cold water before use.	Bologna, cappicola, Lebanon, salami
Beef rounds 38–40 mm	Salt or brine. Rinse in cold water before use.	Liver sausage, mettwurst, salami
Beef rounds 40–42 mm	Salt or brine. Rinse in cold water before use.	All ring sausage and looped sausage

Please note:
1. All natural casings are ordered in hanks. There are about 24 yards of casings per hank.
2. The casings are packed either in dry salt or brine.
All casing must be stored in a soft brine under refrigeration. They must be systematically washed and rinsed in cold water before use.
These casings can be found in The Sausage Maker catalog. See Appendix, p. 271.

Table 3.2. Man-made Casings

Name and Sizes	Storage Tips	Typical Uses
Beef stick 2 in. to 24 in.	Keep dry and soak before use	Beef stick, salami
Deer salami 3½ in. to 24 in.	Keep dry and soak before use	Venison salami
Cooked salami 5 in. to 24 in.	Keep dry and soak before use	Salami, braunschweiger
Bologna casings 8 in. to 24 in.	Keep dry and soak before use	Bologna
Mahogany color 2 in. to 20 in.	Keep dry and soak before use	Small salamis of all types
Flat collagen 60 mm 2.3 × 24	Keep dry and soak before use	Pepperoni beef sticks
Flat collagen 90 mm 3.5 × 24	Keep dry and soak before use	Genoa salami
Flat collagen 100 mm 3.9 × 24	Keep dry and soak before use	Thuringer, mortadella
Collagen casing 19 mm	Keep dry and soak before use	Slim jims, jerky
Collagen casing 22 mm	Keep dry and soak before use	Fresh sausage, hot Italian
Collagen casing 26 mm	Keep dry and soak before use	Spanish chorizo, bratwurst
Collagen casing 32 mm	Keep dry and soak before use	Country sausage, bangers
Collagen casing 36 mm	Keep dry and soak before use	Polish, pepperoni, melton mobray
Protein lined casing 2 in. to 24 in.	Keep dry and soak before use	Salami and some liver sausages
Protein lined casing 3½ in. to 24 in.	Keep dry and soak before use	Salami

Please note:
1. All man-made casings must be soaked in cold water for at least 30 minutes prior to use.
2. All soaked casings that are not used must be stored under refrigeration in cold water between applications.
3. Use natural, not man-made casings for all grilling variety sausage.
4. Man-made casings are ordered by size, and not normally by yardage. They are packed in standard count packages.

These casings can be found in The Sausage Maker catalog. See Appendix B, p. 271.

Preparing Casings

All natural casings come in hanks, rolls, or packs of some kind. The simple procedure is to unpack the casings, wash off the salt or saline solution, and separate each strand into a container of cold water. Leave a "tail" of each strand hanging over the rim of the container; this will serve as a handle to retrieve the strand when you are ready to stuff.

Man-made casings, both collagen and plastic, require a soak in warm water to condition them for use. For example, salami skins must be soaked for at least 30 minutes in tap water. Each type of casing has its own requirements. Specific instructions will be in the recipe and/or on the pack of casings. See Tables 3.1 and 3.2 for general information about the storage and preparation of various casings.

Stuffing Sausage Casings

Photos showing proper techniques for preparing and stuffing cases are on pages 33 to 40. Before stuffing, one end of the casing must be secured with a butterfly knot to prevent a ruptured sausage. To tie a butterfly knot (Fig. A):

1. Use stout butcher's twine to tie a double knot around the casing at least 1 inch from the end of the skin.
2. Spread out the tail with the two ends of twine free; run two loops around the double knot. Then crisscross a loop over each wing of the butterfly.

Always slide a wet casing onto a stuffing tube that has been generously lubricated with water (Fig. B). Casings that are too dry will cause stuffing problems. Load the stuffing horn

Metal and plastic stuffing tubes. (Photo courtesy of The Sausage Maker, Buffalo NY)

Techniques for Stuffing Casings

The following illustrations show proper techniques for preparing and stuffing casings, as described on pages 32 and 41 (photos by Jon Macamy, Learning Resource Center, Cincinnati Technical and Community College).

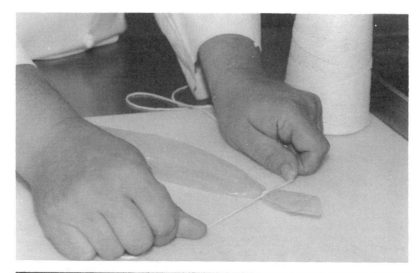

Fig. A-1 *Tying a fibrous casing.*

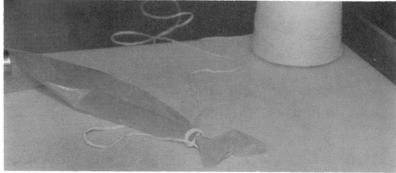

Fig. A-2 *A butterfly tie.*

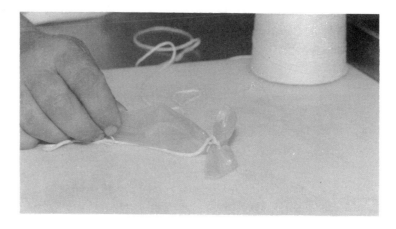

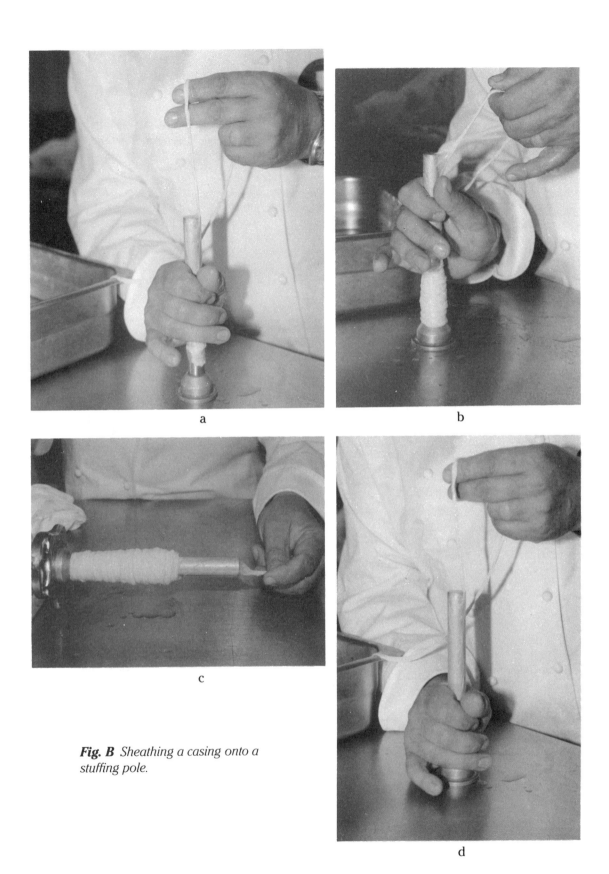

a

b

c

Fig. B *Sheathing a casing onto a stuffing pole.*

d

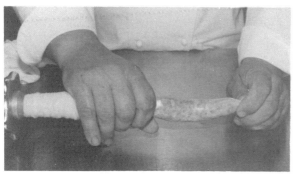

Fig. C Stuffing a casing to make a rope sausage.

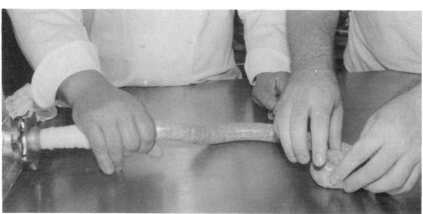

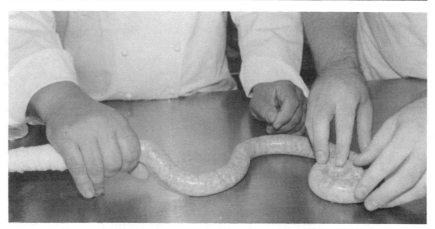

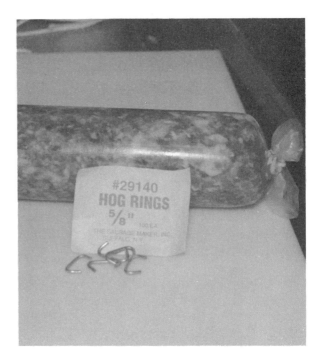

Fig. D Hog Rings.

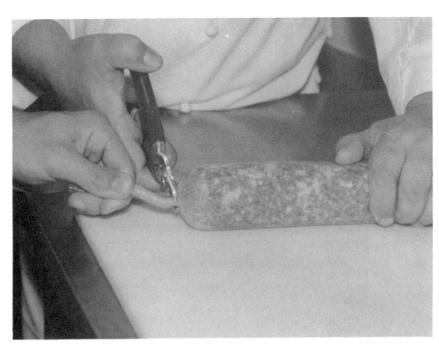

Fig. E Closing a salami with hog ring clippers.

Fig. F *Rope sausage.*

37

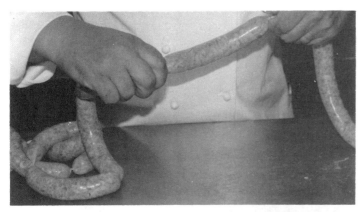

Fig. G *Linking sausage.*

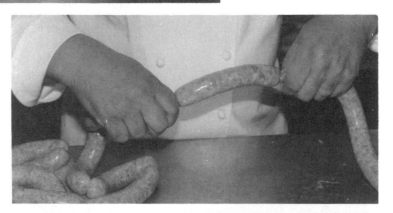

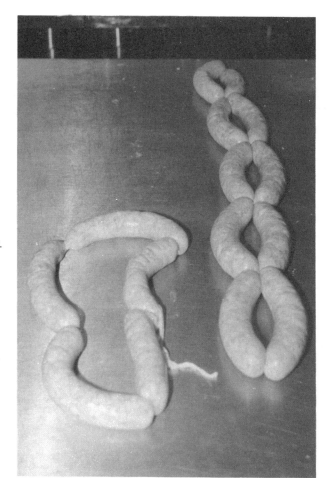

Fig. H *Links and chains.*

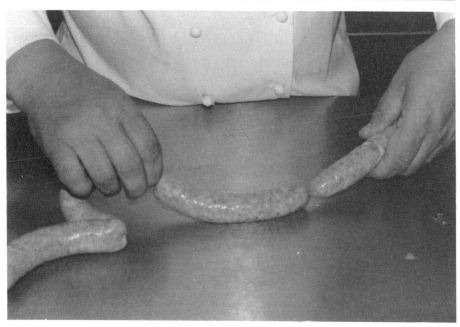

39

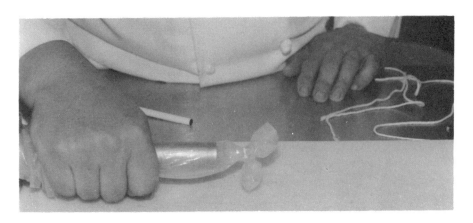

Fig. I *Preparing to stuff a salami.*

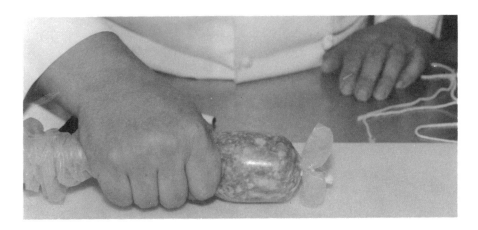

Fig. J *Stuffing a salami.*

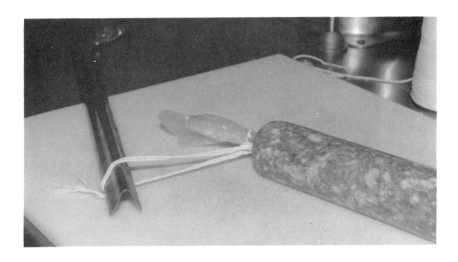

Fig. K *A salami prepared to be hanged for smoking.*

40

carefully to prevent air pockets. Air pockets will not only detract from the finished appearance, they will also interfere with the safe processing of the sausage. The casing must be held in place on the stuffing tube with enough pressure to pack the sausage firmly, but not too full. It takes practice to acquire the skill for stuffing properly (Fig. C). Fortunately, most students do this in a very short time.

The open ends of large sausages are secured either with a hog ring (Fig. D) and hog ring tool or with a Clark clip and pliers (Fig. E). There are four basic styles for finishing other sausages:

- **Coiling (or Roping):** This is the simplest method (Fig. F). The entire length of sausage falls into a neat coil on a tray like rope on a ship deck. The sausage is not linked or tied off. This presentation can be very attractive in a butchershop case.
- **Linking:** Stuff-coil-link is the usual procedure (Fig. G). Pinch off and twist links of uniform length in the coiled sausage. Since the casing is of uniform diameter, the weight of each link will automatically be uniform. Appearance and convenience are the main advantages to linked sausages.
- **Chaining:** This is the joining of one skin of links to another (Fig. H). Use butcher's twine to join two or more groups of links; this facilitates processing and display. Allow extra casing for chaining.
- **Looping:** This is an optional step, appropriate for sausages such as kielbasa. The sausage is loosely stuffed into the casing until it is large enough to tie the ends together. For processing and display, smaller loops may be placed on a hanging stick.

See Figures I, J, and K for steps in preparing a salami.

OFFAL

For centuries, offal has been fully utilized in charcuterie. Here, we present basic guidelines for its use in the recipes given in this book. Follow them. They will assure safe, profitable utilization of this highly diversified, valuable ingredient. We may define offal as *edible organ meats.* For the purposes of this book, a few other specific parts of common slaughter animals are included.

Every variety of offal is by nature, highly perishable. Thus it is extremely important to handle them properly from the slaughterhouse to finished product distribution. Often, the steps in this process are unique to the particular offal variety. We recommend following the instructions very faithfully. Consider them absolutely necessary for safe and flawless production.

Commonly, all orders for offal are handled and subsequently labeled by the supplier as "special order goods." Your own products, when using this commodity, should always carry that same label. Incidentally, *offal* is correctly pronounced like *awful*. Be assured that the many fine products produced using offal are anything but that!

Constant, safe levels of refrigeration, proper packaging, and well planned, rapid utilization by the charcutier is absolutely mandatory for all offal. Listed below are specific methods, and some practical tips. Remember, most are specific for each variety. Diligently apply this information. Do this long before starting, and while working with the recipe. You will find that it is not difficult to work with offal, and your product line will benefit greatly.

Brains

Use within one day of delivery. Brains, when received, should be bright pinkish-white, firm and plump. **Preparation:** (1) Soak in chilled, acidulated water for 1 to 2 hours. (2) Soak in several changes of plain, cold water to remove all traces of blood. (3) Simmer for about 20 minutes in acidulated water. (4) Cool at once in an ice water bath. Source: beef, sheep, hogs.

Tongue

Preparation: (1) Scrub and wash, with running tap water. (2) Simmer 15 to 20 minutes in acidulated water. (3) Quickly chill in an ice water bath. (4) When cooled, skin the tongue. (5) Remove any small bones and gristle found in the root of the tongue and proceed with the recipe.

Tongues may be smoked, boiled, or pressed. Note: If brining, do not skin—tongue should be dressed and skinned *after* brining. Smaller beef tongues (less than 3 lbs) and those from a full range of slaughter animals are especially desirable for many delicious applications.

Heart

Heart is a muscle meat, not an organ meat. **Preparation:** (1) Wash very well to remove excess blood. (2) Remove fat, veins, and arteries. (3) Trimmed muscle may be marinated in a chilled, acidic marinade (wine or lemon juice) to tenderize. (4) Simmer the heart in good stock, until tender.

Marinated heart may be stuffed with sausage forcemeat, wrapped with caul fat, then braised. All poultry hearts are easily trimmed, and are very tender without marination (although they may be marinated for added flavor). Use hearts of all sorts freely in forcemeats and pâtés. Source: All hoofed animals and poultry.

Kidney

Use kidneys the day of delivery. Look for uniform color and freedom from dry or dull spots. Older kidneys are acceptable, and are deep reddish-brown. Younger kidneys are more pale, tender, and milder in flavor. Choose either, depending upon the flavor characteristics required. The recipe and flavor preferences will always determine the selection of kidney variety. **Preparation:** (1) Soak any variety of more mature, *and all pork kidneys,* in salted or acidulated water for 2 hours. (2) Blanch to reduce the characteristic odor. (3) Proceed with the recipe.

Commonly, kidneys are simmered, braised, or baked. Note: Kidneys from vealers, pork, and sheep should simply be washed, patted dry, then sautéed for just 1 minute. This aids in the removal of membranes. Trim any kidney fat. Distinguish multi-lobed beef and veal kidneys from lamb or pork kidneys, which appear smooth, being single-lobed organs. Lamb kidneys are very tender. They readily absorb water, and should not be soaked. All varieties of kidneys are used in classic charcuterie.

Liver

Liver is the most popular and widely used offal. **Preparation:** (1) Drain the liver of the abundant excess blood. If desired, reserve this blood for blood sausages, etc. (2) To set and firm the texture, sauté or blanch all liver, always cooling quickly. Overcooking toughens liver. (3) Trim the liver. For many, this is easier after cooling.

Poultry livers, and those from younger animals of every sort, have a higher demand and price, owing to their milder flavor and usually lighter color. Liver should have a fresh clean aroma, bright color, and a moist (not slick) surface. Poultry livers should be uniform in color, free of irregularities, and plump. Inspect them carefully and discard any small green or bluish colored bodies. These contain gall, and are extremely bitter. Trim the livers to remove any tough membranes or obvious larger vessels. Freezing of livers to lengthen holding time is satisfactory for many charcuterie applications. Choose from the wide range of liver flavors available, according to recipe requirements. Stronger flavored livers, such as pork, are often augmented in popular recipes, such as braunschweiger. These also may be utilized whenever more dominant liver qualities are desired. Sources: Beef, veal, lamb, pork, and commercial poultry of all sorts.

Sweetbreads

Universally prized by gourmets, sweetbreads are the thymus glands of lamb, pork, younger beef, and veal animals. **Preparation:** (1) Soak in several changes of acidulated water. (2) Remove the outer membrane. (3) Blanch briefly, then use at once. After blanching the sweetbreads may be held briefly if necessary.

Milk-fed vealers supply the top grade glands. Older sweetbreads are no longer white but have a reddish hue. All should be plump and firm. Sweetbreads have two distinct parts, the heart gland and the throat gland, which in the animal was connected by a tube. This tube is generally removed and is not marketed. Heart sweetbreads are preferred for overall quality, and bring the highest prices. The best flavor and texture are, as with other offal, primarily dependent upon the breed and age of the slaughter animal. Charcuterie uses center around classic pâtés and related items.

Pig's Feet

Inspect any shipment of pig's feet for absolute freshness. **Preparation:** (1) Just before use, wash in cold water. (2) Lightly scrub skin surfaces if needed. (3) Proceed with recipe.

Pig's feet are very often split lengthwise in the packing house. When ordering, specify whole or split. This economy cut is very high in valuable flavor and gelatin. Accordingly, it is excellent for goetta, and in the production of rich stocks to enrich and bind other pork sausages and specialties. This cut is very sinewy and bony. After boiling, often done to cook and tenderize, pig's feet are easily brined (spicy-hot and plain), or may be smoked. In all forms, well prepared pig's feet enjoy remarkable and steady support in many regional market areas. Great quantities of pig's feet are processed in a variety of ways to supply this demand. To many loyal consumers, there is no substitute!

Blood

Blood is a special order item. Depending on varying local regulations, it may not always be readily available from the packing house. Extremely perishable, this item should be worked straight from the cooler. Simply strain it, to assure freedom from any foreign matter, and combine it with well-chilled ingredients in the batch. Blood is employed in much traditional charcuterie. It is a prime ingredient for black puddings, tongue and blood sausage, and all other specialty blood sausages.

Caul Fat

Caul fat, or simply caul, is a very interesting, highly useful item. It has long been a favorite tool in the authors' charcuterie. Spread flat and viewed, caul is a large, translucent, delicately laced, fatty membrane. Anatomically, it is the *mesenteric lining* of the abdominal cavity of many animals. Sheep and hogs are the two animals generally sourced for caul, with the pork caul being considered superior. Caul is supplied in large sections, just as it grew. It requires initial separation into single layers for use. When used to wrap pâtés, as well as variously formed shapes of forcemeats, and crepinettes, it eventually melts during cooking but the intended shape of the item is preserved. It adds to the fatty elements of the product, contributing little, but certainly a measure, of desirable flavor. Caul fat is a fine, and fully natural, "shrink wrap." Always handle this delicate offal with extra care to avoid tearing. **Preparation:** Soak briefly in tepid, salted water to facilitate separation of the layers of the packaged caul.

Although caul is not so widely known or used today, it has exceptional properties. When you have used it once or twice, you will also appreciate its unique and reliable properties.

SEASONINGS

If meat is the body of a sausage, then seasoning is the spirit—its character, energy, and finesse. Before refrigeration became commonplace, heavy-handed seasoning was too often used to disguise aging meat and game. Some butchers still fear their customers will suspect inferior meats if they use more than minimal seasoning. Today we have access to fresh, aromatic seasonings and excellent meats; we are free to season our products without worrying about masking disagreeable flavors.

Most experienced chefs season to enhance the main ingredients. In the best salamis or delicate boudins and pâtés, numerous seasonings are subtly blended and balanced; it should be difficult to identify one particular flavor. In a different style, some popular sausages are famous for one dominant note, such as garlic or fiery cayenne pepper. While obligated to season some classical sausages in traditional style, a charcutier has more scope for invention with personal creations. Exercise good judgment; remember that even small adjustments can make a big difference in the finished product. Whether complex or simple, give full attention to use of all seasonings.

To ensure consistency in your products, buy high-quality seasonings from a reliable vendor. Buy in practical quantities that won't go stale on the shelf, and store them away from light, heat, and potential contamination.

Below we list the important seasonings—herbs, spices, and blends—that are used most frequently in the charcuterie kitchen. They may be used fresh, dried, whole, granulated, ground, or powdered. Follow the specific recipe instructions because the form will affect the flavor, appearance, and texture of a product. In general, we advise against using a dried herb if it is available fresh. For example, a dry-cured salmon is outstanding with fresh dill, but much less remarkable with dried dill. Garlic, parsley, and mint are some of the herbs that should always be used fresh. To heighten the flavor of dried herbs, rub them lightly with your fingers or palms before adding them to a dish.

For each entry, we list the common name and form, the country or region of origin, the Latin botanical name, and some application suggestions. Additional seasonings may appear in the recipes; where necessary, sources and instructions will be indicated.

Allspice: Whole or ground pungent berries from West Indies and Latin America; *Pimenta dioica*. Use in blood sausage, pepperoni, and braunschweiger.

Anise: Whole or ground seeds from Greece and the Middle East; *Pimpinella anisum*. Resembles licorice in flavor, sweetish; use in pepperoni and other sausages.

Bay Leaf (Laurel Leaf): Whole or powdered leaves from Mediterranean region and California. California bay leaves are narrower and longer than Turkish; Turkish leaves have more subtle flavor than Californian and are often preferred. Bay's mellow flavor is very versatile, but can be bitter when overused. Use in many recipes, including marinades, terrines, and poaching liquids.

Caraway: Whole or ground seeds from Europe and North America; *Carum carvi*. Resembles licorice in flavor; use in various sausages.

Cardamom: Green or roasted whole pod, whole or ground shelled seeds, from India; *Elettaria cardamomum*. The world's second most expensive spice. Distinctively spicy, pungent; a main ingredient in curry powder.

Celery Seed: Whole or ground seeds, worldwide; *Apium graveolens*. Use in mettwurst, wieners, and many other sausages.

Chili Powder: Ground red chili peppers with herbs and spices. Flavors and the intensity of heat will vary.

Cloves: Whole or ground flower buds from Indonesia; *Syzgium aromaticum*. Very strong and pungent; use in various sausages. Use whole cloves as garnish on hams and other meats.

Coriander: Whole or ground seeds from southern Europe; *Coriandrum sativum.* Sweet and pungent; fresh leaves are known as Chinese parsley or cilantro.

Cumin: Whole or ground seeds from the Mediterranean; *Cuminum cyminum.* Pungent, aromatic flavor which resembles caraway.

Curry Powder: Variable blends, some very hot, of up to 20 Indian herbs, spices, and seeds; best if ground fresh daily. Vindaloo is the hottest curry powder mixture. Valuable for flavor and color, curry powders are used in sausages, forcemeats, terrines, pâtés, and sauces.

Fennel: Whole, cracked, or powdered seeds and cut leaves from southern Europe; *Foeniculum vulgare.* Also known as sweet fennel. To avoid a bitter taste, use cracked instead of whole seeds in Italian sausages.

Garlic: Bulb from the Northern Hemisphere; *Allium sativum.* Strong, unique flavor; available fresh, granulated (dry) or canned (moist). Use in various sausages.

Garlic, Powdered: A convenient and reliable product from California; do not confuse with garlic salt. Use for garlic flavor with a fine texture. Stores well if kept dry.

Ginger: Whole, powdered, or crystallized rhizomes from Southeast Asia; *Zingiber officinale.* Aromatic, pungent; use in some bratwurst, liverwurst, and salami recipes.

Juniper: Whole or ground berries. Obtained from shrubs in North America, Europe, and Asia; *Juniperus communis.* Slightly bitter and haunting flavor; use in schinkenspeck sausage.

Mace: Ground cover of nutmeg from Indonesia; *Myristica fragrans.* Rich, smooth flavor; use in wieners and various wursts.

Marjoram: Whole or crushed leaves from North Africa and southwestern Asia. Mild-sweet, complex, and inviting flavor, sometimes slightly bitter. Combine with other herbs for liver, fish, poultry, and meats; use in marinades for pork, veal, and beef. Indispensable for smoked or fresh Polish sausage (kielbasa).

Mustard: Whole, ground, or prepared seeds from Europe and Asia; *Brassica.* Pungent flavor, sometimes sharp and hot. One of the most widely used seasonings for sausage; use in krakowska, summer sausage, braunschweiger, weisswurst, souse, and others.

Nutmeg: Whole or ground seed from Indonesia; *Myristica fragrans.* Fragrant, sweetish, slightly bitter flavor; use in breakfast sausages and many others.

Onion: Dehydrated chopped bulbs from the Northern Hemisphere. Distinct flavor, ranging from sweet and heavy to strong and hot. Reliable product; good for sausage where fine texture is not required. Use onion powder for fine-textured varieties.

Paprika: Ground fruit pods from North and South America; *Capsicum.* Flavor is sweet, aromatic, and pleasantly spicy; this pepper is very mild compared with cayenne and chili peppers. It can be used for color as well as flavor. Sometimes paprika is added to signal a very spicy item. Use in various sausages, including Hungarian paprika sausage.

Pepper, Black: Whole or ground unhusked berry from India and Ceylon; *Piper nigrum*. All varieties of the pepper vine are grown within 20 degrees of the equator. Black pepper is picked earlier than white pepper, and it has a pungent and aromatic flavor. We recommend #64 mesh for recipes that require finely ground pepper such as bratwurst, wieners, and bologna. Use whole black peppercorns for products such as salami where appearance and full flavor are important.

Pepper, Cayenne: Ground mature seed pods from North and South America; *Capsicum annuum*. This is a very hot pepper. The heat in the commercial brands varies; for uniformity, stick with one brand from the same supplier. Hot sausages continue to grow in popularity, but they must be seasoned skillfully. Don't allow hot pepper to overpower other flavors. Use in various sausages, especially in Cajun, Creole, and Italian products.

Pepper, Red: Flakes of dried seed pods of various hot chili peppers from North and South America; several varieties of *Capsicum frutescens*. As with cayenne pepper, buy the same brand for uniformity of heat.

Pepper, White: Whole or ground husked berry from India and Ceylon; *Piper nigrum*. Mature berry with a milder, less imposing flavor than black pepper; the flavor can be complex and delicate. It is often used finely ground to remain invisible in sausages such as wieners and bologna.

Peppercorns, Green: Whole underripe unhusked berries from India and Ceylon; *Piper nigrum*. Soft berries are available freeze-dried and packed in brine or water. Less pungent than black or white pepper. Usually used whole to lend flavor, color, and texture to terrines, forcemeats, and sauces.

Peppercorns, Pink: Whole berries of the Baies rose from Madagascar. These slightly sweet berries are not a true peppercorn. They are very high-priced, and are available freeze-dried and packed in brine or water. Use for their color in meat and fish terrines and pâtés.

Pickling Spices: Mixture of whole leaves, berries, pods, etc. Purchase small quantities for freshness. Gives a fine bouquet of flavors to numerous pickled items such as corned beef.

Quatre Épices (Four Spices): Variable blends of finely ground spices such as nutmeg, ginger, white pepper, cinnamon, and cloves. Avoid high heat as it can cause unpredictable results. Adds a distinctive, traditional flavor and aroma to many charcuterie items.

Sage: Whole or ground leaves and small stems, worldwide; various *Salvia* species. Sage has a distinctive, aromatic flavor. Because it is so fluffy, rubbed sage must be measured by weight. Some people seem to crave ever-larger amounts of sage, a phenomenon that is observed with hot peppers also; seek to balance sage properly with other seasonings. A very popular ingredient in breakfast sausage, sage is used in many other sausages also.

Tarragon: Stem tips and leaves from Europe; *Artemisia dranunculus*. Fresh is superior to dried; preserve small quantities in vinegar. Anise flavor is valued in French cuisine as one of the fines herbes and the main flavor ingredient in Sauce Béarnaise. Use in marinades, vinegars, terrines, sausages, and sauces.

Thyme: Leaves from Europe and Asia; various *Thymus* species. This is a versatile herb that can season almost any meat, poultry, or fish. Recommended for blending with other herbs such as sage, marjoram, and bay leaf.

OTHER INGREDIENTS

Curing Agents

Three main ingredients are used to cure sausages: sodium chloride, sodium nitrite, and sodium nitrate. Sodium chloride, or common salt, is used to flavor and preserve sausages. Sodium nitrite and sodium nitrate also preserve sausages and their rosy color, although the chemical action of these compounds is complex and not entirely understood. Necessary for safe and wholesome sausages, they are the industry standard and are accepted by the proper authorities. They are used in very small amounts and, to be fully safe and effective, they must be measured accurately.

Preserving compounds are sold premixed as "Prague powder." Prague powder #1 contains salt and sodium nitrite in a ratio of 16 ounces salt to 1 ounce sodium nitrite. It is used in wet cures for products that will subsequently be smoked or canned. Prague powder #2

is the mixture to use for dry cures. It contains the same ratio of salt to sodium nitrite, but it has an additional ingredient, 0.0625 ounce of sodium nitrate. Its delayed-action cure makes it suitable for uncooked products such as salami and summer sausage, which need long drying and smoking times. **The two Prague powders have different applications and are *not* interchangeable.**

Binding Agents

Agents such as corn syrup solids, soy protein concentrate, and nonfat dry milk solids not only bind ingredients together, they contribute other valuable properties to the finished sausage. Corn syrup solids, suitable for sausages which are cured at lower temperatures, foster the necessary fermentation. Properly controlled, this action gives a unique flavor to the finished product. Soy protein concentrate and nonfat dry milk solids retain the natural meat juices and flavor which would otherwise be lost during smoking. This enhances the appearance and yield of the sausage. To avoid undesirable flavor changes, limit the soy protein concentrate to 5 percent and the dry milk solids to 12 percent of the sausage weight.

Sweeteners

Sweetening agents not only flavor and sweeten, they also promote browning, nourish the beneficial bacteria that are active during the curing process, and reduce any harshness from a salt cure. Natural sugars that are commonly used include maple sugar, caramelized sugar, brown sugar, honey, and molasses.

Dextrose is the principal sweetener used in sausage making. It is the best form of sugar for sausage mixtures, brines, and marinades. It penetrates more quickly and effectively than white granulated sugar. Because dextrose has only 70 percent of the sweetening power of white sugar, formula adjustments must be made.

Corn syrup solids, mentioned above as a binding agent, are also used as a sweetener. They enhance the color-holding ability of a sausage; under fluorescent shop lights, products without corn syrup solids bleach out more quickly.

Artificial sweeteners may be used in a sausage formula, marinade, or cure. However, they will not provide bacterial nourishment, enhance browning, or add any additional flavor.

Other Additives

The sausage kitchen employs a relatively modest number of additives that have been in use for many years. Both producers and consumers have an understandable interest in the effects of chemical additives. We often feel confused by conflicting advice and information overload; foods we have eaten all our lives suddenly become our mortal enemies. We advise following a policy of moderation. Keep informed by reading labels and industry reports rather than inconclusive and sensationalized allegations. We recommend that all sausage producers keep up-to-date with the regulations and guidelines of the Food and Drug Administration.

Ascorbates (Vitamin C): When used with sodium nitrite, ascorbic acid inhibits the effectiveness of a brine. Although it improves the color of a product, it has limited use for the average sausage maker.

Disodium phosphate: This retains fluids in sausages and meat products, and shrinkage can be reduced to levels as low as 5 percent. Widely used in commercial production, this compound has limited use in the chef's kitchen.

Monosodium glutamate (MSG): MSG is produced by the fermentation of natural food products and resembles granulated sugar. It is used as a flavor enhancer; it adds no appreciable flavor of its own when used in reasonable quantities (one half the amount of the salt in a recipe). Our bodies produce glutamates; they are also available in many foods such as meat, seafood, vegetables, and dairy products.

Potassium chloride: This has similar properties to sodium chloride, but has a bitter taste. Research is underway on how to use potassium chloride in sausages without the bitterness.

C H A P T E R

4

Wet and Dry Curing

The object of curing meat or fish is to dry and thereby preserve it. This happens through the dehydrating action of sodium chloride (salt) with small amounts of sodium nitrite and sodium nitrate. Curing is a separate process, the necessary first step before drying or smoking. *A product may be safely cured without smoking, but a product should never be smoked without curing.*

Any charcuterie product, except one intended for immediate consumption such as fresh breakfast sausage, must be fully cured to avoid spoilage. The curing compound may be a dry mixture or a wet brine solution (also called a pickling solution). To be successful, a cure must have an adequate amount of evenly distributed curing ingredients and sufficient time to complete the chemical process. Seasonings such as herbs and spices are usually incorporated with the curing elements. **Remember that the two premixed compounds, Prague powders #1 and #2, are *not* interchangeable.** It is critical to measure curing ingredients accurately and to observe sanitation practices throughout the curing process.

WET CURES

Corned beef, bacon, and ham are some of the best-known products that are made with wet cures. Prague powder #1, a compound of salt and sodium nitrite, is used in wet cures. Before using, it is generally mixed with dry seasonings and additional salt as directed in a recipe.

To make a wet brine, mix the dry ingredients into a liquid and stir well to dissolve thoroughly; the brine will be not only worthless but dangerous unless the full amount of cure ingredients are dissolved. A brine must be agitated to prevent the solids from settling out of solution. Always check for settled material on the bottom of any wet cure container as you empty it; add it to the rest of the batch at once.

The simplest way to apply a liquid cure is to soak the meat in the brine, turning it from time to time. For larger items such as hams, bacon, and large birds, the soak method must be combined with an injection technique that pumps the brine directly into the meat. Because proper placement of the needles is important with this method, knowledge of the animals' anatomy is necessary. A variation of the injection technique is arterial pumping; this method uses the arteries and veins as conduits for the curing solution. Meats may be pumped as often as twice a day during the cure period; reliable recipes will indicate the appropriate method and frequency.

Small kitchens find a single-needle injector useful, but large commercial operations spray pump with multiple-needle injectors. This fast, automated procedure accomplishes complete and even saturation.

Wet Brine Formula

2 oz Prague powder #1

8 oz canning or kosher salt

5 qt simmering water (or other liquid)

Appropriate seasonings

This formula makes a good basic brine and is sufficient for 25 pounds of meat. Use it on various meats for products like Canadian bacon that will be fully cooked after curing. You can make a different amount of brine, but always use the same proportions of Prague powder, salt, and water.

Because a wet cure can be vulnerable to bacterial contamination, we strongly advise against reusing any brines. The curing process will dilute and exhaust a brine, and it will not be effective for multiple uses.

DRY CURES

Throughout history, military rations have depended on many dry-cured meats; beef jerky is a centuries-old example. Dry cures are fast and efficient for fish that is going to be smoked; wet cures cause fish to lose flavor, color, and texture.

Mix Prague powder #2, a compound of salt with sodium nitrite and sodium nitrate, with the seasonings and additional salt called for in the recipe. It is as important to thoroughly mix a dry cure as it is to thoroughly dissolve a wet cure. A standard commercial mixer performs this task very efficiently with the paddle at low speed. Run the machine long enough to ensure complete mixing; take care not to inhale dust particles.

Some of the dry mixture is often rubbed by hand into the surface of the meat or fish. (Of course, a salmon will get a more gentle rub than a side of bacon.) To fully expose the product to the cure, it is then surrounded with the remaining cure mixture and refrigerated in a packing box for the prescribed time. A different method is used for salamis and similar sausages; the dry mixture is spread throughout the ground sausage meat before stuffing, often using ice water as the carrier for the cure. Using water that is truly ice cold (33–35°F or 1–2°C) will help prevent smearing, an undesirable mixing of the fatty particles with the lean portion of the mix. It will also keep the sausage meat at a safe temperature during the mixing. Some warming, due to the friction of processing, is to be expected; rechill the mixture before proceeding.

Dry Cure Formula

2 oz Prague powder #2

12 oz canning or kosher salt

6 oz dextrose or brown sugar

This general dry cure formula is enough for 25 pounds of meat. Add a suitable amount of herbal seasonings such as bay leaf, thyme, marjoram, and allspice.

OTHER CURING METHODS

Marination, the oldest method of flavoring and tenderizing meat, is accomplished by means of a raw or a cooked solution. Cooked marinades are recommended, especially for fresh game such as venison or moose. The formula below will make 1 pint, enough to marinate meat for six portions:

Marinade

6 oz carrots

12 oz onions

Peppercorns, parsley stalks, thyme, bay leaf

¼ pt vinegar

¾ pt red wine

2 oz vegetable or virgin olive oil

For Raw Marinade: Combine ingredients and pour over meat in a container of inert material. Marinate 2–3 days in the refrigerator, turning meat every 8 hours.

For Cooked Marinade: Combine ingredients in a pan of stainless steel or other inert material; simmer for at least 1 hour. Add fresh liquid to bring the volume back to 1 pint. Pour the hot marinade over meat; cool and refrigerate. The heat of the cooked marinade speeds the process. Small pieces of meat will be ready in 5 hours; marinate larger pieces for 24 hours.

Oil and vinegar can be used successfully as a marinade for meat, fish, and fowl. Many flavor variations are possible by adding herbs and seasonings to made-from-scratch (or commercially prepared) dressings. A good ratio to use is three parts oil to one part vinegar. If you always record the formula as you make a dressing, it will be easy to duplicate or modify your recipes.

A unique *oriental marinade* can be made from teriyaki sauce, sake, pineapple juice, and turmeric. Soak fish briefly in a marinade like this before making fish sausage; this is one of several outstanding ways to handle fish in the sausage kitchen.

Carbonnade, a beer marinade, gives sausage great flavor. An early reference to this practice is mentioned in a letter from medieval England at the time of Richard I. It describes the "soaking of scrawny beef" in malted ale. Just as French and Italian sausages call for a wine marinade, many German and Austrian sausages call for beer. Carbonnades enjoy limited favor today, but they can be delicious and should be in every sausage maker's repertoire. Choose a flavorful malt beer, ale, or stout for meat and poultry; use a light lager for fish. This is not the place for "lite" beer. Cut the meat in reasonably small pieces; you need only enough beer to cover. Heavy cuts of pork and beef need about 24 hours to become tender and well-flavored; thinner and more delicate meats and fish will require less time. Experiment to establish the timetable necessary for the end result you want. One Swedish chef soaks herring in beer for only 30 minutes to get the flavor he wants before grilling it; it's delicious with hot dill mustard, new potatoes, and buttered savoy cabbage.

Sausage of *Jugged Hare* is another traditional dish from the past that can be successfully made today. You must clean and skin a young, freshly killed hare or rabbit; carefully retain the blood and hold it in the refrigerator. Soak the hare in wine for 6 hours, refrigerated, and then strip the meat from the bones. Use the meat to prepare the Rabbit Sausage on page 208. To make a sauce, add the marinade wine to a thin demi-glace and reduce by half; thicken with the reserved blood. Strain the sauce, and serve it with the grilled sausage.

CURING PORK

Even though trichinosis has been almost eradicated, many of the cases that still occur are traced to improperly cured sausage products (usually due to nonprofessional processing). The chemical action of a properly applied cure will effectively eliminate the danger of the trichina larva. Consequently, we must take special care in the curing of pork. For full safety, always follow recipe procedures and use the indicated amounts of curing ingredients. As a general guideline, a cure mixture should contain 2½ teaspoons of Prague powder #2 for each 10 pounds of fresh pork.

HAMS

An excellent ham may be the most distinctive of all cured products, the mark of a master charcutier. Hams may be delicate or robust, and they are eaten raw, braised, boiled, and roasted. They are universally popular in both haute cuisine and everyday fare. The *Larousse Gastronomique* credits the French with being the first to salt and smoke pork to make ham;

something so good spread quickly, and today almost every pork-eating region of the world has its own variety of ham. Many different curing, seasoning, and smoking methods produce myriad tastes, textures, and colors.

Hams, like bacon, can be made with either a wet or dry cure. The dry cure is hand-rubbed into hams, and they are cured for no less than 45 days before being smoked. Although the flavor and quality of dry-cured hams is second to none, today the wet cure is more popular, partly to reduce the potential for spoilage. The deep interior of the ham near the bone is prone to spoil; often the aitchbone and the lower thigh bone are removed to minimize this risk. But with either bone-in or boneless ham, the deep penetration provided by the brine pump needles ensures that the cure solution is distributed throughout the meat. This gives optimal flavor and quality to the wet-cured ham. Because a ham is pumped several times with solution, it will lose virtually no weight during the cure period.

The words "water added" on a ham may indicate that a solution of water, disodium phosphate, and ascorbic compounds has been pumped into the ham. By law, it may be added to bring the ham to 110 percent of its weight; when the ham is subsequently smoked, this extra weight becomes the shrink. The ham, in effect, finishes at its original weight, boosting its profitability. This device is widely used by large packing operations.

After curing, the hams should be soaked in cold water for 15 hours, then thoroughly air-dried before smoking and wrapping for cold storage.

Curing Data

Product	Country of Origin	Cure Used	Cure and Smoke Process Time
Bacon, Canadian	Canada	Wet cure	16 days
Bacon, Pea-Meal	Canada	Wet cure, hand rubbed	16 days
Beef, Corned	Universal	Wet cure, hand rubbed	16 days
Beef, Dried	Europe United States	Wet cure Dry cure	15 days 50 days
Capicola	Italy	Wet cure	48 days
Gammon Rashers	Ireland England	Dry/wet cure	14 days
Pastrami	Italy	Wet cure	16 days
Slowina Papkrykowa	Poland	Wet cure	16 days
Venison Jerky	Europe United States	Dry cure	30 days

Ham Curing Data

Product	Country of Origin	Cure Used	Cure and Smoke Process Time
Beer Ham (Scotch Ham)	France	Wet cure	50 days
Country Ham (Jambon de Campagne)	France	Dry cure	50 days
Italian Ham	Italy	Wet cure Dry cure	14 days 60 days
Parisian Ham	France	Wet cure	10 days
Parma Ham	Italy	Dry cure	60 days
Prosciutto	Italy	Dry cure	50 days
Roscrea Ham	Ireland	Wet cure	14 days
Shinkenspeck Ham, Bacon	Germany England	Wet cure	12 days
Smithfield Ham	United States	Dry cure	60 days
Virginia Ham	United States	Dry cure	Up to 50 days
Westphalian Ham	Germany	Dry cure, rub in	50 days

CHAPTER

5

Hot and Cold Smoking

Cooking or drying with wood smoke is the finishing touch for many charcuterie items. It is an ancient and universal way to flavor and preserve food. Smoking improves flavor, aroma, color, and texture. Because smoking is always combined with a curing process, it helps to preserve food and extend its keeping quality. If you are new to smoking, start with a simple recipe like andouille. As you gain experience, move on to more complex preparations such as hams and salamis. Always carry out the smoking in a well-ventilated area.

Foods that are *cold smoked* are smoked at very low temperatures to prevent them from cooking. Products that are *hot smoked* are processed at higher temperatures so they are cooked during the smoking process. Smoking is usually preceded by or combined with a period of air drying.

AIR DRYING

Charcuterie products are hung to air dry in an environment of controlled temperature and humidity. The drying time may be an hour or two, or it may last for several weeks. Some meats are smoked only at the end of this period, while others require smoke from start to finish.

This process causes several desirable changes in a product: moisture is lost, first from the surface and then, more slowly, from the interior; the cure matures and finishes; some fermentation occurs; and flavors have time to blend and mellow. Drying prepares certain items for the smoking process; a thin skin, or pellicle, forms which helps the product acquire the proper smoke finish. Some products such as jerky and genoa are not smoked. They are ready to be eaten after an extended air drying which gives them their traditional texture, flavor, and appearance.

57

Drying can be accomplished in the refrigerator or the smoker. Because ambient temperature and relative humidity vary seasonally and geographically, these factors are easier to control in a closed environment. This will achieve consistent results for every batch. The capacity of the refrigerator or smoker must not be overloaded; to provide adequate air circulation, hang products so that pieces do not touch each other. Keep drying products well away from other refrigerated foods to avoid cross contamination and transfer of flavors and aromas.

Although drying may sound easy, it's important to follow recipe directions carefully. The details about time, temperature, and damper adjustments will guide you around potential problems. For example, moisture will be blocked inside a sausage whose case has been hardened by being dried too quickly. On the other hand, mold will appear on the surface of a product if the drying rate is too slow. Both situations will create products that are inferior, if not totally unusable.

COLD SMOKING

The cold smoke method, which does not cook the product, is used primarily for items that have been preserved with a dry cure. In this method, the smoking is less important to the preservation than the cure, but it contributes color, aroma, and flavor. Before refrigeration, cold smoking was done only during the winter months, a custom practiced by many people including Native Americans, Norsemen, Saxons, and Celtic tribes in Ireland, Scotland, and Wales. If your smoker does not have adequate temperature controls, cold smoking during the winter months is still a good idea.

Smoked salmon is one of the most famous cold-smoked dishes. After dry curing, the salmon is typically hung in a cold smoker set at 70°F (21°C); the temperature is gradually raised to 90°F (32°C), the maximum temperature for cold smoking fish. At higher temperatures, the fish will cook; this will dry it out and ruin the texture. Although some smoked fish are also cooked, in general it is advisable to keep the smoker set at 90°F (32°C) or lower when processing fish.

Many meat products are cold smoked, and they can also be overcooked at too-high temperatures. Prosciutto di Parma and Westphalian are but two examples of cold-smoked hams; the temperature limit for cold smoking hams is 120°F (49°C).

Chorizos and pepperonis are examples of cold-smoked sausages. Sausages should be cold smoked at 65–90°F (18–32°C).

HOT SMOKING

The basic purpose of conventional or hot smoking is to impart flavor while simultaneously cooking the product. Hot smoking also coagulates the proteins near the surface of a sausage; this creates a physical barrier that protects the sausage and prevents mold from forming on the skin.

Smoking is a personal art, and you can make some changes if you prefer. For example, you can reduce the intensity of the smoke taste by reducing the smoking time. However, it is very important to fully cook the product to the temperature required by the recipe. A tolerance of plus-or-minus 5 degrees is implied in the recipes in this book. We stress this precision to assure safe and wholesome products.

Our experience has taught us that, when smoking, haste will indeed make waste. If there is any possibility of overheating, it is always better to reduce the smoker temperature and extend the process time accordingly.

THE SMOKER

The smokehouse unit is the most important factor in successful processing. The smoke must circulate evenly around the food. Time, temperature, and moisture are the three elements that must be regulated properly for good results. Precise temperature regulation is essential for the

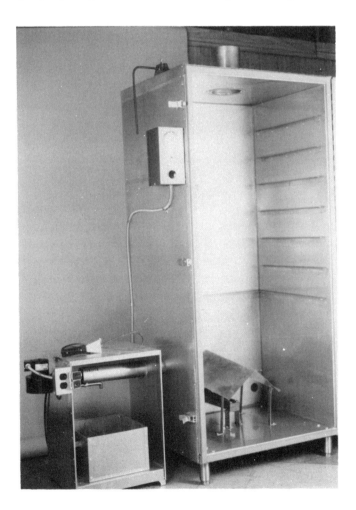

100-pound convection smoker. (Photo courtesy of The Sausage Maker, Buffalo, NY)

50-pound convection smoker. (Photo courtesy of The Sausage Maker, Buffalo, NY)

quality and safety of both hot-smoked and cold-smoked products. For this reason, we recommend using professional equipment obtained from an established supplier. Homemade or makeshift devices cannot give you the temperature control to process foods safely. Like other equipment, smokers are not all alike; with experience, you will use your judgment to adapt procedures to get the results you want from your smoker. Follow the manufacturer's directions.

If you have purchased a brand-new smoker, you must cure it before you use it. Break it in with medium-level smoke for 24 hours. This will give the equipment a fine smoke aroma, and it will be ready for the first batch of product.

The damper device, which regulates the flow of air, is one of the most important ways to control heat and moisture. Damper settings determine the efficiency of your processing, and this translates into wise use of your time and dollars. For instance, if the heat and moisture are

Standard 20-pound smoker. (Photo courtesy of The Sausage Maker, Buffalo, NY)

too high for a sausage like kielbasa, fat smearing can occur. The fat bleeds into the lean meat, and the sausage will be wrinkled, greasy, and overcooked. In our recipes, we emphasize the damper settings in relation to the temperature; check the instructions and use the damper with care. Keep complete notes about damper settings and file them with your recipes.

Countless woods are used for smoking. Some examples are apple, cedar, cherry, hickory, lime, mesquite, oak, orange, rose, and willow. Some regions are known for unique smoking materials such as swamp wood and burlap bags in Louisiana Cajun country and camphor trees in India. We especially prefer apple, cherry, hickory, mesquite, and oak. Wood must be aged for at least 2 to 3 months before it is used as smoker fuel. Some woods, like mesquite, burn very hot; to maintain even temperatures, it must be carefully watched and moistened frequently. Oak and apple burn slowly and are easier to control with the damper device and an occasional spray of water.

STEPS FOR SMOKING

- Check the smoker for leaks and mechanical problems before each use.
- Preheat smoker manually or automatically.
- Bring the product to room temperature, then hang it in the smoker.
- Ignite the dry wood, then adjust dampers for a slow and steady smoke.
- Frequently check the temperature of the product in several areas of the chamber.
- Moisten the wood with a cold water spray if it flares or burns too hot.
- Be prepared to spray the product from time to time after it has reached the desired internal temperature or if it becomes too hot.
- Remove the product from the smoker. If the recipe calls for it, give the sausages a cold water shower. This will improve the appearance of the sausage by shrinking loose casings and removing any external fatty deposits. Do not shower salamis and other hard sausages which develop a characteristic bloom like the rind on a Brie cheese.

    Repair any air pockets in the sausages before a cold water shower by pricking them. If air pockets persist after the shower, they can be repaired again by dropping them in hot water; remove at once and the skins will shrink back onto the sausages.

PAN SMOKING

In most kitchens, a large smoker is not available. It is possible to smoke small items for immediate use with the following standard kitchen equipment: one 4-inch deep hotel pan and cover, one cake rack to fit inside the hotel pan, and four metal Bavarian molds. Lay 8 ounces of dampened wood shavings on the bottom of the hotel pan and ignite. Place one mold in each corner and put the lightly oiled cake rack on top of them. When the wood starts to smolder and smoke, put the food on the rack, cover with the lid, and place in a preheated 300°F (149°C) oven. Cook and smoke the food, checking the internal temperature. This pan can accommodate about eight chicken breasts or halibut filets.

CHAPTER

6

Traditional Charcuterie

"**W**ho does *that* anymore?" is a question we occasionally hear about traditional charcuterie. "Anyone who seeks the pleasure and distinction of making outstanding haute cuisine dishes," is our response. Highly specialized and admired, these preparations call for skill, creativity, and attention to detail. National and international culinary competitions have improved both the products and their presentations. Although elegant, these recipes were very labor-intensive in the past; they are less so today, thanks to recent technical innovations such as powerful food processors that make light work of the most demanding tasks. We have chosen to highlight only a few of the traditional dishes, especially terrines and pâtés, to serve as an introduction to classical terms, techniques, and ingredients. We hope working with these recipes will engender an appreciation of the charcutiers of the past and a desire to perpetuate this classic artistry.

FORCEMEATS

Forcemeats are nearly infinite in number and variety. Most often, they are made of meat (with a certain percentage of fat), but forcemeats can also be made of poultry, fish, and vegetables. Depending on the recipe, the forcemeat ingredients are chopped, minced, finely ground, or puréed. A mousseline is a very fine, creamy forcemeat.

    Classic forcemeats are seasoned with a wide variety of herbs and spices. Whole spices such as green peppercorns add texture, flavor, and eye appeal. A persillade, chopped parsley with onion and garlic, is often used to season a terrine. Wine and spirits such as brandy can contribute to the complexity of flavors.

A forcemeat can be bound with various sauces such as a thick béchamel. A starch paste called a panada, made from flour, bread, rice, or potatoes, is a common binder for forcemeat. The starch is cooked, sieved, and mixed until very smooth with milk, cream, and sometimes eggs. The usual ratio is two parts main ingredient to one part panada.

After the forcemeat has been assembled and seasoned, it should be tested for taste and texture before being used. Make a small dumpling and cook it. Taste it and correct the seasoning of the forcemeat accordingly. Then proceed with the recipe. Remember, once the forcemeat has been cooked in a terrine or pâté, the seasoning cannot be changed.

FATS AND BUTTER

The superb products of classic charcuterie rely on a certain amount of fat and butter. We recommend that you become familiar with the classic recipes and their traditional ingredients before you try to alter a recipe to reduce the fat content. We believe that moderate consumption of the traditional dishes is the best policy. Stay mindful of genuine health concerns as you strive to make excellent products.

Pork Fatback: Thin strips of fatback are used to garnish the forcemeat or line a terrine or pâté mold. In addition to enhancing flavor and texture, they add a haute cuisine finish to a slice of terrine.

Pork Caul Fat: The caul is a membrane, the mesentery, from the abdominal cavity of a hog. It is very useful for wrapping sausages and forcemeats because it shrinks onto the meat when cooked. It is laced with high-quality white fat which protects and flavors the meat. It has been used extensively over the years in French and Italian cuisines, less so in Britain, Canada, and the United States.

Veal and Beef Fat: These two fats are used extensively in garde-manger work, in forcemeats, as garnish, and for tallow sculpture. Some of the finest lard is made from veal and beef fat.

Chicken and Duck Fat: We highly recommend these fats as they add very rich flavor to a product.

Butter: Butter's superb flavor, aroma, and texture cannot be surpassed, and it will give you reliably uniform results. If you decide that you must replace some or all of the butter, there are some acceptable substitutes with reduced cholesterol and fewer saturated fats. This may require formula changes because margarines and oils do not behave exactly like butter; you may find that products are greasy or that your sauces break more easily. Expect to do some trial-and-error adjustments until you get the results you want.

TERRINES

Meat Terrines

A terrine, often constructed in layers for visual effect, is made from seasoned forcemeat. It is molded in an ovenproof earthenware or china vessel ("terrine" means a container made of earthenware). Nuts, meats, vegetables, or fats may be added for contrasting texture, flavor, and color. Although we use a terrine for a buffet or elegant mirror work today, it was originally an everyday meal of the poor, made from tough cuts of meat, trimming scraps, and fat. Because terrines require much handling and processing, the ingredients must be very fresh; food-handling rules are especially important.

The mold is usually lined, first with standard plastic wrap, then with an appropriate food such as ham, poultry, fish, fatback, caul fat, or vegetable paste. The main element of the terrine, the forcemeat, is then added. Whole pieces or strips of appropriate garnish may be layered with the forcemeat. The lining and plastic wrap are folded over the top to seal in the contents. To settle the ingredients and prevent air pockets from ruining the finished terrine, tap it lightly several times on the table. The terrine is covered and baked in a deep water bath. After cooling, weight and refrigerate meat, game, and poultry terrines for a minimum of 24 hours to mellow and mature the flavors and to develop the proper texture. To allow for this aging, it is wise to start meat terrines several days before you need them. Meat terrines are served cold.

The terrine may be served directly from its container or removed and presented more formally. To unmold the terrine easily, surround it with warm wet towels for several minutes; turn out and remove the plastic wrap. Decorate and finish with aspic or chaudfroid sauce, then chill to set. Slice the terrine, leaving some unsliced for display. Put the unsliced piece on a serving platter and fan the slices around it in a decorative manner.

Terrine forcemeats can easily be made into small balls or dumplings which are poached or gently sautéed. They make fine borders or garnish for platter presentations, and can add a classic touch to soups or broths. This is an excellent way to use up any leftover forcemeat.

Fish and Seafood Terrines

These terrines are known for their delicate flavor, silky texture, and subtle pastel colors. A typical forcemeat is made by blending one or more kinds of fish with seasonings, panada, cream, eggs, and butter. It is much lighter and smoother than a meat or game forcemeat. More than one forcemeat may be used; an attractive pattern can be designed with forcemeats of contrasting colors, such as salmon and sole. Fish filets and whole shellfish are often used as garnish to create decorative patterns in a terrine.

We recommend thoroughly cooking and then freezing the fish or shellfish to be used as garnish. Assemble the terrine by layering the frozen pieces in a raw forcemeat, and then bake as usual. By the time the forcemeat is cooked, the frozen garnish pieces will be thawed. This method allows both the garnish and the forcemeat to be completely cooked, but not overcooked and dried out.

Use the same technique to achieve a decorative effect of one forcemeat surrounded by another of a different color. Cook one forcemeat in a small mold. Cool, unmold, and then freeze. Prepare the terrine and fill with the second (raw) forcemeat. Embed the frozen piece in the raw forcemeat and bake as usual. After chilling, the texture will be smooth and the two colors will be nicely separated.

Fish terrines are often garnished with fresh herbs and vegetables. Herbs can bleed color into a forcemeat. Wash and chop them very fine; then squeeze them gently in a tammy cloth to remove excess moisture. To prevent vegetables from smearing in the same way, blanch them before puréeing. This will set the color in the vegetable fibers.

Refrigerate cold fish terrines 24 hours before serving. This allows the flavors to mellow and improves the texture for slicing. Fish terrines are not weighted while they chill.

Vegetable Terrines

The best vegetable terrines convey a very natural, fresh, and delicate impression. They may be made of one or several vegetables; use care and imagination to combine flavors successfully. Use only the freshest high-quality vegetables. As before, blanch to fix the vegetables' colors. Vegetable forcemeats can be made with panadas, mousselines, or just bread and eggs.

An imaginative vegetable terrine can be made in the shape of its main ingredient. Countless vegetables can be used for garnish and decoration, but be sure to use only natural and edible items. Unlike meat terrines, vegetable terrines do not benefit from aging for several days. Twenty-four hours is usually enough time to improve the texture and make slicing easier.

PÂTÉS

Pâtés and terrines are both made from forcemeat, and they share a common ancestry. Although the words are often used interchangeably, a *terrine* is forcemeat that is baked in a dish (a terrine). *Pâté* often refers to the forcemeat itself which may be used in various preparations. It especially describes forcemeat that is baked in a pastry crust (which may also be called *pâté en croûte*). To make it even more confusing, the menu item *pâté à la maison* may mean a hot or cold item of meat, fish, or vegetable that is baked with or without pastry.

The pastry used to wrap a pâté must be able to withstand a lot of handling. Some chefs like a hot water paste, others prefer a cold water paste; either will give you good results. To make a pâté en croûte, line a traditional tinplate pâté mold with the pastry and fill with the prepared forcemeat. Be sure the lining has no rips or tears. Moisten the sealing surfaces of the lining and the top crust. Put the top crust into position without delay, and seal by crimping the edges with a decorative design. To allow steam to escape during baking, cut three or four vents in the top crust and fit in small funnels made of aluminum foil (or use pastry bag tips). Working the vent holes into the overall design, decorate the pâté with pieces cut from pastry scraps; secure the decorative pieces with water or egg wash. Brush the whole top crust with egg wash, and bake.

After cooking and cooling, a gap will exist between the top of the meat and the crust. Use the vent holes to fill the interior with a savory aspic. When the pâté has been chilled, the slices will be solid meat and aspic from top to bottom. Similar to a terrine, give the pâté time to mature by aging it in the refrigerator. Always serve it cold.

RAISED PIES

Throughout the centuries, especially during the Hundred Years' War, the French and English cultures intermingled, and they became familiar with each other's food, drink, and customs. Over time, French game pâtés became English raised pies, and English herbs were introduced into French foods. The most famous raised pies today are certainly English, but they seem to share a common history with some modern French specialties.

English raised pies, served hot or cold, are commonly made of pork, veal, ham, or game wrapped in pastry or brioche dough. The fillings and pastry can include herbs, nuts, spices, and vegetables. A fresh leafy salad contrasts with the rich pie, and the combination makes a splendid meal.

CHAPTER
7

Sauces

A well-chosen and properly made sauce can transform a good food product into an extraordinary one. However, if it's the wrong sauce or if it's poorly made, it will ruin even the best dish. So we must learn more about the basic sauces and how to use them.

We can describe *sauce* as a hot or cold thickened liquid that moistens food, enhances its appearance, and adds flavor. The flavor of the sauce may *harmonize* or *contrast* with the dish; both are acceptable. This makes selecting a sauce even more interesting and challenging.

Where and when did sauces originate? References to sauces turn up in ancient Greek writing such as Homer's *Iliad* and in descriptions of lavish Roman feasts. But it was not until the seventeenth century that the word *saucier* appeared and the separate art of sauce-making began to emerge. Auguste Escoffier, the grand master of the early twentieth century, organized sauce recipes in a precise way that is still useful for the *saucier* of today.

Sauces that appeal to the eye and to the palate will add a wonderful touch to your fine products; they are well worth the modest investment of time and effort. To maximize your success with sauces, use only fresh ingredients and clarified stocks. Always use clean pots and utensils. Never use a metal whip in an aluminum pot; a white sauce will turn gray. It is best to use pans and utensils of inert materials such as stainless steel, ceramic, porcelain, or glass. As always, follow the recipes carefully.

SAUCE THICKENERS

We describe five basic thickening agents for sauces: roux, vegetable starches, eggs, beurre manié, and blood. We have not included *"reduction"* in this list because this term describes a process rather than an ingredient. A reduction is made by boiling a liquid to decrease the quantity. This concentrates flavors and thickens the liquid to sauce consistency.

68

Roux

Roux, a mixture of flour and fat, is basic to many fine sauces. The fat may be butter, oil, or margarine; in the past, even rendered animal fats were widely accepted. To make a roux, heat the fat until it sizzles and blend in the flour. Cook, stirring, until the roux reaches the desired color. There are three degrees of color used for sauces—white, blond, and brown.

White Roux: Cook the roux for only a few minutes; it must remain white. It is used to make the basic white sauce, béchamel.

Blond Roux: Cook the roux until the flour becomes very lightly browned or blond. This roux is used in velouté sauces, tomato sauce, and many Italian sauces.

Brown Roux: This roux is cooked until it turns nut brown. Brown roux is very versatile and used primarily for Sauce Espagnole, the base for the great meat sauces.

Roux can be cooled and refrigerated for later use. To avoid making a lumpy and watery sauce, always add cold liquid to a hot roux or hot liquid to a cooled roux. Fully cook the sauce for the prescribed time to develop a desirable sheen and a translucent quality. Consistency is a critical factor; a properly cooked sauce will lightly coat the back of a spoon so that you can see the metal through the sauce. This allows the food beneath the sauce to be seen.

Vegetable Starches

Cornstarch, arrowroot, and tapioca are typical thickeners made from vegetable starches. Arrowroot, used to make delicate gravies and sauces, gives the best results. When used properly, it is almost neutral; it is sometimes added to speed a reduction process. Slurries, simple but effective mixtures of starch and water, have been widely used in the past. A slurry of flour and water known as "Liverpool roux" was extensively used during World War II when butter and oils were in short supply.

Eggs

Eggs are the thickening agent for hot and cold emulsion sauces such as hollandaise, mayonnaise, and their variations. To encourage the eggs to produce the maximum amount of sauce, add liquids or oils to the eggs very slowly. These sauces are losing favor due to concern about dietary cholesterol and the harmful bacteria that may be present in raw eggs, but there is still a place for them in the repertoire of the charcutier. A grilled Italian sausage with béarnaise is always appreciated, and the mayonnaise sauces are excellent condiments for sausages and pâtés.

Beurre Manié

"Kneaded butter" is equal amounts of butter and flour worked with the fingers to make a soft paste that is, in essence, an uncooked roux. Small amounts are whisked into sauces, gravies, and soups to finish and adjust the thickness. Although use of this thickener seems to be diminishing, it can be very convenient to have on hand, especially during hectic service hours. Don't overlook beurre manié as a practical way to "fine tune" your sauces.

Blood

When blood is added to a warm liquid, it will thicken quickly and effectively as the protein coagulates; it will make a very fine sauce. Be sure to fully cook and strain a blood sauce. It is the only thickener used in many game sauces.

SELECTED SAUCES

We recommend the following sauces because they are especially well suited to the recipes in this book. Try some of these sauces and then branch out; look for other sauces that will enhance your creations.

Albert: Butter sauce with poached horseradish, cream, and bread crumbs. Boil, strain, and mix with egg yolks, mustard, and vinegar. Serve with cured meats, poultry, and all types of smoked sausages.

Albuféra: Sauce Suprême finished with pimento butter. Serve with cured pork products, smoked turkey, and other poultry offerings.

Allemande: Reduced velouté with eggs, lemon juice, and (a) tomato paste, or (b) mushroom purée and cream. Season to taste with lemon or nutmeg. This thick sauce is also used as a coating for deep-frying such items as faggots, rissoles, and kebabs.

Anchois: Normandy sauce with anchovy paste. Serve with fish sausages and pâtés.

Apple: Apples cooked soft with sugar and cloves. Especially recommended for pork products.

Aspic: Flavored gelatin used to coat pâtés and terrines.

Bâtarde (Butter Sauce): Made from a white roux and water, this sauce is bound with butter and optional egg yolks, seasoned with salt and lemon juice, and strained. It can be modified with herbs or capers and is thus very versatile; fine on fish and seafood products.

Béarnaise: Hollandaise variation; in place of lemon juice, substitute a reduction of vinegar, wine, shallot, tarragon, and pepper. Strain and finish with chopped tarragon and chervil. This is one of the best sauces to serve with grilled meats, poached fish, chicken, and hot pâtés.

Bercy: Sautéed shallots reduced with white wine and fish, chicken, or veal stock, and topped with butter. Serve with fish or meats.

Bigarade: Reduced duck gravy with orange and lemon juices, thickened with arrow-root. Several variations make it quite useful. Serve hot with game birds such as teal, wild duck, and turkey.

Bordelaise: Demi-glace mixed with a strained reduction of red wine, shallots, thyme, pepper, and bay leaf. Serve with any red meat, venison, or grilled smoked ham.

Caper: Sauce Bâtarde with capers and cream. Serve with veal, fish, pork, and sausages.

Cardinal: Béchamel sauce with fish glaze, truffle, lobster, and cayenne pepper. Serve with hot fish products.

Champignon: Demi-glace with sautéed button mushrooms.

Charcutière: Sauce Robert with julienne of gherkins. Serve with spiced sausages and meats.

Chasseur: Reduction of shallots, tarragon, and minced mushrooms added to a demi-glace. Finish with tomato concassée and chopped parsley. Serve with all types of game, grills, sautés, and braises.

Chateaubriand: Sauté of shallots, mushroom trimmings, thyme, and bay leaf, reduced with white wine and added to a demi-glace. Finish with tarragon butter and chopped parsley. Serve with grilled sausages, meats, chops, and steaks.

Chevreuil (Venison): Mirepoix and game meat trimmings sautéed in butter, reduced with red wine, and mixed with **Sauce Poivrade**. Strain and finish with cayenne pepper. Serve with all game sausages and warm pâtés.

Chevreuil (Roebuck Sauce): Paysanne of onion and ham, lightly colored in butter. Add vinegar and reduce; mix with demi-glace and add red currant jelly. Serve with smoked venison and all game and hot sausages.

Choron: Sauce Béarnaise finished with tomato purée. Serve with all fish sausages.

Cumberland: Red currant jelly dissolved in port wine and garnished with blanched shallots, orange zest, and lemon juice. Add mustard, cayenne pepper, and ground ginger. This traditional game and sausage sauce is also excellent for cold pâtés.

Curry: Velouté made with various stocks. The level of heat can be changed to taste. Serve this versatile sauce hot or cold with all types of meats and fish.

Diable: Reduction of chopped shallots, black pepper, white wine, and vinegar; demi-glace and chopped parsley. Serve this spicy sauce with all sausages. When made with a tomato demi-glace, it is an excellent accompaniment for hot Italian sausage. The commercial brand Sauce Escoffier is a diable sauce.

Estragon: (a) Thickened gravy with chopped tarragon; or (b) velouté with tarragon purée, finished with chopped tarragon. Serve with English raised pies, hot pâtés, and white sausages.

Fennel Sauce: Beurre blanc with diced fennel. Serve with smoked pastrami.

Fines Herbes: Demi-glace with an infusion of fines herbes. After straining, add finely chopped fines herbes. This sauce is delicious with corned beef, baked ham, and kielbasa.

Fish Velouté: Our choice with any hot fish pâté.

Génoise: Mayonnaise made with a base of herbs, almonds, and pistachios. Serve to advantage with cold sausages and pâtés.

Gloucester: Mayonnaise with sour cream, fennel, and **Sauce Diable** (Sauce Escoffier). Serve with cold meat and poultry dishes.

Gooseberry: Uncooked purée of sweetened gooseberries finished with apple cider. This has a tantalizing affinity for smoked fish and meats.

Grand Veneur: Sauce Poivrade with a venison stock reduction. Add red currant jelly and cream. Serve this full-flavored sauce with game sausages and meats.

Gratin: Fish stock demi-glace with a reduction of white wine, shallots, duxelles, and finely chopped parsley; fine with game, fish, and most pâtés.

Gribiche: Mayonnaise with cooked egg yolks and mustard; garnish with gherkins, capers, chervil, and fresh tarragon. Finish with julienne of cooked egg white. May accompany cold meats, fish, and sausages.

Hachée: Fish velouté with anchovy paste and cream. Serve with poached seafood sausage, fish pâté, or terrine.

Hussarde: Diced shallots in a white wine reduction, demi-glace, raw chopped garlic, and ham. Cook for 30 minutes and strain. Garnish with brunoise of smoked ham, fine julienne of horseradish root, and chopped parsley. This textured sauce is wonderful with mettwurst, jagwurst, or any grilled smoked sausage.

Lyonnaise: Sliced onions lightly fried in butter, deglazed with white wine, mixed into a demi-glace, and strained. We highly recommend this adaptable sauce; serve with grilled sausages or smoked venison.

Madeira: Demi-glace with Madeira wine; satisfying when served with grilled ham and roasted meats.

Mayonnaise à la Russe: Mayonnaise with tarragon vinegar and horseradish. A soft aspic is whipped in for consistency. Serve with cold meats, especially chicken and turkey pâtés.

Mousquétaire: Mayonnaise with chopped, blanched shallots in a reduction of white wine. Cayenne pepper and a touch of meat glaze further enhance this sauce. Garnish with chopped chives and parsley. Serve with dressed crab and cold lobster; it can also accompany chicken terrines, cold fish, or meat pâtés.

Nantua: Fish velouté with sautéed crayfish, burnt brandy, tomato purée, and cream. Serve with fish pâtés and sausages.

Paloise: Béarnaise with a reduction of mint instead of tarragon.

Piquante: Chopped shallots, reduced in wine vinegar, added to a demi-glace and sieved. Garnish with gherkins, chervil, tarragon, and finely ground black pepper. Can be served with many sausages and smoked meats; highly recommended.

Poivrade: Mirepoix lightly sautéed with game trimmings previously marinated in wine vinegar. Add to demi-glace and cook gently for 30 minutes. Strain and serve with grilled or roasted meats.

Porto: Demi-glace and port wine reduced until rather thick. Serve this rich sauce with game charcuterie.

Portugaise: Sautéed onions and tomato concassée with garlic, added to a thin tomato sauce with glace de viande. Cook lightly, and serve with fish, pork, and other meats.

Raifort: Fold together whipped cream and freshly grated horseradish root with some fresh lemon juice; excellent served with any cold meat or fish preparation.

Rémoulade: Mayonnaise with mustard, capers, parsley, chervil, gherkins, and tarragon. Finish with anchovy paste. This well-known cold sauce accompanies many foods.

Robert: Cook chopped onions in butter and add white wine to reduce. Combine with demi-glace and finish with dry mustard. Serve with grilled meats and game.

Romaine: Light caramel dissolved with vinegar and game stock. Add demi-glace, reduce, and strain. Garnish with pine nuts and plumped sultanas at time of service. This sauce is wonderful served with grilled venison sausage.

Rouennaise: Sauce Bordelaise and raw duck livers. Cook to blend, then pass through a fine strainer. Add lemon juice, pepper, and a reduction of red wine and chopped shallots. Sauces game or other hearty sausage very well.

Russe: Mayonnaise with caviar purée, lobster meat, and mustard. **Sauce Diable** (Sauce Escoffier) is added at time of service. Serve with cold fish pâtés and terrines.

Salmis: Mirepoix sautéed with game carcasses, skin, and trimmings. Add wine and reduce; add demi-glace. Cook to thicken, strain, and finish with butter. Serve with smoked game fowl.

Solférino: Glace de viande whisked with shallots and maître d'hôtel butter. Add tomato essence and cayenne pepper, and finish with lemon juice to taste. This is outstanding with Italian sausage or in a pepperoni pie.

Suédoise: Mayonnaise with apple purée and grated horseradish; great to serve with cold pork or turkey products.

Tartare (American version): Mayonnaise with chopped capers, gherkins, parsley, and shallots.

Tartare (original version): Mayonnaise with chopped egg yolks, diced onions, and chives. Both sauces are widely known and appreciated; serve with fish and salads.

Verte: Mayonnaise with a purée of blanched herbs such as spinach, watercress, parsley, chervil, and tarragon. Pass through a sieve and serve with a variety of fish and meats.

Yorkshire: Combine Sauce Espagnole and red currant jelly; add a touch of finely ground cinnamon and cayenne pepper. Simmer briefly; strain and add orange juice. Finish with orange zest that has been simmered in port wine. A wonderful, traditional sauce to accompany ham and duck.

Zingara: Tomato sauce and demi-glace with julienne of pickled tongue, ham, truffle, mushroom, and cayenne. Add a Madeira wine reduction and paprika. Serve warm, but do not boil the finished sauce. Serve with poultry and other mild-to-medium-flavored meat products.

PART TWO

Recipes

Common Links

Some of these tips apply to all sausages. Others are specific for only one type of sausage. Become familiar with them all. Just be sure to use them appropriately.

Understand and fully read each and every recipe. Never hesitate to ask for, or take time to research, the method that is presented. Small variations are always significant in sausage production. Never generalize from one familiar recipe to another. Secure and assemble all ingredients and equipment before starting the procedure. Follow every recipe carefully, realizing that time and temperature, along with very accurate measurement of all ingredients are the main keys to your success in production of an excellent product.

The use of cures containing sodium nitrate, sodium nitrite, and in fact, all other additives must be carefully undertaken. This translates to accuracy of measurement and complete adherence to curing times, temperatures, and procedures as outlined in any recipe. Strive always to assure rewarding, fully safe, and therefore profitable production at all times. Your success requires strictly following established culinary practice in all that you undertake.

Keep a permanent log of your timing and other procedures. This provides a useful, accurate record of equipment performance, and will make possible consistent excellence in all your products. Do this faithfully for all your sausage production.

Smoking

Smoking time is a very important factor in all sausage processing. It will generally vary from smoker to smoker. Optimum time, damper settings, and temperatures for smoking must be established *for your combinations of equipment* by the process of careful observation. Follow up your observation with accurate record keeping, combined with a thorough evaluation of the finished product. This added effort will soon establish excellent uniform quality and assure your full success.

Casings

All sausages must be properly linked, tied or clipped, for consumer satisfaction. If the casings are not perfect, the storage, cooking, and eating qualities of a sausage are seriously compromised. *The casing is the ultimate package.* It influences the total quality of the product. Be sure to select and use every casing and closure with thought and skill.

Grilling, Pan Frying, Sautéing, and Baking

Learn and practice good grilling and sauté procedures for cooking all link sausages. Grilling temperature should not be excessive. Many casing varieties cook to perfection if placed into the skillet with a small amount of water. Heat is then applied, and by the time the water has quickly evaporated, the sausage links have been uniformly heated. Very little additional time is then needed to brown them to perfection—without bursting or overcooking. We suggest starting at about 350°F (177°C).

Contrary to some instruction that has crept into the culinary literature and also into retail packaging of late, we do not recommend piercing the casings before grilling or pan frying. The marked flavor superiority of casing sausages is adversely affected by intentional destruction of the casing! Well-stuffed sausage products will not burst when cooked as described above.

Whenever possible, "cook to order." This holds true for all cooking methods. By arranging to avoid excessive holding time, you will greatly enhance overall appeal and eating qualities of all sausage products. For example, the many popular English fresh herb sausage varieties will greatly benefit from extra care and thought in their cooking and presentation.

To cook larger quantities, simply bake them on sheet trays in a moderate oven, set at 325°F (163°C) for 12 or 15 minutes. Most sausage varieties, when baked in this manner, do not require further attention or turning. Some varieties may be quickly and easily "marked" on a hot grill, then sheet-tray baked to fully finish cooking to satisfactory internal temperature. Oven cooking is very efficient, and should appeal to any busy chef

Poaching

Any recipe which specifies that the product be "poached in stock" implies that sufficient stock will be used to fully cover the product during such cooking. (Allowance should be made for some loss due to evaporation.) The exact quantity of stock will vary with the amount of sausage product and the cooking vessel used. Remember to record and make accurate note of such quantities, however, for your future quick reference.

The type of stock (chicken, beef, fish, etc.) to use for poaching will always be indicated in the recipe. Proper, gentle poaching calls for a bath in the 160°F (71°C) range for all pork/beef sausages, with 140°F (60°C) for fish and seafood sausages. Always maintain these lower temperatures to preserve taste and texture and to assure very best and most attractive finish of the product. Remember that poaching, as a production step or for final cooking or service, is always a gentle cooking. It is accomplished in a bath of water, stock, court bouillon, or other liquid. It should uniformly bring the sausage in the liquid to a required temperature. The bursting of casings, or various undesirable texture changes, will occur in products that are not properly poached. Note, and follow carefully, specific recipe recommendations for bath starting temperatures, total cooking time, and internal finishing temperatures.

Stuffing

Every sausage mixture you prepare must be kept well chilled during all steps of production. Frequently check the batch to maintain its temperature well below 40°F (4.4°C). Always complete full preparation of casings ahead of stuffing time. Casings should be kept supple, chilled, and properly moistened to assure efficient and proper stuffing. Stuffing is quick and easy. It is a reward for your effort, and many chefs consider it fun. Prechilled mixing tubs and other equipment will aid in maintaining a low temperature at all times.

Cooling after Smoking

A cold or hot water shower, upon removal of the product from the smoker, is called for in many recipes. This step is critical for high quality and best finish of the product. A very rapid cooling of the product is essential. This calls for cold water, and attention to full coverage of the sausages. When indicated, the hot water spray will remove fatty deposits on the casing. Major faults, including internal smearing and excessive wrinkling, are greatly reduced or fully eliminated by the careful, timely application of these showers.

Identifying Sausages

It should be easy to identify different varieties of sausages, in storage, while on the grill, or at the table. To do this, establish different link lengths for those types that would be otherwise difficult, if not impossible, to tell apart. This simple method is commonly used by many producers. It avoids guesswork for the cook and the guest, and enhances the presentation of your products.

Temperature

The frequent use of accurate, quick-read type thermometers is highly recommended for all stages of sausage production, storage, cooking, and final presentation. Remember: it is high-quality, consistent, and fully wholesome sausage products that will establish and maintain your reputation. Temperature control is essential to achieving these goals.

The "Bloom"

Semi-dry and dry-cure sausages will often exhibit a natural "bloom." This is a very visible, whitish, powdery coating which soon appears upon the surfaces of the casings while sausages are hanging to cure. It is harmless, and it should be recognized by the informed consumer as a "mark of quality" for many varieties. Efforts to remove the bloom are not necessary, but if desired, simply wipe the surfaces lightly with a clean, damp cloth.

Acidulated Water

Water, prepared by adding small amounts of vinegar or lime or lemon juice, is used for whitening and efficient cleansing of a number of foods. Regarded and valued widely as a natural bleach, it can also serve as a soak to retard discoloration of cut fruits and vegetables. Use it as a cooking medium for offal meats, including brains and sweetbreads, for charcuterie items. Specific details are included in the recipes.

Seasoning and Flavoring

Mix herbs, seasoning and curing agents, and other additions to the meat ingredients of a batch of sausage into the water or other liquid specified in the formula one hour prior to blending into the meats. This greatly enhances flavor and improves quality. After mixing with the meats, always check the temperature of the batch. It is generally advisable to rechill and hold the mixture for at least one-half hour before stuffing. After stuffing, all sausages will benefit from a maturation of flavor which is achieved by holding for 24 hours minimum. (Note: semi-dry and dry cure types will often call for specific holding times or other temperature and humidity settings. Follow these instructions fully.)

A *bouquet garni,* useful in flavoring many soups, stews and broths, has numerous applications in sausage production. The classic equal-parts trio is a bundle of parsley, thyme, and bay leaf. Tie it into a celery stalk, leek leaf, or cheesecloth packet for easy removal after cooking preparation.

Sausage recipes commonly require a final adjustment of the seasoning, before stuffing. All seasoning must be considered highly subjective, but do remember these points:

- Mixing must be complete and very thorough before tasting.
- Generally, there is *raw meat* in the batch to be tasted. Therefore *always fully cook (usually by a quick sauté) a small patty, before tasting or offering samples to anyone!*
- Make allowances for the fact that some flavors will intensify upon completion of the full processing of many varieties. Your continuing experience, aided by accurate note keeping, will make seasoning skills easy and pleasant to acquire.

Terrines

All terrines will be cooked to a specified temperature. Some, but not all, will require a surrounding water bath (*bain-marie*). Subsequent cooling, decoration, and other treatment is always detailed in the recipe. It is necessary to hold many terrines and similar preparations for at least 8 hours (refrigerated) to bring the complex flavors to an acceptable degree of maturation. Pressing, or top-filling with aspic after cooling, and final decoration are all important details, not to be overlooked.

A FINAL WORD

The authors sincerely offer this admonition: Take pride in your work. This may appear to state the case all too easily, but pride of workmanship will allow you to fully explore, and personally enjoy, the fascinating culinary specialty of charcuterie. Sausages of all sorts do have a universal appeal, and with care you will become skilled, consistent, and uniquely knowledgeable in their production. Our sincere hope is, that with some time, you will have gained your own ever larger list of "Common Links." This valuable information will remain in your head and will serve to fortify your efforts. You will experience great satisfaction as you advance and continue exploring the many areas of charcuterie.

BEFORE YOU BEGIN

Read these 12 steps carefully before you launch into any recipe. Every step is equally important.

1. **Read the entire recipe all the way through.**

2. **Check your supply of all ingredients.**

3. **Weigh and measure the ingredients as precisely as possible.**

4. **Follow the step-by-step instructions in order.**

5. **Grind, dice, or chop exactly as instructed.**

6. **Mix thoroughly.**

7. **Always preheat your equipment.**

8. **Cook at the recommended temperature for the required time.**

9. **Test for doneness with accurate thermometers.**

10. **Keep perishable ingredients refrigerated during all stages of a recipe.**

11. **Follow recommendations carefully for storage, reheating, and serving.**

12. **Develop the habit of keeping precise notes.**

Alligator Smoked Sausage

Yield: 25 pounds (11 kg)

U.S.		Ingredients	Metric		Preparation
22	lb	alligator meat	10	kg	trimmed and cubed
3	lb	fatback	1.4	kg	
40	oz	ice water	1.2	l	
3	oz	granulated sugar	85	g	
1½	oz	Prague powder #2	42	g	measured accurately
3	oz	fine salt	85	g	
1	oz	#10 black pepper	28	g	coarsely ground
2	oz	fresh jalapeño pepper	57	g	finely chopped
2	oz	cayenne pepper	57	g	ground
1	oz	dry red pepper flakes	28	g	
3	T	fresh sage	18	g	finely chopped
2	T	fresh onion	12	g	finely chopped
8	T	fresh garlic	48	g	minced
10	oz	soy protein concentrate	284	g	powdered
		casings	38–40	mm	

1. Pass the meat once through a ⅜ in. (0.95 cm) plate. Dice the fatback uniformly and chill. Do not combine the meat and fatback at this time.

2. Put the water into a container and stir in the remaining ingredients. Mix the solution into the ground meat. When mixing is nearly complete, add the chilled fatback.

3. Stuff the prepared casings moderately tight, avoiding air pockets. Tie into 3–4 in. (8–10 cm) links (or a size that you prefer).

SMOKING

1. Preheat the smoker to 130°F (54°C). Place the sausages on sticks and hang in the smoker with dampers one-half open. Gradually increase the temperature to 165°F (74°C) over several hours.

2. Remove from the smoker when the internal temperature of the sausages reaches 155°F (68°C). Shower at once with cold water until the internal temperature has cooled to 100°F (38°C) or less.

3. Refrigerate for use as a grilling sausage.

Aspic

Yield: 4 quarts (3.9 l)

U.S.		Ingredients	Metric		Preparation
FOR STOCK:					
4	lb	veal bones	2	kg	strictly fresh
3	lb	beef stew meat	1.5	kg	
3	ea	calves' feet	3	ea	strictly fresh
8	oz	pork skin	225	g	
2	gal	water	8	l	
6	oz	mirepoix (celery, carrot, and leek)	170	g	equal parts mixture, coarsely chopped
6	oz	onion	170	g	coarsely chopped

1. Blanch and drain the veal bones, stew meat, calves' feet, and pork skin.
2. Add the water and vegetables. Bring to a gentle boil and skim once or twice. Reduce heat and simmer 6 hours.
3. Cool briefly and strain. Cool completely and refrigerate.

U.S.		Ingredients	Metric		Preparation
FOR ASPIC:					
1	lb	extra lean beef	450	g	finely ground
6	lg	egg whites	6	lg	beaten until frothy
8	oz	mirepoix (as above)	225	g	diced medium
6	ea	black peppercorns	6	ea	
1	gal	cold stock	4	l	recipe above
8	oz*	granulated gelatin	225	g	
3	oz	cold water	89	ml	

1. Mix the beef with the egg whites, vegetables, and peppercorns. Add to the stock and allow to rest for 30 minutes.
2. Bring slowly to a simmer, stirring once or twice. *Do not allow to boil.* Simmer 1 full hour.
3. After 30 minutes, soften the gelatin in the cold water.
4. After 1 hour of simmering, add the gelatin and simmer for another 15 minutes. Stir once or twice.
5. Strain carefully through a chinois lined with cheesecloth.
6. Refrigerate, covered, in a nonreactive container.

*Use 12 oz (340 g) of gelatin per gal (4 l) for aspic that must hold up in warm conditions such as a culinary competition.

SOME TIPS FOR MAKING AND USING ASPIC:

1. Substitute any sound meat, to gain the flavor you require.

2. Reheat stored aspic gently, using due caution (a double boiler is good) to avoid scorching. Bring to at least 110°F (43°C), then cool to near 75°F (24°C) for use. *Aspic handles best for pouring and dipping when kept near this temperature.*

3. Cool pies, terrines, and similar pieces before filling with aspic. Work with pieces on a rack placing dipped items onto a grid with a drip pan below. This saves much clean-up and will add to the high-quality finish of any pieces.

4. Small items may be dipped on skewers, then placed into styrofoam blocks to set.

5. "Bloom" granular or leaf gelatin: Mix granular or soak the sheets in a small quantity of tepid water for 10 to 20 minutes. Use a whisk to assure absorption of water into the gelatin. After this, it may be poured and mixed with the main body of liquid, without fear of lumping or other problems.

6. Do not be tempted to add excessive granulated or sheet gelatin to a recipe. This will result in undesirable flavor.

7. Full clarification of the aspic, with close attention to procedure, is paramount for achieving excellent results with any aspic work. Aspic coating must be crystal clear, and should present a flawless appearance.

Dry-Cured Bacon

Yield: Over 20 pounds (9 kg)

U.S.		Ingredients	Metric		Preparation
25	lb	pork belly	11.25	kg	scraped and trimmed
12	oz	pickling salt	340	g	
6	oz	brown sugar	170	g	
2	oz	Prague powder #2	57	g	measured accurately
1	oz	pâté/terrine spices	28	g	see separate recipe (p. 193)

1. Cut the pork into uniform squares.

2. Mix the salt, sugar, Prague powder #2, and pâté spices well.

3. Working in a nonreactive tub, rub the dry cure into the lean side of one piece of pork. Turn the piece over and rub the fatty side. Arrange another piece on top of the first and repeat. Rub and stack all pieces.

4. Arrange a light weight on top of the meat. Cover and place in the cooler to cure undisturbed for 10 days.

SMOKING

1. Hang the meat securely and load it into a preheated smoker at 120°F (49°C). Maintain a moderate smoke for 10 or more hours. Check progress from time to time. Remove the bacon when desired smoke finish is attained.

2. Refrigerate, unwrapped, for use. (Never wrap the bacon in plastic; hanging on a hook in the cooler is preferable.)

VARIATIONS

Irish bacon: Replace the pâté spice with 1 oz of sage, onion powder, and thyme in equal parts.

English bacon: Replace the pâté spice with 1 oz of sage, ginger, and coriander in equal parts.

Scottish bacon: Replace the pâté spice with ½ oz of sage and medium-grind black pepper.

Basic Poultry Sausage

Yield: 10 pounds (4.5 kg)

U.S.		Ingredients	Metric		Preparation
8	lb	poultry meat	3.6	kg	
1	lb	poultry fat	450	g	
1	oz	salt	28	g	
⅛	oz	Prague powder #1	3.5	g	measured accurately
16	oz	poultry broth	475	ml	
12	oz	bread panada	340	g	
½	oz	ground white pepper	14	g	
3½ in. × 24 in.		fibrous casings	9 cm × 60 cm		

1. Grind the meat and fat through a ⅛ in. or ³⁄₁₆ in. (0.3 cm or 0.5 cm) plate.
2. Dissolve the salt and Prague powder #1 in the broth.
3. Add the broth solution, panada, and pepper to the meat; mix thoroughly.
4. Stuff the prepared casings.

SMOKING

1. Place in a preheated smoker at 130°F (54°C). Hold for 30 minutes with dampers wide open.

(Continued)

2. Introduce a heavy smoke, raise the temperature to 150°F (65°C), and hold for 1 hour.
3. Increase the temperature to 180°F (82°C). Hold until the internal temperature is 165°F (74°C).
4. Remove from the smoker and shower with cold water to reduce the temperature to under 100°F (38°C).
5. Refrigerate, well wrapped, for use.

Beef Brisket Sausage

Be sure to use brisket for this sausage. Leave a fair amount of fat with the lean meat. Cook on the grill.

Yield: 10 pounds (4.5 kg)

U.S.		Ingredients	Metric		Preparation
10	lb	beef brisket	4.5	kg	boiled and chilled
2	T	fine salt	30	g	
1½	oz	black pepper	43	g	
¾	oz	ground mace	21	g	
¼	oz	ground nutmeg	7	g	
2	oz	ground coriander	57	g	
1	t	fresh marjoram	2	g	finely chopped
16	oz	ice water	475	ml	
		sheep casings	32–35	mm	
		or			
		collagen casings	32	mm	

1. Grind the meat through a ⅜ in. (0.95 cm) plate.
2. Add the spices and herbs. Mix very well.
3. Regrind the mixture using a ⅛ in. (0.3 cm) plate.
4. Add the water.
5. Stuff the prepared casings and tie into 3 in. (8 cm) links.
6. Refrigerate, well wrapped, for use.

Bierwurst

We have somewhat modified this savory sausage from *Great Sausage Recipes and Meat Curing* by Rytec Kutas. It makes fine sandwiches on rye bread with mustard and cheese.

Yield: 25 pounds (11.3 kg)

U.S.		Ingredients	Metric		Preparation
15	lb	pork butt	6.8	kg	trimmed
7	lb	trimmed lean beef	3.2	kg	
3	lb	fresh bacon	1.4	kg	diced
1	oz	Prague powder #1	28	g	measured accurately
3	oz	kosher salt	85	g	
2	oz	powdered dextrose	57	g	
1	oz	#34 mesh black pepper	28	g	
½	oz	ground nutmeg	14	g	
¼	oz	ground cardamom	7	g	
3		garlic cloves	3		crushed
1	oz	yellow mustard seed	28	g	whole

3½ in. or 5 in. × 24 in.   synthetic fibrous casings

1. Grind the pork butt and the beef through a ¾ in. or 1 in. (1.9 or 2.5 cm) plate. The meat may also be diced by hand.

2. Dice the bacon and return to the cooler. Keep the bacon separate from the beef/pork mixture.

3. Add the Prague powder #1 and all the seasoning ingredients to the beef/pork mixture. Mix lightly and pack, avoiding air pockets, into pans not deeper than 6 in. (15 cm). Cover and refrigerate for 12 hours.

4. Grind the beef/pork mixture using a ⅛ in. (0.3 cm) plate. Grind the bacon using a ¼ in. (0.6 cm) plate. Combine the bacon with the beef/pork mixture. Mix again to assure a uniform forcemeat.

5. Stuff the prepared casings. Tie ends or use clips and hanging ties. Hang to dry at room temperature for a full hour after stuffing.

SMOKING

1. Preheat the smoker to 130°F (54°C) with dampers wide open.

2. Hang the sausages in the smoker and dry for another hour or until the bierwurst begins to color. Adjust the dampers to one-quarter open and the temperature to 165°F (74°C). Monitor the bierwurst and remove it from the smoker when the internal temperature is 152°F (67°C).

3. Hang briefly to cool, then wrap for refrigerated storage. The bierwurst is ready for consumption after resting for 1 day.

Biltong

We found this popular jerky in a South African government publication. It is made from beef or other red meat. It may be used like bacon (in a quiche, for example). Store in a cool, dry place in glass or heat-seal plastics. Excessive moisture will shorten its storage life and may induce a mold.

Yield: 7 pounds (3.1 kg)

U.S.		Ingredients	Metric		Preparation
10	lb	venison	4.5	kg	
8	oz	salt	227	g	
2	oz	mixed spice	57	g	
¾	oz	red pepper flakes	21	g	
1	t	black pepper	2	g	finely cracked
1	oz	Prague powder #2	28	g	measured accurately

1. Remove as much fat from the meat as possible. Cut the meat into thin strips about 1 in. (2.5 cm) wide.
2. Mix the salt, mixed spice, red pepper, black pepper, and Prague powder #2.
3. Working in a nonreactive tub, layer the strips evenly while sprinkling the dry cure over all. Repeat the layers until all the meat is well covered. Place a clean cloth over the tub and allow to cure for 24 hours in a cool place.
4. Remove the strips from the tub and gently brush off the excess cure.

SMOKING

1. Preheat the smoker to 100°F (38°C) and drape the strips over hanging sticks or secure them to hangers. Process for about 8 hours with dampers one-half open. The biltong is finished when it bends with some resistance but is not completely brittle.
2. Remove and cool quickly.
3. Store in a cool, dry location.

Block Sausage (Plockwurst)

This sausage is a rare sight in today's kitchens. It is known as "Dublin Brawn" in Ireland. It must not be consumed before the cure is fully accomplished; the characteristic bloom on the casings indicates it is ready to eat.

Yield: 8 pounds (3.6 kg) after drying

U.S.		Ingredients	Metric		Preparation
6	lb	lean pork	2.7	kg	trimmed and cubed
2	lb	smoked ham	900	g	cubed
1	lb	lean beef	450	g	trimmed and cubed
2	oz	fine salt	57	g	
2	T	dextrose	45	g	powdered
2	T	corn syrup solids	30	g	powdered
2	T	white pepper	12	g	freshly ground
1	T	onion powder	9	g	
2	t	Prague powder #2	10	g	measured accurately
3½	in.	casings	9	cm	

1. Grind the meats through a ¼ in. (0.6 cm) plate. Do not allow the mixture to become warm. Check and chill as necessary.

2. Mix all the seasoning ingredients; stir in the Prague powder #2. Sprinkle the seasonings over the meat and work in very well by hand.

3. Stuff the prepared casings and tie each end. (A clip on one end and a secure butterfly knot on the other end work well.)

4. Hang to cure at 65–70°F (18–21°C) and 70–80% relative humidity for 48 hours.

5. Hang in the cooler at 45–50°F (7–10°C) for 70–80 days.

Bologna

This bologna is made from a ground forcemeat. Purée the sausage in a food processor if a completely smooth bologna is desired. Include the optional garlic for Garlic Bologna.

Yield: 10 pounds (4.5 kg)

U.S.		Ingredients	Metric		Preparation
5	lb	lean stew beef	2.25	kg	trimmed and cubed
5	lb	pork shoulder	2.25	kg	trimmed and cubed
16	oz	ice water	475	ml	
1	oz	fine salt	28	g	
1	T	ground white pepper	6	g	
1	T	ground paprika	6	g	
1	T	ground nutmeg	6	g	
1	T	ground allspice	6	g	
2	oz	crushed fresh garlic	57	g	optional
1	oz	soy protein powder	28	g	
		natural beef bung casings			
		or			
		beef rounds (for ring bologna)			

1. Put the ice water in a container and stir in the seasonings and soy protein powder. Return to the cooler to keep well chilled.
2. Grind the beef and pork, first with a ⅜ in. (0.9 cm) plate, then with a ⅛ in. (0.3 cm) plate. Mix in the seasoning solution and chill for 1 hour.
3. Stuff the prepared casings. Use clips or butterfly knots to close the large beef bungs. Loop the beef rounds and tie with string for ring bologna.

SMOKING

1. Place in a preheated 135°F (57°C) smoker. Hold at this temperature with the dampers wide open for 1 hour.
2. Adjust the dampers to one-third open and increase the temperature to 165°F (74°C). Process until the internal temperature is 150°F (66°C).
3. Remove the bologna and hang at room temperature until cooled to under 100°F (38°C).
4. Hold refrigerated for use.

Boston Pork Sausage

This Irish-American grilling variety was developed from an old Dublin link sausage. Because freezing can alter the delicate flavor of this sausage, it is best consumed fresh.

Yield: 5 pounds (2.25 kg)

U.S.		Ingredients	Metric		Preparation
7	lb	pork shoulder	3.25	kg	trimmed and cubed
16	oz	ice water	475	ml	
2	lb	soft bread crumbs	1	kg	fine crumbs
2	t	fine salt	10	g	
1	T	fresh thyme	6	g	
1	T	fresh sage	6	g	finely minced
1	T	ground mace	3	g	
		fresh collagen casings	22 or 32	mm	

1. Pass the pork through a ³⁄₁₆ in. (0.5 cm) plate. Place in a pan, cover, and chill for 1 hour.

2. Put the ice water in a container and stir in the crumbs, salt, thyme, sage, and mace. Chill.

3. Working in a suitable mixing tub, distribute the seasonings over the meat and hand mix very well. Return to the cooler and chill for 1 hour.

4. Stuff the prepared casings rather loosely. Link into 3–4 in. (8–10 cm) lengths. Arrange on trays or pans and cover tightly.

5. Refrigerate at once. The sausage is ready to use the next day when flavor has fully developed.

Boudin Aux Epinards
(Spinach Boudins)

These savory blood sausages are delicious grilled and served with linguine and roasted pepper sauce. Accompany with salad, a good loaf, and some Chianti.

Yield: 6 pounds (2.7 kg)

U.S.		Ingredients	Metric		Preparation
2	lb	fatback	900	g	
½	oz	ground nutmeg	14	g	
½	oz	fine black pepper	14	g	or fine white pepper
½	oz	ground cloves	14	g	
1½	lb	stale bread crumbs	680	g	crusts trimmed
1	pt	heavy cream	475	ml	
1	oz	salt	28	g	
2	oz	light brown sugar	57	g	
4	oz	Grand Marnier liqueur	118	ml	Cordon Jaune
2	oz	fresh chives	57	g	finely diced
2	lb	spinach	1	kg	washed, dried, chopped
5	pt	pig blood	2.25	l	fresh
		hog casings	32–35	mm	
		light chicken stock			cold

1. Grind the fatback, first with a ¼ in. (0.6 cm) plate, then with a ⅛ in. (0.3 cm) plate. Return to the cooler.

2. Combine the nutmeg, black pepper, cloves, and bread crumbs. Pour over the cream and allow to soften completely. Add the salt, brown sugar, and Grand Marnier; mix lightly.

3. In 4 oz (113 g) of the ground fatback, sauté the chives to soften. Add the chopped spinach and sauté briefly to wilt.

4. Add the spinach to the soaked crumb mixture. Add the remaining fatback and blood. Mix lightly but thoroughly. Cover and chill for 1 hour.

5. Stuff the prepared hog casings loosely. Tie in rings approximately 9 in. (23 cm) in diameter.

6. Place the rings in a cooking pot and cover with the cold chicken stock. Gently heat to 155°F (68°C). Watch and maintain the temperature. When the internal temperature of the sausages is 155°F (68°C), remove from heat. Leave the boudins in the poaching bath.

7. Place the pot with sausages into the cooler and chill for 24 hours.

8. Pull the sausages from the broth, drain briefly, and wrap. Hold refrigerated for use.

Boudin Blanc

This is a popular variety of traditional Creole sausage. To prepare as hors d'oeuvre, slice on the bias and serve with cocktail picks. These sausages are fragile, and they require gentle handling.

Yield: 3 pounds (1.4 kg)

U.S.		Ingredients	Metric		Preparation
1	lb	white chicken meat	450	g	
1	lb	lean pork	450	g	
1	lb	fat pork	450	g	
1	t	salt	5	g	
1	t	white pepper	2	g	freshly ground
1	t	cayenne pepper	2	g	ground
1	med	onion	1	med	minced
1	t	minced fresh garlic	1	g	
½	c	stale white bread	118	g	trimmed, torn in pieces
1	pt	heavy cream	473	ml	chilled
2	lg	egg yolks			beaten
¾	t	pork & veal blend	2.8	g	Chef Paul Prudhomme's Magic
		hog casings	28–32	mm	
		milk-water bath			50% each

1. Mince all of the meat. Season with the salt, white pepper, and cayenne pepper. Add the onion and garlic.
2. Moisten the bread pieces with water and squeeze out. Add to the meat and mix well.
3. Add the cream. Stir the mixture over medium heat for about 15 minutes to reduce. Remove from heat. Briskly stir in the egg yolks and the Chef Paul seasoning. Cool.
4. Stuff the prepared casings. Tie with cord at both ends to make 3–4 in. (8–10 cm) links.
5. Immerse the links in a milk-water bath and poach 15–20 minutes.
6. Finish by broiling on a nonstick surface. Prick lightly if necessary to minimize bursting.

VARIATIONS

Leftover turkey, partridge, or other fowl may be used. Rabbit, crawfish, and crab are also excellent. Color may vary, but the flavor is superb.

Boudin Noir

Black pudding is served grilled for breakfast in Ireland and England. It is often part of a mixed grill platter which can also include lamb chops, chipolatas, gammon rasher, veal liver, tomatoes, and mushrooms. Hot coleslaw is a good accompaniment for grilled boudins.

Yield: 6 pounds (2.7 kg), approximately 6 rings of sausage

U.S.		Ingredients	Metric		Preparation
2	lb	pork fat	900	g	
1	pt	heavy cream	475	ml	
1½	lb	white bread crumbs	675	g	
2	lb	red onion	900	g	diced
1	oz	fresh chives	28	g	chopped
1	oz	kosher or canning salt	28	g	
½	oz	ground black pepper	14	g	
1	oz	brown sugar	28	g	
½	oz	ground nutmeg	14	g	
½	oz	ground cloves	14	g	
5	pt	pig blood	2.25	l	
3	oz	Jamaican Navy rum	88	ml	dark
		hog casings	32	mm	
3	qt	chicken stock	3	l	cold

1. Mix the cream and bread crumbs. Set aside to soak for 1 hour.

2. Pass the pork fat through a ¼ in. (0.6 cm) plate.

3. Render 4 oz (113 g) of the pork fat in a heavy skillet. Add the onions and sauté until soft.

4. Remove from heat and cool to room temperature. Add the chives, remaining pork fat, salt, pepper, sugar, nutmeg, and cloves. Mix lightly, but well.

5. Fold in the soaked bread crumbs; add the blood and rum. Mix lightly but thoroughly to achieve a uniform mixture.

6. Stuff the prepared hog casings; stuff without air pockets, but not too tightly. Tie into rings, allowing sufficient string to handle and hang the rings.

7. Place the sausages in a heavy pan and cover with the cold chicken stock. Over moderate heat, bring slowly to an internal temperature of 150°F (65°C). Note that sausages will burst if cooked at too-high temperatures.

8. Remove the sausage rings from the stock and spread out to cool rapidly. When cool, refrigerate for 24 hours to mellow.

Boudin with Apples

We recommend grilling these boudins, turning them frequently. As with other boudins, poach them over low-to-moderate heat. Excessive heat will cause the sausages to burst. A curry mango relish is an excellent match.

Yield: 10 pounds (4.5 kg)

U.S.		Ingredients	Metric		Preparation
8	oz	dry bread crumbs	227	g	
1½	pt	heavy cream	700	ml	
5	lb	cooking apples	2.25	kg	peeled, cored, diced
8	oz	butter	225	g	
4	oz	apple brandy	120	ml	
2	oz	kosher or canning salt	57	g	
1	oz	cracked black pepper	28	g	#6 mesh
½	oz	ground nutmeg	14	g	
½	oz	ground cinnamon	14	g	
½	oz	dry, rubbed sage	14	g	
4	oz	brown sugar	113	g	
3½	lb	fatback	1.5	kg	brunoise (⅛ in. dice)
1½	lb	shallots	680	g	finely chopped
5	pt	pig blood	2.4	l	
		hog casings	32–35	mm	
		chicken stock			cold

1. Soak the bread crumbs in the cream.
2. Sauté the apples in butter until tender; do not overcook. Remove from heat and cool slightly. Add the brandy, salt, pepper, nutmeg, cinnamon, sage, and brown sugar. Set mixture aside.
3. Render 1 lb (450 g) of the fatback. Add the shallots and sauté briefly to sweat. Set the mixture aside to cool.
4. Combine the soaked bread crumbs, apples, shallots, remaining fatback, and blood. Mix lightly but thoroughly.
5. Stuff the prepared hog casings. Tie into rings, allowing sufficient strings for handling.
6. Immerse the sausages in the cold chicken stock. Heat the stock to 150°F (65°C). Maintain the temperature carefully over low-to-moderate heat.
7. When the internal temperature of the sausages reaches 152°F (67°C), remove from stock with care. Cool rapidly, then refrigerate 24 hours to mature flavor before serving.

Bratwurst

Bratwursts are prime grilling sausages. Sliced into small diagonal pieces, they make tasty appetizers to dip in mustard or horseradish sauce. Or present them on a platter with other sausages like kielbasa, mettwurst, wieners, and frankfurters. During service, bratwursts are often held in hot water and quickly grilled to order. When grilling, always turn the bratwursts frequently for uniform color. Although they can be made with a fine grind, we prefer the slightly coarse texture obtained with the ⅜ in. (0.95 cm) plate.

Yield: 10 pounds (4.5 kg)

U.S.		Ingredients	Metric		Preparation
3	lb	trimmed veal	1.35	kg	
7	lb	trimmed pork shoulder	3.15	kg	
1	pt	milk	475	ml	cold
1	oz	fine salt	28	g	
½	oz	ground white pepper	14	g	
2	oz	mace-ginger-nutmeg	56	g	equal parts mixture
1	lb	soy protein concentrate	450	g	powdered
4	lg	whole eggs	4	lg	well-beaten
5	oz	fresh parsley	141	g	finely chopped
		collagen or hog casings	32–35	mm	
		veal stock			cold

1. Grind the veal and pork with a ⅜ in. (0.95 cm) plate.
2. Place the ground meat into a mixing tub and add all remaining ingredients. Mix very thoroughly. Return to the cooler and chill at least 1 hour.
3. Stuff the prepared casings. Tie into 4 in. (10 cm) links.
4. Poach the sausages in good veal stock for the best flavor. Cover with the cold stock and heat gently. Maintain a temperature of no more than 160°F (71°C). When the sausages reach an internal temperature of 140°F (60°C), remove from the stock.
5. Cool quickly. Dry, wrap, and refrigerate for use.

Braunschweiger

Braunschweiger is also known as "chicken liver" or "liver sausage." Because freezing will alter its flavor and texture, it is best consumed fresh.

Yield: 20 pounds (9 kg)

U.S.		Ingredients	Metric		Preparation
10	lb	pork shoulder	4.5	kg	
10	lb	pig or chicken liver	4.5	kg	
20	oz	ice water	592	ml	
4	t	salt	20	g	
⅛	oz	black pepper	4	g	
1	oz	granulated onion	28	g	
½	t	ground cloves	2	g	
½	t	marjoram	2	g	
½	t	sage	2	g	
½	t	ginger	2	g	
½	t	nutmeg	2	g	
½	t	allspice	2	g	
¼	oz	dried mustard	7	g	
1	t	powdered dextrose	4	g	
1	oz	Prague powder #1	28	g	measured accurately
5–6	oz	soy protein powder	142–170	g	
3½ in. × 24 in.		fibrous casings	9	cm × 60 cm	
		or			
2–3	in.	casings	5–7.5	cm	
		rich meat stock			

1. Grind the pork shoulder and liver separately using a ⅝ in. (1.6 cm) plate. Steam or sauté the meat and liver separately. Mix the meat and liver and regrind together using a 3/16 in. (0.5 cm) plate. Chill.

2. Put the ice water in a container and stir in the salt, pepper, onion, cloves, marjoram, sage, ginger, nutmeg, allspice, mustard, dextrose, and Prague powder #1. In a large mixing tub or bowl, mix the meat and the seasoning solution. Add enough soy protein powder to bind properly and to give a good texture. The mixture should hold small peaks. Make sure the ingredients are well blended. Chill for 1 hour.

3. Stuff the prepared casings.

4. Preheat the stock to 165°F (74°C). Immerse the sausage in the stock and cook 2–3 hours. The cooking time will depend on the quantity of sausage. Check and maintain the cooking temperature carefully.

(Continued)

5. When the center of the sausage reaches 155°F (68°C), remove from the stock. Handle with care to avoid rupturing casings.

6. Place into an ice water bath or cold stock. Cool quickly to 35°F (2°C).

SMOKING

1. Wash off any excess fat with hot water spray. Place the sausages securely on hanging sticks. Hang and dry very well at room temperature before smoking.

2. After approximately 2 hours of drying, place in a preheated smoker at 110°F (43°C) with heavy smoke for 1 hour to ensure good flavor. Smoke a bit more if you prefer.

3. Wrap and refrigerate for use.

Lancashire Brawn

This sausage, also known as "head cheese," is made with brains. Read about preparing and cooking brains, p. 42. Allow for about 10 percent trim and cooking loss. The brawn should be used soon after production. It is more perishable than other sausages and does not freeze well. Compare with the Oxford Brawn.

Yield: 10 pounds (4.5 kg)

U.S.		Ingredients	Metric		Preparation
10	lb	beef or calves' brains	4.5	kg	prepared and chilled
2	oz	fine salt	57	g	
2	T	ground white pepper	12	g	freshly ground
1	t	ground cayenne pepper	1	g	
1	t	ground cloves	2	g	
1	t	ground ginger	2	g	
1	t	ground mace	2	g	
1	pt	ice water	475	ml	
		beef bung or hog stomach casings			

1. Grind the poached brains using a ⅜ in. (0.9 cm) plate. Add all the dry seasoning ingredients and mix in a tub. Regrind using a ⅛ in. (0.3 cm) plate. Add the ice water and mix.

2. Stuff the prepared casings.

3. Wrap and refrigerate for storage. To cook, grill gently until just done.

VARIATION

Poach the brains in a rich veal stock instead of acidulated water; cut them into ¼ in. dice. Mix them with all of the ingredients above and pack the forcemeat into greased bread pans. Pour 1 pt of aspic over the forcemeat. Chill to set and unmold the following day. Slice and serve cold.

Oxford Brawn

This sausage, also known as "head cheese," is made with brains. Read about preparing and cooking brains, p. 42. Allow for about 10 percent trim and cooking loss. The brawn should be used soon after production. It is more perishable than other sausages and does not freeze well. This is a good variety to grill. Compare with the Lancashire Brawn.

Yield: 10 pounds (4.5 kg)

U.S.		Ingredients	Metric		Preparation
10	lb	beef or calves' brains	4.5	kg	prepared and chilled
2	oz	fine salt	57	g	
1	T	ground white pepper	7	g	freshly ground
1½	t	ground cayenne pepper	2	g	
1	t	ground mace	2	g	
1	pt	ice water	475	ml	
1½	t	pimento, canned	8	g	¼ in. (0.6 cm) dice
		lamb casings	24–26	mm	

1. Grind the prepared brains using a ⅜ in. (0.9 cm) plate. Add the salt, pepper, cayenne pepper, and mace; mix in a tub. Grind again using a ⅛ in. (0.3 cm) plate. Add the ice water. Mix in the diced pimento.
2. Stuff the prepared casings. Tie into 3 in. (9 cm) links.
3. Wrap and refrigerate for use.

Cajun Pork Sausage

A lively fresh sausage for panfrying or grilling. Use pork butt or pork scraps that are not too fatty. Stuff into casings or freeze in patties separated with waxed paper.

Yield: 5 pounds (2.25 kg)

U.S.		Ingredients	Metric		Preparation
5	lb	pork butt or scraps	2.2	kg	diced
3	c	dried onion	288	g	finely chopped
1½	c	green onion	144	g	finely chopped
2	T	garlic	12	g	finely minced
		salt			to taste
		cayenne pepper			to taste
1	T	dried mint	3	g	crumbled

1. Finely grind the meat into a large bowl. Mix in the onions, green onions, garlic, salt, cayenne pepper, mint, and any other seasonings you have chosen. Mix by hand.
2. Fry a small patty; taste and adjust seasoning. Pass the mixture through the meat grinder again to mix very well.
3. Form into patties or stuff into casings as desired.
4. Refrigerate or freeze for use.

VARIATION

Add or substitute other seasonings such as Chef Paul Prudhomme's Magic Cajun Spice mix.

Chicken Liver Braunschweiger

This is a great Cincinnati flavor. It makes a delicious sandwich with sweet onions on rye bread.

Yield: 10 pounds (4.5 kg)

U.S.		Ingredients	Metric		Preparation
4	lb	pork butt	1.8	kg	trimmed and cubed
6	lb	chicken livers	2.7	kg	trimmed
2	t	Prague powder #1	10	g	measured accurately
1	oz	salt	28	g	
1	oz	granulated onion	28	g	
½	t	ground allspice	0.5	g	
½	oz	ground white pepper	14	g	
¼	oz	powdered dextrose	7	g	
¼	t	marjoram	0.25	g	
½	t	ground nutmeg	0.5	g	
½	t	ground ginger	0.5	g	
½	t	ground sage	0.5	g	
½	t	ground cloves	0.5	g	
1	T	ground mustard	3	g	
1	pt	ice water	475	ml	
5	oz	soy protein powder	142	g	more if needed
4	ea	synthetic fibrous casings	4	ea	
		chicken stock			

1. Grind the pork and livers with a ³⁄₁₆ in. (0.5 cm) plate. Add all the remaining ingredients and mix well. Chill for at least 30 minutes.

2. Grind again using a ¹⁄₁₆ in. (0.2 cm) plate. Adjust the texture with more soy protein if necessary.

3. Stuff the prepared casings immediately. Tie and secure with hog rings. Chill well for 12 hours.

4. Immerse the braunschweigers in 165°F (74°C) chicken stock. Cook until the internal temperature reaches 165°F (74°C). This will take 3–4 hours. Do not increase the temperature of the cooking stock above 165°F (74°C).

5. Remove the sausages and chill in an ice water bath. Use a large tub and add more ice as needed to chill the braunschweiger as quickly as possible.

SMOKING

1. Hang securely on smoke sticks. These heavy sausages can slip easily. Hang to dry at room temperature before smoking. This may take several hours.

(Continued)

2. Place in a preheated smoker at 110°F (43°C). Apply a heavy smoke after the first 30 minutes. Hold at this temperature for about 3 hours or until a medium mahogany color is attained.
3. Refrigerate for use.

Chicken Liver Pâté

Serve this pâté with buttered toast or crackers. This recipe was passed on to Chef Kinsella by his mother.

Yield: Serves 20–24

U.S.		Ingredients	Metric		Preparation
4	oz	onions	113	g	
¼	t	garlic	0.5	g	
1	lb	butter	450	g	
2	lb	chicken livers	1	kg	trimmed
2	oz	brandy	60	ml	
⅛	t	salt	0.63	g	
⅛	t	pepper	0.25	g	
1	t	pâté spice	2	g	

1. Chop the onions and garlic; sauté in 8 oz of the butter.
2. Add the livers and sauté for at least 5 minutes over low heat.
3. Grind the mixture once through a coarse plate, then grind again through a fine plate.
4. Add the remaining butter, brandy, salt, pepper, and pâté spice. Mix very well.
5. Turn into a china mold and chill in the refrigerator to set.

Chicken Sausage with Tarragon

These sausages, Chef Kinsella's personal favorites, are delicate and perishable; use them within a few days. Poach them in a well-flavored chicken stock. They are delicious served on a bed of spaetzle coated with a Sauce Bretonne.

Yield: 10 pounds (4.5 kg)

U.S.		Ingredients	Metric		Preparation
8½	lb	boned chicken	3.9	kg	white meat only
1½	lb	chicken fat/skin	680	g	fatty skins
3	oz	green bell pepper	85	g	finely diced
3	oz	red bell pepper	85	g	finely diced
4	oz	shallots	114	g	finely diced
2	oz	garlic	57	g	minced
3	oz	dried tarragon	85	g	or 1½ oz fresh, chopped
2	oz	oil	59	ml	
8	lg	whole eggs	8	lg	well-beaten
2	oz	salt	57	g	very fine
1	pt	heavy cream	475	ml	35–40% fat content
2	T	white pepper	12	g	
		sheep casings	24–26	mm	
		or			
		hog casings	29–32	mm	

1. Lightly sweat the peppers, shallots, garlic, and tarragon in the oil to impart a sheen. Set aside in the cooler.

2. Pass the chicken meat and fatty skins through a ⅜ in. (0.95 cm) plate. Grind again using a ¹⁄₁₆ in. (0.15 cm) plate.

3. Put the ground chicken into a mixing tub. Add the eggs, salt, and cooled pepper/tarragon mixture; blend well.

4. Pour the cream onto the forcemeat and blend well. Cover the pan tightly with plastic film. Chill.

5. Stuff the prepared casings. (We prefer the sheep casings as they are more tender.) Tie into 4 in. (10 cm) links. Chain the sausage links; place in layers in a pan or on a tray.

6. Cover tightly and refrigerate.

Chinese Wine Sausage

We have designed this partly cooked sausage to be finished with a light grilling. This will fully cook it and preserve its subtle flavor. Pay particular attention to the sizes of the dice for the ham and the fatback; they create the sausage's unique texture.

Yield: 10 pounds (4.5 kg)

U.S.		Ingredients	Metric		Preparation
3	lb	fatback	1.4	kg	cut into ¼ in. dice
7	lb	fresh pork ham	3	kg	cut into ⅛ in. dice
3	oz	powdered dextrose	85	g	
1	pt	soy sauce	475	ml	
1	pt	Samsu wine	475	ml	or sake
½	oz	Prague powder #2	14	g	measured accurately
1	oz	corn syrup solids	28	g	
1	oz	salt	28	g	
12	oz	soy protein concentrate	340	g	
		hog casings	35–38	mm	

1. Place the fatback cubes into a pasta strainer and immerse in boiling water for a few seconds. Drain and chill the cubes for 3 hours.

2. Mix the pork with the dextrose, soy sauce, wine, Prague powder #2, corn syrup solids, and salt. Let stand 5 minutes.

3. Add the blanched fatback and soy protein concentrate. Mix well. Chill 25 minutes before stuffing.

4. Stuff the prepared casings. Tie in 4–6 in. (10–15 cm) links.

SMOKING

1. Place in a smoker without smoke; dry 5–6 hours at 100°F (38°C). Vary the time to obtain the desired color and texture.

2. Remove the sausages.

3. Wrap, label, and refrigerate for use. Finish cooking the sausage on the grill before serving.

Chipolata Sausage

The ultimate cocktail sausages, chipolatas may be lightly grilled or cooked in the oven. The English banger evolved from this variety. They may be served as garnish with main course roasts.

Yield: 100 small links

U.S.		Ingredients	Metric		Preparation
7½	lb	pork butt	3.4	kg	trimmed
1	lb	fatback	450	g	diced
2	c	ice water	473	ml	
6	oz	dry bread crumbs	170	g	fine crumbs
1	T	fine salt	15	g	
1	t	fine black pepper	2	g	
3	t	rubbed sage	3	g	
1	t	onion flakes	1	g	
1	t	ground thyme	1	g	
1	t	ground mace	1	g	
		sheep casings	22–26	mm	

1. Combine the meat and fatback; grind through a ⅜ in. (0.95 cm) plate. Chill.
2. Put the water into a container and stir in the bread crumbs and all of the seasoning ingredients.
3. Purée the chilled ground meat in batches in a food processor. Keep bowls, mixing tubs, and ingredients well chilled while processing.
4. Combine the processed meat with the crumbs/seasoning mixture. Mix very well in a power mixer.
5. Chill for at least 1 hour.
6. Stuff the prepared casings. Make small links of 1–1½ in. (3–4 cm).
7. Wrap or tightly cover the links. Refrigerate for use.

Spanish Chorizos

These highly seasoned sausages are particularly identified with Spanish and Philippine cuisine. *Olla Podrida,* a Spanish stew, is a one-dish meal that calls for this hot, coarsely textured sausage. Chorizos are fresh; fully cook them before eating.

Yield: 10 pounds (4.5 kg)

U.S.		Ingredients	Metric		Preparation
6¼	lb	lean pork	2.8	kg	cut in 1 in. dice
3⅛	lb	fatback	1.4	kg	cut in ½ in. dice
3¾	t	whole cumin seed	8	g	
25–40		small hot red chilies*	25–40		seeded and finely chopped
1	t	ground coriander	1.5	g	
16	ea	whole cloves	16	ea	
3	T	honey	44	ml	light, mild flavored
¼	c	fine salt	60	g	
6	T	hot paprika	36	g	
1½	t	black peppercorns	1.5	g	whole
1	T	fresh garlic	6	g	minced
2	c	dry red wine	475	ml	good quality
10	yd	hog casings	9	m	washed and rinsed

1. Combine the cumin seed, chilies, coriander, and cloves in a small pan. Toast lightly over medium heat. Shake constantly as the spices burn easily.
2. Blend the toasted spices with the honey, salt, paprika, and peppercorns. Use a spice mill or mortar to grind them to a coarse but uniform texture. Add the minced garlic and set aside.
3. Have the meats well chilled. Combine the pork, fatback, and seasonings with the wine in a mixing tub. Mix very well.
4. Grind the meat using a ½ in. (1.37 cm) plate; grind again with a ⅜ in. (0.95 cm) plate. (The mixture should be quite coarse, but a ¼ in. (0.63 cm) plate may be used if you prefer.)
5. Pack, with no air pockets, into shallow pans not deeper than 4 in. (10 cm). Cover and chill for at least 1 hour.
6. Stuff the prepared casings. Twist into 3–4 in. (8–10 cm) links.
7. Loop the sausages onto hanging sticks. Hang to air dry, chilled, for 8–12 hours. The sausages must appear uniformly dry and smooth on the surface.
8. Hold at 32–35°F (0–2°C) up to 5 days. Wrap for freezing; they will keep several weeks with minimal loss of quality.

---

*You may substitute 2½ T (7.5 g) dried hot pepper flakes for the fresh small red chilies.

Mexican Chorizos

This hot and spicy sausage, which is dry-cured and smoked, is great for grilling. The recipe calls for several temperature changes during the smoking period; follow the instructions carefully.

Yield: 10 pounds (4.5 kg)

U.S.		Ingredients	Metric		Preparation
7½	lb	pork	3.4	kg	
2½	lb	pork fatback	1.1	kg	
3	t	coarse salt	12	g	
3	t	sugar	13	g	
1	oz	Prague powder #2	28	g	measured accurately
2	t	ground cumin	4	g	
2	t	turmeric	5	g	
2	t	basil	2	g	
2½	t	cayenne pepper	5	g	
5		garlic cloves	5		finely chopped
2½	c	Mexican red wine	600	ml	
5		red bell peppers	5		finely chopped
5		small chili peppers	5		finely chopped
		hog or collagen casings	38	mm	1 hank

1. Mix the salt, sugar, Prague powder #2, cumin, turmeric, basil, cayenne pepper, and garlic cloves into the red wine. Add the bell peppers and chili peppers and marinate for 4 hours.

2. Coarsely grind the pork and fatback together. Mix with the marinade ingredients in a large mixing bowl.

3. Stuff the prepared casings. Tie in 5–6 in. (13–15 cm) links and hang on smoke sticks.

SMOKING

1. Put the sausages into a preheated smoker at 70°F (21°C). Lightly cook them to an internal temperature of 75°F (24°C).

2. Hold the sausages in the smoker for 72 hours at 70°F (21°C) with 70–80% relative humidity.

3. Increase the smoker temperature to 110°F (43°C) for 12 hours.

4. Increase the smoker temperature to 115°F (46°C) for 1 hour. The internal temperature of the sausage must reach 110°F (43°C).

5. Remove from the smoker; wrap or vacuum seal. Refrigerate for use.

Cincinnati Sausage

This good grilling sausage shares the flavors of the German and Irish cultures of Cincinnati.

Yield: 5 pounds (2.25 kg)

U.S.		Ingredients	Metric		Preparation
5	lb	pork butt	2.25	kg	
1	lb	pork belly	450	g	
½	pt	ice water	235	ml	
¼	oz	salt	7	g	
1	T	ground black pepper	6	g	
1	T	sage	3	g	
1	T	thyme	3	g	
1	t	ground mace	1	g	
		hog casings	32–35	mm	

1. Grind the pork and pork belly separately. Combine them and pack into shallow pans no deeper than 6 in. (15 cm). Chill for at least 1 hour.

2. Shortly before removing the ground meat from the cooler, put the water in a container and stir in the dry seasoning ingredients.

3. In a tub or electric mixer, work the seasoning solution into the meat thoroughly.

4. Stuff the prepared casings, avoiding air pockets. Tie in 3 in. (8 cm) links.

5. Cover or wrap well and refrigerate immediately. Use the sausage within 5 days. Grill gently until no longer pink to an internal temperature of 160°F (71°C).

Cognac Sausage

This superb grilling sausage is a good one to have on hand.

Yield: 12 pounds (5.4 kg)

U.S.		Ingredients	Metric		Preparation
7	lb	beef, venison, or lamb	3.2	kg	one or a combination
3	lb	lean pork	1.4	kg	
2	lb	fatback	1	kg	
3	oz	salt	85	g	
1	oz	pepper	28	g	
1	oz	sugar	30	g	
2¼	t	Prague powder #1	11.25	g	measured accurately
8	oz	cognac	235	ml	
6	oz	beer	178	ml	
1	hank	hog casings	32–35	mm	

1. Finely grind all of the meats together. Keep the meat cool; rechill as needed.
2. Dice the fatback and freeze for 1 hour to stiffen.
3. Combine the salt, pepper, sugar, and Prague powder #1 and work into the ground meat.
4. Add the cognac and beer and mix thoroughly.
5. Add the diced fatback. Mix very well, but avoid smearing the fatback. Refrigerate for 1 hour.
6. Stuff the prepared casings and make 3 in. (7.5 cm) links.

SMOKING

1. Put the sausages into a preheated smoker at 135°F (57°C) and cook until the internal temperature reaches 155°F (68°C). A light smoke is an option for this variety.
2. Spray the sausage with cold water to cool quickly.
3. Refrigerate 1–2 days to mature the flavor before serving.

Cold Water Paste

Cold water pastes are used for meat pies and other charcuterie items that require pastry. See also the recipe for Hot Water Paste.

Yield: 2 pounds (900 g)

U.S.		Ingredients	Metric		Preparation
2	lb	bread flour	900	g	
6	oz	lard	170	g	
2	oz	dried milk powder	57	g	
1½	t	salt	7	g	
6	oz	ice water	178	ml	

1. Using an electric mixer fitted with a dough hook, mix the flour and lard until it resembles fine bread crumbs. Mixing small batches by hand is acceptable.
2. Add the milk powder and salt.
3. Add the water and mix until smooth.
4. Wrap well and refrigerate. Rest at least 1 hour before use.

Cooked Salami

This is a *cotto* or cooked salami. For best flavor, slice it thinly and serve at room temperature. It combines well with other meats for submarine-style sandwiches. It is very useful for hors d'oeuvre and antipasto platters. Chop and add it to soups and salads.

Yield: 10 pounds (4.5 kg)

U.S.		Ingredients	Metric		Preparation
6½	lb	very lean beef	2.9	kg	
3½	lb	very lean pork butt	1.5	kg	
1	pt	ice water	475	ml	
6	T	salt	90	g	
2	T	ground black pepper	12	g	
1	T	whole black pepper	9	g	
1	T	cardamom	6	g	
4	lg	cloves fresh garlic	4	lg	finely chopped
6	T	corn syrup solids	90	g	
2	t	Prague powder #1	10	g	measured accurately
2	c	soy protein concentrate	192	g	
3½ in. or 5 in. × 24 in.		synthetic fibrous casings	9 cm × 61 cm		

1. Grind the beef through a ⅛ in. (0.3 cm) plate. Grind the pork through a ³⁄₁₆ in. (0.5 cm) plate.

2. Put the water into a container and stir in the remaining ingredients. Mix the solution into the ground meat and blend well. Pack the meat into tubs, avoiding any air pockets. Put in the cooler overnight at 38–40°F (3–4°C).

3. Stuff the prepared casings evenly; use moderate pressure to get a solid pack. Close with a clip and a butterfly knot. Make a sturdy loop for hanging.

SMOKING

1. Place into a preheated smoker at 130–135°F (54–57°C) for 1 hour.

2. After 1 hour, you may apply a light or medium smoke. During the next 30 minutes, gradually increase the smoker temperature to 155°F (68°C); hold at that temperature until the desired color is attained. The salami *must* reach a minimum internal temperature of 155°F (68°C).

3. Remove the salami from the smoker and shower at once with cold water until the internal temperature reaches 120°F (49°C). You may allow the salami to hang at room temperature for 30–60 minutes until a bloom appears.

4. Store, unwrapped, refrigerated for use.

Corned Beef

The classic dinner accompaniment for corned beef is cabbage. Cook it until just tender in the same broth used to cook the corned beef. When served with mashed potatoes and a white sauce, this dinner is known as Bully Beef.

Yield: 5 pounds (2.3 kg)

U.S.		Ingredients	Metric		Preparation
BRINE:					
1	gal	water	3.8	l	
8	oz	salt	225	g	
½	oz	Prague powder #1	14.2	g	measured accurately
4	oz	light brown sugar	113	g	
1	oz	pickling spice	28	g	
6	lb	beef silverside	2.8	kg	brisket or bottom round
RUB:					
3	ea	bay leaves	3	ea	broken, whole leaf
1½	oz	grated garlic	42	g	
1	oz	mustard seeds	28	g	crushed
2	oz	black pepper	57	g	cracked
2	oz	red pepper flakes	57	g	
¼	oz	coriander seed	7	g	crushed

1. Make the brine by mixing the water, salt, Prague powder #1, brown sugar, and pickling spice in a nonreactive container. Stir to dissolve well.

2. Place the well-dissolved mixture in a stainless steel pot and bring to the boil. Simmer for 5 minutes and cool to room temperature.

3. Put the beef in a nonreactive container and cover with the brine. Refrigerate.

4. Allow the beef to stand in the brine for 14 days. Turn the meat every 2 days to ensure complete and uniform brining.

5. Remove the beef from the brine. Combine the bay leaves, garlic, mustard seeds, pepper, red pepper, and coriander; rub this mixture into all surfaces of the beef. Place the beef in a plastic bag with any excess rub; seal the bag well.

6. Hold the meat in the cooler at 35–38°F (2–3°C) for 5 days. Turn the bag once each day.

7. To cook, remove the beef from the bag; do not discard the juices. Put the beef and juices in a large pot with water to cover. Bring quickly to the boil. Reduce the heat and simmer for 4 hours or until the meat is fork-tender. Add water if necessary to keep the meat covered.

8. Refrigerate the meat in the cooking liquid (in a fresh bag if desired) until needed for service.

Coulibiac of Salmon

The French adapted this pastry-encased creamy mélange from the Russian *kulebiaka*. Serve this special salmon presentation as a first or main course.

Yield: 1 buffet piece serving 12–15

U.S.		Ingredients	Metric		Preparation
1½	lb	salmon or sturgeon	700	g	skinless filets
⅓	c	clarified butter	158	ml	
2	oz	onions	60	g	
3	oz	mushrooms	85	g	diced
3		hard-boiled eggs	3		chopped medium

1. Cut the salmon into thick slices. Melt the clarified butter and cook the salmon. Remove the salmon and reserve.

2. Lightly sauté the onions and mushrooms in the same skillet. Stir in the hard-boiled eggs. When this mixture is cool, fold it into the cooked salmon.

BRIOCHE DOUGH:

1	oz	granulated sugar	28	g	
⅓	c	warm water	158	ml	98°F (37°C)
½	oz	dry yeast	14	g	
8	oz	butter	227	g	melted and cooled
2	c	bread flour	227	g	
5	lg	whole eggs	5	lg	beaten
¼	oz	fine salt	7	g	

1. Dissolve the sugar in the warm water. Add the yeast and proof for 10 minutes.

2. Add the butter and one third of the flour to make a paste.

3. Let this sponge rise to about double in volume.

4. Add the eggs, the rest of the flour, and the salt. Knead the dough, using additional flour as needed.

5. Allow to rise again until double in volume. Punch down. The dough is now ready for use.

(Continued)

ASSEMBLY

U.S.		Ingredients	Metric		Preparation
		cooked salmon/mushroom/hard-boiled egg mixture			
1	recipe	brioche dough	1	recipe	
7	oz	medium grade kasha	200	g	cooked
½	t	mixed salt and pepper	3.5	g	optional
1	t	fresh cilantro	2	g	optional

1. Working on a lightly floured surface, roll the dough into a 15 × 8 in. (38 × 20 cm) rectangle. Cut two pieces shaped in the outline of a fish. Set aside one piece to use as the top layer.

2. Leaving a small margin around the outside for sealing, spread an even layer of kasha on the dough. Follow with a layer of the salmon/mushroom/egg mixture. Sprinkle with some salt and pepper, and cilantro. Repeat these layers several times, using all of the kasha, salmon, and seasonings.

3. Moisten the edge of the dough. Top with the other piece of dough and seal the edges well. Cut two slits in the top and insert funnels.

4. Transfer carefully (a pizza peel works well) to a lightly oiled baking sheet. Complete the fish detail with fins, eyes, and scales made from dough trimmings. Brush with butter or egg wash and sprinkle with fine bread crumbs.

5. Bake at 375°F (190°C) for about 40 minutes. Reduce the temperature slightly if the fish browns too rapidly.

6. Remove from the oven and add more melted butter through the funnels. The dish may be served hot or cold.

ABOUT POACHING FISH

Poaching in a good court bouillon is the best way to cook fish for sausage. Textures are at their best, and the subtle flavors of the bouillon are very desirable.

To poach a whole fish, place the cleaned fish into cold court bouillon in a nonreactive fish poacher. Bring to a gentle simmer and cook the fish 5 minutes per pound. Let the fish cool in the poaching liquid. The skin is easy to remove when the fish is still slightly warm. Refrigerate the fish until needed. Discard the bouillon; make a fresh bouillon for each whole fish.

Fish can also be poached in salted or acidulated water with no other flavoring ingredients. To 1 gallon of water, add *either* 2 tablespoons of kosher/canning salt *or* 2 tablespoons of distilled vinegar. Use this in the same way as a court bouillon.

Court Bouillon #1

This is a court bouillon to use for *oily fish* such as salmon.

Yield: 1 gallon (3.8 l)

U.S.		Ingredients	Metric		Preparation
1	gal	water	3.8	l	
8	oz	malt vinegar	237	ml	
12	oz	carrot	340	g	scrubbed, diced
1	sprig	fresh thyme	1	sprig	
3	lg	bay leaves	3	lg	
2	oz	fresh parsley	57	g	chopped
15	ea	black peppercorns	15	ea	whole

1. Combine all ingredients except the peppercorns in a nonreactive pot. (Do not use aluminum.) Bring to the boil. Reduce heat, cover, and simmer gently for 1 full hour.
2. Add the peppercorns and simmer for 10 minutes.
3. Strain into a clean nonreactive storage container and cool.
4. Refrigerate for use.

Court Bouillon #2

Following the method below, use this bouillon to poach *nonoily fish* such as turbot and brill for sausage recipes.

Yield: 1 gallon (3.8 l)

U.S.		Ingredients	Metric		Preparation
1	gal	water	3.8	l	
1	pt	whole milk	475	ml	
2	oz	kosher or canning salt	57	g	
1		lemon	1		juiced
1		small onion, optional	1		stuck with 2 cloves
1	rib	celery, optional	1	rib	coarsely chopped
1		bouquet garni	1		optional
		3–4 sprigs parsley			
		2 sprigs fresh thyme			
		½ large bay leaf			
1		whole fish	1		dressed

1. Combine the bouillon ingredients in a nonreactive fish poacher or a pan large enough to hold the fish.
2. Place the fish in the cold bouillon and bring quickly to a gentle simmer.
3. Maintain a simmer for 5 minutes per pound of fish.
4. Allow the fish to cool completely in the bouillon. Skin and bone the fish while it is still slightly warm.
5. Refrigerate the fish in poaching liquid until needed.

Court Bouillon #3

Use this court bouillon to poach *freshwater fish.*

Yield: 1 gallon (3.8 l)

U.S.		Ingredients	Metric		Preparation
2	qt	white wine	1.9	l	
2	qt	water	1.9	l	
½	lb	onions	225	g	peel and slice
2	lg	bay leaves	2	lg	
2	sprigs	fresh thyme	2	sprigs	
2	oz	salt	57	g	kosher or canning
24	ea	black peppercorns	24	ea	

1. Bring all of the ingredients except the peppercorns to a boil in a nonreactive pot. (Do not use aluminum.) Reduce heat and simmer for 20 minutes.

2. Remove from heat and add the peppercorns. Cool and strain.

3. Refrigerate in a tightly covered container.

Crayfish and Oyster Sausage

Chef Kinsella found the recipe for this rich Creole sausage in Baton Rouge, Louisiana. We recommend serving it with a fish sauce and pasta. The links can also be grilled and served with mustard mayonnaise.

Yield: Serves 20

U.S.		Ingredients	Metric		Preparation
2½	lb	crayfish meat	1.1	kg	
2	lb	oysters	900	g	shucked, drained
1	lb	catfish	450	g	skinned
3	oz	best butter	85	g	melted
2	oz	green onions	57	g	finely chopped
2–3	t	fine salt	10–15	g	
1	t	ground mace	1	g	
1	t	dried thyme	1	g	
1	t	Cajun spices	1	g	Chef Paul's Magic blend
1	t	curry powder	1	g	
½	oz	fresh garlic	14	g	finely minced
1	pt	whole milk	475	ml	
4	lg	egg whites	4	lg	lightly beaten
1	lb	white bread crumbs	450	g	very fine
		lamb casings	26–28	mm	
		fish stock			

1. Grind the prepared crayfish, oysters, and catfish through a ¹⁄₁₆ in. (0.15 cm) plate. Refrigerate immediately for 1 hour.

2. Heat the butter gently and sweat the green onions without coloring.

3. Remove the pan from heat. Add the salt, mace, thyme, Cajun spices, curry powder, and garlic. Stir well to blend while adding the milk. Cool. When the mixture is cool, add the egg whites.

4. Pour the seasoning solution at once into the chilled ground fish mixture. Mix lightly but well.

5. Fold in the bread crumbs to bind the mixture. Chill if necessary.

6. Stuff into the prepared casings. Link 5 sausages per pound (450 g).

7. Poach the links at once in a good fish stock. Check the internal temperature frequently, removing the links at 150°F (65°C).

8. Wrap the links well and refrigerate. Use within 3 days.

Creamed Herring

This is a very popular Scandinavian fish preparation. We give three cream variations because each changes the dish. We recommend making it ahead in small quantities.

Yield: 2 pints (1 kg)

U.S.		Ingredients	Metric		Preparation
2	pt	pickled herring	1	kg	
1	c	light sour cream	240	ml	
		or			
½	c	light sour cream	118	ml	
½	c	heavy cream	118	ml	
		or			
1	c	yogurt	240	ml	unflavored

1. Strain the herring over a bowl to capture the pickling liquid. Measure and reserve half of the liquid.
2. Combine the reserved pickling liquid and sour cream. Add the herring and any accompanying spices and onions. Mix gently but thoroughly. Return the creamed herring to the empty jars.
3. Mellow in the refrigerator for at least 12 hours before serving.

Creamed Truffle Sausage

This "King of Sausages" is best served grilled. We suggest serving it with a rich Sauce Suprême. It can be accompanied with roasted red peppers and pasta with a fresh tomato-basil sauce.

Yield: 10 pounds (4.5 kg)

U.S.		Ingredients	Metric		Preparation
8	lb	skinless chicken breast	3.6	kg	
1	lb	chicken fat	450	g	skins and body fat
4	oz	salt	113	g	
½	oz	ground white pepper	14	g	
2	oz	ginger, mace, nutmeg	58	g	equal parts mixture
3	oz	white sugar	85	g	granulated
4	oz	brandy	118	ml	good quality
2	oz	garlic	57	g	very finely minced
4	lg	whole eggs	4	lg	
1½	pt	heavy cream	709	ml	
2	oz	truffles	57	g	very finely minced
1	in.	sheep casings	2.5	cm	
		strong chicken stock			cold

1. Grind the chicken breasts and fat twice with a ⅜ in. (0.9 cm) plate.
2. Mix in the salt, pepper, ginger, mace, nutmeg, sugar, brandy, and garlic. Pack into a shallow pan, cover, and chill for at least 1 hour.
3. Beat the eggs and add to the forcemeat. Add the cream and mix well.
4. Make a smooth paste of this mixture in a food processor, stirring down once or twice.
5. Add the truffles and fold in to obtain a very uniform mix. Pack into shallow pans and cover. Return to the cooler for 1 hour.
6. Stuff the prepared casings carefully, avoiding air pockets. Twist into 4 in. (10 cm) links.
7. Place the sausages in a pan and cover with the stock. Poach very gently to an internal temperature of 165°F (74°C). Remove the sausages with care and drain.
8. Keep well chilled for 24 hours. Separate the links, grill, and serve.

Crépinettes

Crépinettes are an ancient sausage. They can be made with various meats, fish, and poultry. Sometimes used as a classic garnish, they are delicious served with a sharp mustard sauce.

Yield: 3 pounds (1.4 kg)

U.S.		Ingredients	Metric		Preparation
2	lb	pork tenderloin	900	g	
12	oz	fatback	340	g	
½	c	thick béchamel sauce	118	ml	cool
3		eggs	3		beaten
1	oz	salt	28	g	
1	oz	black pepper	28	g	
2	oz	brandy	60	ml	
1	t	parsley			finely chopped
		caul fat			cut into 16 rectangles

FOR BREAD CRUMB COATING:

1		egg	1		beaten
8	oz	bread crumbs	225	g	

1. Grind the pork and fatback together. Chill.
2. To the béchamel, add the eggs, salt, pepper, brandy, and parsley.
3. Add the seasoning mixture to the chilled meat.
4. Let the mixture stand for 1 hour in the refrigerator.
5. Shape the mixture into 3-oz (85 g) flat rectangles.
6. Wrap them in the pieces of caul fat.
7. Coat lightly with the egg and bread crumbs. Return to the cooler for about an hour to set up.
8. Sauté or deep-fry the crépinettes for 3–5 minutes and serve.

Desros Sausage

We thank Marta Atkocaitis for this wonderful Lithuanian sausage. We think it works well for breakfast, brunch, dinner, or picnic.

Yield: Serves 30

U.S.		Ingredients	Metric		Preparation
10	lb	pork shoulder	4.5	kg	cubed
2	lb	onions	1	kg	finely diced
4	oz	butter substitute	114	g	
2	c	ice water	475	ml	
2	oz	salt	57	g	
3	t	black pepper	6	g	
3	t	ground allspice	6	g	
		casings	28–32	mm	

1. Sauté the onions in a light butter substitute.
2. Grind the meat once through a ⅜ in. (0.9 cm) plate.
3. Put the ice water into a container and stir in the salt, pepper, and allspice. Mix this solution into the ground meat.
4. Stuff the prepared casings. Tie into 3 in. (8 cm) links. Chill for 24 hours.
5. Grill or roast this sausage to order.

Dry-Cured Farmer's Sausage

Although this sausage takes a long time to make, it keeps well for over 6 months.

Yield: 10 pounds (4.5 kg)

U.S.	Ingredients	Metric		Preparation
8 lb	lean beef	3.6	kg	boneless
1½ lb	lean pork trimmings	680	g	
½ lb	fatback	220	g	
8 T	salt	120	g	
2 t	Prague powder #2	10	g	measured accurately
1 oz	powdered dextrose	28	g	
3½ in. × 20–24 in.	beef middles	9 × 50–60 cm		

1. Have the meats chilled to 32–34°F (0–1°C). Grind the beef using a ⅛ in. (0.3 cm) plate. Grind the pork trimmings and fatback using a ½ in. (1.3 cm) plate. Mix the beef, pork, and fatback; grind again using a ¼ in. (0.6 cm) plate.

2. Combine the salt, Prague powder #2, and dextrose and mix into the meat very well by hand. Pack the mixture into shallow tubs or pans. Eliminate all air pockets. Cover and refrigerate. Hold at 34–38°F (1–3°C) for 3 days.

3. After 72 hours, firmly stuff the prepared beef middles with no air pockets.

4. Hold the sausages for 12 hours at 75°F (24°C) with 70–80% relative humidity.

SMOKING

1. Using a very heavy smoke, smoke for 3 days at 70°F (21°C).

2. After smoking, dry the sausages at 52–56°F (11–13°C) with 65% relative humidity for at least 30 days. The sausages are then ready for use.

Dry-Cured Hard Salami

We give Poland the credit for this salami which is very popular in the northeastern and mid-western regions of the United States.

Yield: 2 salami sausages of 2¼ pounds (1 kg) each

U.S.		Ingredients	Metric		Preparation
2	lb	lean pork	1	kg	trimmed and diced
2	lb	lean beef	1	kg	trimmed and diced
1	lb	fatback	450	g	diced (½ in. and frozen)
8	oz	ice water	237	ml	
1	t	salt	5	g	
½	t	black pepper	1	g	freshly ground
1	t	pure garlic powder	1	g	
¼	t	ground ginger	1	g	
¼	oz	powdered dextrose	7	g	
1	oz	corn syrup solids	28	g	powdered
½	oz	Prague powder #2	14	g	measured accurately
		fibrous salami casings			

1. Grind the pork and beef through a ⅛ in. (0.3 cm) plate.
2. Grind the frozen fatback pieces through a ³⁄₁₆ in. (0.5 cm) plate. Return the fatback to the freezer until mixing time.
3. Put the ice water in a container and stir in the salt, pepper, garlic powder, ginger, dextrose, corn syrup solids, and Prague powder #2. Add this seasoning solution to the meat.
4. Fold in the frozen fat.
5. Press the forcemeat into a container, avoiding air pockets. Cover and refrigerate for a full 48 hours.
6. Stuff the prepared salami casings, packing quite firmly. Tie a butterfly knot at one end and use a hog ring to close the other end.
7. Air dry in the smoker for 5 days at 70°F (21°C) and 80% relative humidity.

Note: A carefully regulated smoker, having steam injection available, can be used to great advantage for this curing time. It is wise to be familiar with your equipment first, before attempting this process.

Dry-Cured Smoked Bratwurst

Bratwurst is a real midwestern favorite. Plan to use this sausage within 6 days as it does not keep well.

Yield: 6 pounds (2.7 kg); serves 25

U.S.		Ingredients	Metric		Preparation
5	lb	pork butt	2.2	kg	trimmed
1	lb	fatback	450	g	cubed
½	pt	ice water	235	ml	
1	T	salt	15	g	
2	T	ground pepper	12	g	
2	T	garlic powder	6	g	
1	t	nutmeg	1	g	
1	t	ground mace	1	g	
1	T	rubbed sage	3	g	
1	T	Prague powder #2	15	g	measured accurately
3	t	powdered dextrose	9	g	
		hog or sheep casings	32	mm	

1. Grind the meat and fatback through a ³⁄₁₆ in. (0.5 cm) plate. Pack into shallow pans and chill for 1 hour.
2. Put the water in a container and stir in the remaining ingredients. Distribute this mixture carefully over the meat and mix thoroughly.
3. Stuff the prepared casings. Make 6 in. (15 cm) links.

SMOKING

1. Place the sausages in a preheated smoker at 75°F (24°C). Maintain a cold smoke to dry cure for a full 36 hours.
2. Wrap the bratwursts well and refrigerate for use.

Duck Salami

This sausage can be made with any game poultry. It is excellent for sandwiches and buffets. *Be aware that this recipe requires a 40-day cure.*

Yield: 10 pounds (4.5 kg); serves 40

U.S.		Ingredients	Metric		Preparation
10	lb	duck meat	4.5	kg	
1	c	brandy	235	ml	
1	pt	ice water	475	ml	
2	T	salt	15	g	
1	T	pepper	5	g	coarsely ground
1	oz	fresh orange zest	28	g	
1	T	Prague powder #2	15	g	measured accurately
1	t	ground nutmeg	1	g	
1	t	ground cloves	1	g	
1	t	garlic powder	1	g	
1	lb	soy protein	450	g	
1	T	powdered dextrose	15	g	
4	ea	salami casings	4	ea	soaked and rinsed

1. Grind the meat using a ³⁄₁₆ in. (0.5 cm) plate. Mix in the brandy and let stand for 1 hour.
2. Put the water in a container. Combine the salt, pepper, zest, Prague powder #2, nutmeg, cloves, garlic powder, soy protein, and dextrose; stir into the ice water and mix well.
3. Mix the seasoning solution into the ground meat and distribute well. Refrigerate overnight.
4. Tie one end of each casing securely with a butterfly knot. Stuff the casings, avoiding air pockets. Close the other end with hog rings.
5. Hang in the refrigerator to air dry for 40 days.

SMOKING

1. Place in a preheated smoker at 135°F (57°C). Hold at this temperature for 1 hour with the dampers three-quarters open.
2. Adjust the damper to one-quarter open and increase the temperature every half hour until the smoker reaches 170–175°F (77–79°C). Provide a heavy smoke fire during this period.
3. Remove the sausages when the internal temperature reaches 165°F (74°C). Spray with cold water to cool to an internal temperature of 90°F (32°C). Hang, unwrapped, in the cooler.

VARIATION

Omit the orange zest and replace half of the ice water with orange juice.

English Beef Bangers

To re-create the famous "bangers and mash," grill these sausages and serve them with mashed potatoes and a rich roast gravy.

Yield: 10 pounds (4.5 kg)

U.S.		Ingredients	Metric		Preparation
10	lb	ground beef	4.5	kg	20% fat
1	pt	ice water	475	ml	
1	T	salt	15	g	
1	T	fresh sage	6	g	chopped
1	t	fresh thyme	2	g	chopped
½	t	ground cloves	0.5	g	
1	t	ground nutmeg	1	g	
1	t	onion powder	1	g	
1	t	dried parsley	1	g	
		sheep casings	24–26	mm	for kosher links
		or			
		hog casings	32–35	mm	

1. Put the water in a container and stir in the seasoning ingredients. Mix this solution into the meat and chill for 1 hour.
2. Grind mixture through a ⅛ in. (0.31 cm) plate and chill again.
3. Stuff the prepared casings. Tie into 3 in. (8 cm) links.
4. Refrigerate for use.

English Beef Sausage

This is an excellent kosher grilling sausage.

Yield: 10 pounds (4.5 kg)

U.S.		Ingredients	Metric		Preparation
10	lb	lean beef	4.5	kg	diced
1	pt	ice water	475	ml	
5	oz	fine salt	142	g	
2	oz	black pepper	57	g	freshly ground
1	oz	nutmeg/sage/ginger	28	g	equal parts mixture
2	oz	sugar	57	g	
		sheep casings	32–35	mm	

1. Grind the beef using a ⅜ in. (0.9 cm) plate.

2. Put the water in a container and stir in the salt, pepper, spices, and sugar. Mix thoroughly into the meat by hand.

3. Grind the mixture again using a ⅛ in. (0.3 cm) plate.

4. Stuff the prepared casings. Twist into 3 in. (8 cm) links.

5. Place the links in a pan and cover. Refrigerate for use.

English Black Pudding

This is a ring sausage to grill or sauté for breakfast.

Yield: 10 pounds (4.5 kg)

U.S.		Ingredients	Metric		Preparation
4	lb	fatback	1.8	kg	¼ in. (0.6 cm) dice
1	lb	pearl barley	450	g	
1	pt	milk	475	ml	
¼	lb	shallots	113	g	finely diced
1	gal	beef or pork blood	3.7	l	strictly fresh
3	oz	salt	85	g	
4	oz	black pepper	113	g	
2–3	oz	dried sage	57–85	g	
1¼	lb	oatmeal	600	g	
		beef rounds	38 × 40 mm or 40 × 42 mm		
		cold meat stock			

1. Soak the barley in the milk for several hours. Cook the barley in the same milk.
2. Render half of the fatback and sauté the shallots until they are soft. Cool slightly.
3. Mix the barley and shallots. Add the blood and mix well.
4. Add the salt, pepper, sage, and the remaining fatback.
5. Gradually fold in the oatmeal to the desired consistency. The mixture should not be too stiff.
6. Allowing some room for expansion, stuff the prepared rings. Tie into 10–12 in. (26–31 cm) rings.
7. Place the rings into cold stock. Bring the stock to 160°F (71°C).
8. Poach the puddings gently to an internal temperature of 155°F (68°C).
9. Cool and refrigerate for 24 hours before use.

English Breakfast Sausage

This sausage has many variations throughout England.

Yield: 10 pounds (4.5 kg)

U.S.		Ingredients	Metric		Preparation
10	lb	pork butt	4.5	kg	trimmed and cubed
2	c	ice water	475	ml	
1	oz	salt	28	g	
¼	oz	black pepper	7	g	
¼	t	ground ginger	0.5	g	
1	t	allspice	2	g	
		sheep casings	32–35	mm	

1. Grind the pork through a ⅜ in. (0.9 cm) plate.
2. Put the water in a container and stir in the salt, pepper, ginger, and allspice. Distribute evenly and mix into the meat.
3. Grind through a ³⁄₁₆ in. (0.5 cm) plate. Chill for 1 hour.
4. Stuff the prepared casings loosely, avoiding air pockets. Tie into 2½ in. (7 cm) links.
5. Refrigerate for 24 hours to develop flavor before cooking.

VARIATIONS

English Pork Sausage II: Omit the ginger and allspice and add: 1 t (1 g) rubbed sage, 1 t (2.5 g) nutmeg, 1 t (1 g) mace, and 1 t (2 g) ginger.

English Pork Sausage III: Omit the ginger and allspice and add: 1 t (1 g) rubbed sage, 1 t (1 g) mace, 1 t (2 g) ginger, 1 t (1.5 g) ground coriander, and ¼ t (0.4 g) cayenne pepper.

Sussex Sausage: Omit the ginger and allspice and add: 1 t (1 g) mace, 1 t (1 g) cinnamon, and 1 t (1 g) rubbed sage.

Chicken Sausage: Substitute 10 lb (4.5 kg) chicken leg meat for the pork.

Beef and Suet Sausage: Substitute 8 lb (3.6 kg) lean beef and 1½ lb (700 g) suet for the pork.

English Fresh Herb Sausage

Like most fresh sausages, these are best when served directly from the pan. Avoid over-cooking or piercing.

Yield: 6 pounds (2.7 kg)

U.S.		Ingredients	Metric		Preparation
6	lb	lean pork butt	2.7	kg	trimmed and cubed
2	lb	fatback	900	g	cubed
1	oz	kosher salt	28	g	
1	oz	black pepper	28	g	#10 coarse grind
1	oz	horseradish	28	g	prepared
2	oz	onion	57	g	finely grated
2	t	fresh sage	4	g	finely chopped
1	t	fresh thyme	2	g	finely chopped
2	t	Prague powder #1	10	g	measured accurately
		sheep or hog casings	28–32	mm	

1. Grind the pork and fatback separately using a ⅜ in. (0.9 cm) plate. Mix them and grind together using a ¼ in. (0.6 cm) plate.

2. Blend the salt, pepper, horseradish, onion, sage, thyme, and Prague powder #1. Sprinkle over the meat and mix very well by hand. Pack into shallow pans without air pockets. Cover and chill for 24 hours.

3. Stuff the prepared casings, avoiding air pockets. Tie into 3 in. (8 cm) links. Place into pans and cover tightly.

4. Refrigerate for use.

5. Panfry gently about 8 minutes until the sausages show no pink at the center.

English Venison Salami

This is an excellent salami to serve with Irish brown bread and red wine.

Yield: 10 pounds (4.5 kg)

U.S.		Ingredients	Metric		Preparation
7½	lb	venison or moose	3.4	kg	trimmed weight, cubed
2½	lb	fatback	1.1	kg	½ in. (1.3 cm) dice
1	pt	burgundy wine	475	ml	
2	t	Prague powder #1	10	g	measured accurately
1	oz	dried sorrel	28	g	
1	oz	ground nutmeg	28	g	
1	oz	fresh garlic	28	g	minced
2	oz	light brown sugar	57	g	
2	oz	corn syrup solids	57	g	
½	oz	onion powder	14	g	
1	t	dried thyme	1	g	
1	t	dried sage	1	g	
4	ea	salami casings	4	ea	

1. Combine the wine, Prague powder #1, and all of the seasoning ingredients. Immerse the meat in the marinade and cover. Marinate in the cooler for 24 hours.
2. Remove the venison from the marinade and grind using a ³⁄₁₆ in. (0.5 cm) plate.
3. Stir the marinade and add it to the ground venison; mix well by hand.
4. Dice the fatback using a ¹⁄₁₆ in. (0.15 cm) plate. Mix into the sausage. Chill for 30 minutes.
5. Close one end of each casing with a butterfly knot. Use a large tube to stuff each casing approximately two-thirds full, allowing room to close with a hog ring. Avoid air pockets.

SMOKING

1. Place the salamis into a preheated smoker at 130°F (54°C) with the dampers wide open to create a pellicle.
2. Close the dampers to one-half open and raise the temperature to 155°F (68°C) for 5 hours.
3. Raise the temperature to 160°F (71°C). Hold until the internal temperature is 155°F (68°C).
4. Remove from the smoker and shower with cold water until the internal temperature reaches 100°F (38°C).
5. Hang the sausages briefly at room temperature to dry thoroughly. Check for secure hanging cords and hang in cooler for storage.

VARIATION

Stuff into 28–32 mm hog casings and tie into 3 in. (8 cm) links. Smoke for approximately one-half the time. Loop the links on hanging sticks to facilitate handling.

European Farmer's Sausage

Serve medium-thick slices of this sausage on dark bread with shaved onion and freshly ground black pepper.

Yield: 10 pounds (4.5 kg)

U.S.		Ingredients	Metric		Preparation
4	lb	baby beef liver	1.8	kg	trimmed
3	lb	beef tripe	1.4	kg	well-washed, trimmed
3	lb	pork belly	1.4	kg	
		rich beef stock			as needed
1	pt	strong ale	475	ml	
5	oz	fine salt	142	g	
3	T	onion powder	9	g	
¼	t	ground ginger	0.25	g	
1	t	dried marjoram	1	g	
¼	t	ground cloves	0.7	g	
2	t	Prague powder #1	10	g	measured accurately
1	oz	dextrose	28	g	or light brown sugar
12	oz	soy protein powder	340	g	
		beef middles			
		stock or weak consommé			

1. Weigh the liver, tripe, and pork belly and record the total weight.
2. Simmer the liver in water until cooked through. (The liver may be diced to speed cooking.) Cool.
3. Cook the tripe for 1 hour in water. Cool.
4. Weigh the meats again and add enough stock to return to the original weight.
5. Grind all of the meat using a ⅜ in. (0.9 cm) plate.
6. Put the ale in a container and stir in the salt, onion powder, ginger, marjoram, cloves, Prague powder #1, dextrose, and soy protein powder. Add this solution to the meat and mix well.

(Continued)

7. Grind again through a ⅜ in. (0.9 cm) plate. Pack into shallow pans and cover tightly. Chill for at least 1 hour.

8. Stuff the prepared beef middles. Do not stuff too tightly.

9. Poach the sausages in stock or weak consommé at 160–165°F (71–74°C) for about 2 hours until the internal temperature reaches 160°F (71°C).

10. Remove carefully and place in a large ice bath. Cool quickly to 75°F (24°C). Spray the sausages with hot water at 180°F (82°C) to remove excess fat from the casings.

11. Hang briefly to dry. Refrigerate for use.

Faggots I

Serve this sausage with English pease pudding and creamed potatoes. This is wonderful winter fare.

Yield: 4 pounds (1.8 kg)

U.S.		Ingredients	Metric		Preparation
2	lb	beef liver	900	g	trimmed
1½	lb	fatty pork butt	700	g	gland removed
		clarified butter			for sauté
8	oz	Spanish onion	226	g	
1	oz	fresh garlic	28	g	finely chopped
1	oz	fresh sage	28	g	finely chopped
1	oz	fresh thyme	28	g	finely chopped
¾	oz	ground mace	21	g	
6	lg	eggs	6	lg	beaten
2	lb	fine bread crumbs	900	g	2 days old
2	oz	good white wine	59	ml	
32	pc	caul fat	32	pc	
3	pt	demi-glace sauce	1½	l	

1. Grind the liver and pork butt using a 3/16 in. (0.45 cm) plate. In a large pan, gently sauté the meat in a little clarified butter.

2. Add the onion, garlic, sage, and thyme. Cook briefly at low-to-medium heat to sweat the onions. Drain and reserve any excess juices. Remove from heat.

3. Stir in the mace, eggs, bread crumbs, and wine. The mixture should be firm enough to hold its shape when formed with a spoon. Adjust, if necessary, using the reserved juices and/or a few more bread crumbs.

4. Shape into uniform 2-oz (57 g) quenelles. Wrap each with caul fat and seal well. Place on a sheet pan and bake briefly to set at 325°F (163°C). Do not overcook.
5. Place in a lidded casserole and cover with the demi-glace. Cover the dish and bake at 275°F (135°C) for 45–60 minutes. The faggots are then ready for service.

Faggots II

Because this sausage is exceptionally delicate, it is important to use the seasonings as described. Grill gently and serve piping hot. Use these faggots within 4 days.

Yield: 10 pounds (4.5 kg)

U.S.		Ingredients	Metric		Preparation
10	lb	calf or beef brains	4.5	kg	
1	pt	ice water	475	ml	
2	oz	fine salt	57	g	
1	oz	black pepper	28	g	freshly ground
¼	oz	cayenne pepper	7	g	
1	t	dried sage	1	g	finely sieved
1	t	dried thyme	1	g	finely sieved
		sheep casings	32–35	mm	

1. Soak, rinse, and cook the brains according to the procedure on page 42.
2. Finely chop the brains. Mix in the ice water and all of the seasonings.
3. Grind using a ⅛ in. (0.3 cm) plate. If the mixture is not uniform in texture, grind again.
4. Chill for 45 minutes if the forcemeat has become too warm.
5. Stuff the prepared casings and tie into 3 in. (8 cm) links.
6. Wrap, label, and store the sausages near 32°F (0°C) to preserve quality.

Fennel and Paprika Links

This sausage has a haunting flavor. For a coarser variety, grind only two times and stuff into hog casings. Use this sausage within 5 days.

Yield: 9 pounds (4 kg)

U.S.		Ingredients	Metric		Preparation
9	lb	trimmed pork butt	4	kg	lean
6	yd	lamb casings	5.5	m	24–26 mm
16	oz	fresh orange juice	475	ml	strained
3½	t	fine salt	17.5	g	
1½	t	ground white pepper	3	g	
2½	t	ground fennel seed	2.5	g	
5	T	sweet paprika	15	g	

1. Wash and thoroughly flush the casings.
2. Place the casings in the orange juice to cover. Soak in the cooler for 24 hours before making the sausage.
3. Dice the pork into 1 in. (2.5 cm) cubes. Grind using a ½ in. (1.2 cm) plate. Grind again using a ¼ in. (0.63 cm) plate. Grind a third time using a ⅛ in. (0.31 cm) plate.
4. Pour the orange juice from the casings and reserve the juice. Cover the casings with cool water and return to the cooler.
5. Thoroughly mix the seasonings into the ground meat; add the reserved orange juice. Chill for 1 hour.
6. Stuff the prepared casings rather firmly. Tie into 5–6 in. (14 cm) links. Coil onto a tray lined with parchment paper or plastic film. Cover tightly and refrigerate at 32–36°F (0–2°C) for use within 5 days.

Fish Sausage

This sausage was inspired by a Rytec Kutas recipe. A mild-to-medium flavored fish works best. Carefully remove any bones or strong-flavored skin. Fish sausage is more perishable than other sausages; store it at 35°F (2°C) or lower.

Yield: 10 pounds (4.5 kg)

U.S.		Ingredients	Metric		Preparation
10	lb	skinless fish flesh	4.5	kg	well-chilled
1	T	salt	15	g	or to taste
12	oz	cornstarch	340	g	
1	pt	ice water	475	ml	
1	t	granulated sugar	12	g	
1	T	white pepper	6	g	finely ground
1	t	onion powder	1	g	
1	t	garlic powder	1	g	
1	t	ground nutmeg	1	g	
1	lb	vegetable shortening	450	g	solid hydrogenated
2–3½	in.	fibrous casings	5–9	cm	

1. Grind the fish through a ³⁄₁₆ in. (0.45 cm) grinder plate. Add the salt and mix thoroughly. Hold for 15 minutes in cooler to promote binding.

2. Stir the cornstarch into the ice water; add all seasonings and the shortening. Mix this solution thoroughly and uniformly into the fish.

3. Working quickly, stuff the prepared casings.

4. Cook the sausage at once in 200–205°F (92–95°C) water to an internal temperature of 140°F (60°C). Cool promptly in an ice water bath or shower to reduce the internal temperature to 70°F (21°C). Immediately immerse the sausages into boiling water for 1 full minute to tighten the casings.

5. Refrigerate at once.

VARIATIONS

1. Add 2 t (10 ml) liquid smoke.

2. This recipe may be cooked in loaf pans. It will slice well and can be used like luncheon meat.

Frankfurters

By tradition, these popular sausages are sold fully cooked. Their flavor and appearance are enhanced by finishing on the grill or under the broiler. They can be stuffed into smaller casings and tied off in various lengths.

Yield: 10 pounds (4.5 kg)

U.S.		Ingredients	Metric		Preparation
8½	lb	pork butt	3.8	kg	
1½	lb	fatback	675	g	
1	lb	dried diced onion	450	g	
2	oz	minced fresh garlic	57	g	
		or			
2½	oz	garlic powder	71	g	
3	oz	kosher or canning salt	85	g	
2	oz	ground coriander	57	g	
1½	oz	ground mace	43	g	
1½	oz	ground white pepper	43	g	
1	oz	ground caraway seed	28	g	
1	oz	sweet paprika	28	g	
2	oz	powdered dextrose	57	g	
10	oz	white bread crumbs	284	g	dry
6	lg	egg whites	6	lg	
24	oz	dried milk	709	ml	reconstituted
		hog casings	32–38	mm	

1. In a food processor, purée the seasoning ingredients, bread crumbs, and egg whites with half the milk. Scrape down the sides of the bowl as necessary. Add more milk to reach a pouring consistency. Process the mixture until it is a very smooth purée. Reserve in the cooler.

2. Grind the pork and fatback, first through a ⅜ in. (0.9 cm) plate, then through a ¼ in. (0.6 cm) plate.

3. Combine the meat and seasoning mixtures and mix well by hand.

4. In batches, thoroughly purée the sausage mixture in the food processor. Pack into shallow pans, cover, and chill.

5. Load the sausage stuffer carefully (the frankfurter mixture can be quite sloppy). Stuff the prepared casings and tie into 4–8 in. (10–20 cm) links.

6. To cook the franks, poach in simmering hot water or stock for about 18 minutes until the internal temperature reaches 165°F (74°C). Use a weight if necessary to keep the links fully submerged. Cool and refrigerate for use.

Fresh Beef Sausage

This is a simple, satisfying sausage that grills well.

Yield: 10 pounds (4.5 kg)

U.S.		Ingredients	Metric		Preparation
10	lb	beef stew meat	4.5	kg	trimmed
1	oz	nutmeg, thyme, sage, and ginger	28	g	equal parts mixture
3½	oz	fine salt	99	g	
2	oz	granulated sugar	57	g	
2	oz	black pepper	57	g	freshly ground
1	pt	cold water	475	ml	
		sheep casings	32–35	mm	

1. Grind the beef using a ⅜ in. (0.9 cm) plate.
2. Mix in the spices, salt, sugar, and pepper.
3. Grind again using a ⅛ in. (0.3 cm) plate.
4. Add the water and mix.
5. Stuff the prepared casings and twist into 3 in. (8 cm) links.
6. Wrap, label, and hold refrigerated for use.

Garlic Sausage

This is a sausage for garlic lovers. It is a good choice for grilling.

Yield: 10 pounds (4.5 kg)

U.S.		Ingredients	Metric		Preparation
10	lb	pork butt	4.5	kg	trimmed, cubed
1	oz	fine salt	28	g	
½	oz	white pepper	14	g	freshly ground
1	t	ground mace	0.5	g	
¼	oz	cayenne pepper	7	g	
2	oz	fresh garlic	57	g	finely minced
1	pt	ice water	475	ml	
		sheep casings	32–35	mm	

1. Grind the pork using a ⅜ in. (0.9 cm) plate.
2. Add the salt, pepper, mace, cayenne pepper, and garlic to the meat and mix well.
3. Grind again using a ⅛ in. (0.3 cm) plate.
4. Mix in the ice water.
5. Stuff the prepared casings. Tie into desired lengths.
6. Wrap, label, and refrigerate for use.

Gayettes

We suggest serving these French sausages covered with a Sauce Diable accompanied by gnocchi and cauliflower au gratin.

Yield: 3 pounds (1.3 kg)

U.S.		Ingredients	Metric		Preparation
2	lb	pork liver	900	g	trimmed and cubed
½	lb	fatback	225	g	diced
½	lb	pork tenderloin	225	g	cubed
1	oz	fresh garlic	28	g	finely minced
2	oz	shallots	57	g	finely chopped
4	oz	cooked fresh spinach	113	g	drained, finely chopped
1	T	salt	15	g	
1	t	ground pepper	2	g	
1	oz	chervil, mace, thyme	28	g	dried, in equal parts
		caul fat			

1. Grind the meats and fatback using a ⅜ in. (0.9 cm) plate.
2. Add the garlic, shallots, spinach, and seasonings. Mix well by hand.
3. Chill for 1 hour to firm.
4. Form the mixture into 2-oz (57 g) flat rectangles.
5. Wrap each in a piece of caul fat. Refrigerate for use.
6. To cook, bake in a casserole at 325°F (163°C) for 30 minutes or until done. Drain excess fat and cover with a Sauce Diable. Serve at once or reheat for later service.

Dry-Cured Genoa Salami

This unsmoked Italian salami can be made with pork, beef, or a combination. This is an adaptation of a recipe from Rytec Kutas' book, *Great Sausage Recipes and Meat Curing.*

Yield: one 10-pound (4.5 kg) salami

U.S.		Ingredients	Metric		Preparation
8	lb	pork butt	3.6	kg	trimmed and cubed
2	lb	stew beef	900	g	cubed
8	oz	dry white wine	237	ml	
½	t	fine salt	7	g	
1	T	black pepper	6	g	#6 mesh (coarse)
1½	T	white peppercorns	9	g	whole
1	t	garlic powder	10	g	
2	t	Prague powder #2	10	g	measured accurately
1	T	powdered dextrose	9	g	
1	oz	corn syrup solids	28	g	
		salami casing			

1. Grind the pork and beef together using a ¼ in. (0.6 cm) plate. Chill for 1 hour.

2. Put the wine in a container and stir in the salt, pepper, peppercorns, garlic powder, Prague powder #2, dextrose, and corn syrup solids. Thoroughly mix this solution into the meat. Pack into shallow pans and refrigerate at 38°F (3°C) for a full 48 hours.

3. Tie one end of the casing with a butterfly knot. Stuff the prepared casing, avoiding air pockets. Close the other end with a clip.

4. Hang for 60 days at a constant temperature of 45–50°F (7–10°C) and 75% relative humidity.

German Bierwurst

This useful sausage is quite highly flavored. You may adjust the seasonings. It is a good variety to grill.

Yield: 10 pounds (4.5 kg)

U.S.		Ingredients	Metric		Preparation
6	lb	pork butt	2.7	kg	trimmed and cubed
3	lb	veal trimmings	1.4	kg	cubed
1	lb	boned smoked ham hock	450	g	cubed
1½	oz	fine salt	43	g	
1	oz	fine black pepper	28	g	freshly ground
1	t	ground nutmeg	1	g	
¼	t	ground cardamom	0.25	g	or to taste
1	oz	fresh garlic	28	g	crushed
1	T	powdered mustard	3	g	
1	oz	dried thyme	28	g	rubbed
2	t	Prague powder #1	10	g	measured accurately
		lamb casings	28–32	mm	
		or			
		beef round casings	40–42	mm	

1. Grind the pork and veal using a ⅜ in. (0.9 cm) plate. Add the seasoning ingredients and the Prague powder #1. Mix very well by hand or in an electric mixer. Pack into shallow pans, cover, and chill for 12 hours.

2. Grind the ham hock through a ¼ in. (0.6 cm) plate. Add it to the chilled forcemeat and mix well.

3. Stuff the prepared casings. (Tie stuffed beef rounds securely and make hanging loops with the string.) Dry at room temperature for 2 hours.

SMOKING

1. Place the sausages in a preheated smoker at 140°F (60°C) with the dampers wide open. Process 1 hour or until the sausages begin to color.

2. Adjust the dampers to one-quarter open and increase the temperature to 160–165°F (71–74°C). Continue at this setting until the bierwurst is dark brown and the internal temperature is 152°F (67°C).

3. Remove the sausages from the smoker and shower briefly with hot water. Chill overnight before use.

German Bologna

This bologna makes excellent sandwiches. It is especially good on rye bread with onion and dill pickles.

Yield: 10 pounds (4.5 kg)

U.S.		Ingredients	Metric		Preparation
6	lb	beef	2.8	kg	not too lean
4	lb	pork	1.8	kg	
2	oz	fine salt	57	g	
1	T	ground white pepper	6	g	
1	oz	powdered mustard	28	g	
1	t	ground celery seed	1	g	
1	t	ground nutmeg	1	g	
1	T	ground coriander	3	g	
1	oz	powdered dextrose	28	g	
12	oz	powdered soy protein	340	g	
2	t	Prague powder #1	10	g	measured accurately
1	pt	whole milk	475	ml	
		beef bungs or rounds			

1. Grind the beef and pork through a ³⁄₁₆ in. (0.5 cm) plate.
2. Add the remaining ingredients and mix well.
3. Purée the seasoned mixture in a vertical cutting machine or food processor. Run the machine as long as necessary to make the mixture completely smooth. Check the temperature and chill if necessary.
4. Stuff the prepared casings. Avoid air pockets but do not pack too tightly.
5. Hang to air dry in the cooler for 12 hours. Be sure the hanging strings are very secure, especially when using the large beef bungs.

SMOKING

1. Place the sausages in a preheated smoker at 130°F (54°C). Set the dampers one-half open. Increase the temperature every 45 minutes to a maximum of 170°F (77°C). Cook to an internal temperature of 155°F (68°C).

German Smoked Sausage

This versatile sausage can be seasoned according to individual preference. Like many other sausages, it is best consumed fresh.

Yield: 10 pounds (4.5 kg)

U.S.		Ingredients	Metric		Preparation
10	lb	pork and veal trimmings	4.5	kg	80% lean or better
1	oz	fine salt	28	g	
½	oz	black pepper	14	g	fresh medium grind
¼	oz	ground mace	7	g	
1	t	ground ginger	2	g	
¼	oz	ground nutmeg	7	g	
¼	oz	dried sage	7	g	rubbed fine
2	t	Prague powder #1	10	g	measured accurately
1	pt	ice water	475	ml	
		sheep casings	32–35	mm	

1. Grind the meat using a ⅜ in. (0.9 cm) plate. Add the salt, pepper, mace, ginger, nutmeg, and sage; mix well by hand or in an electric mixer.
2. Thoroughly dissolve the Prague powder #1 in the ice water. Set aside.
3. Grind the forcemeat again using a ⅛ in. (0.3 cm) plate.
4. Sprinkle the Prague powder #1 solution over the meat and blend thoroughly.
5. Stuff the prepared casings. Tie into 5 in. (13 cm) links.

SMOKING

1. Place the sausages in a preheated smoker at 135°F (57°C). Raise the temperature of the smoker 5°F (2–3°C) every 30 minutes until it reaches 165°F (74°C).
2. Remove the sausages from the smoker when the internal product temperature is 155°F (68°C). Spray with cold water until the internal temperature drops to 100°F (38°C).
3. Refrigerate for use.

Goetta

This is an original recipe developed by Chef Harvey over many years in his search for the perfect goetta. It can be served with fried or scrambled eggs or with syrup.

Yield: 2 loaf pans, about 7 pounds (3 kg)

U.S.		Ingredients	Metric		Preparation
1	lb	baby beef liver	450	g	trimmed and cubed
2	lb	beef chuck	900	g	coarsely ground
2	lb	pork shoulder	900	g	coarsely ground
3	T	vegetable oil	45	ml	
4	c	Spanish onion	385	g	finely chopped
2	gal	tap water	8	l	
1½	oz	granulated gelatin	43	g	
4	oz	cold water	118	ml	
1½	oz	table salt	43	g	
3	T	commercial beef base	45	ml	
1½	t	black pepper	3	g	freshly ground
1	T	MSG	13	g	
1	c	white cornmeal	131	g	
1½	T	whole mustard seeds	15	g	
10	c	pinhead oatmeal	1.8	kg	
2	t	fresh sage	4	g	finely chopped
7–8	ea	Turkish bay leaves	7–8	ea	finely ground

1. Select a 16-quart or larger pot with a heavy bottom and tight-fitting lid. Sauté the liver in the vegetable oil over moderate heat until off-pink. Cool, finely chop, and set aside.

2. Sauté the beef and pork in the same pot over medium-high heat until off-pink. Add the liver and onion. Cook 5–7 minutes over high heat, stirring constantly. Pour in the water and mix.

3. Soften the gelatin in the cold water for 5 minutes. Set aside. Combine the salt, beef base, pepper, MSG, cornmeal, and mustard seeds. Add the gelatin, combined seasonings, and oatmeal to the meat.

4. Bring to a full boil over high heat. Cover the pot and reduce the heat. Simmer very gently for 1 hour. Check often and stir to prevent sticking. The mixture should be very thick and heavy.

5. Add the sage and bay leaves. Stir from the bottom to mix well. Cook for another 30 minutes. Remove from heat and cool 10–15 minutes.

6. Lightly oil two or three 8 in. loaf pans. Pack the goetta into the pans. Cover loosely with a towel and allow to cool completely.

7. The finished goetta may be stored in the pans, especially if they are made of glass. Alternatively, unmold after running hot water over each pan and loosening the edges of the goetta with a hot knife.

8. Wrap well with plastic film and refrigerate for up to 10 days. Goetta will freeze well for up to 6 months if properly packaged in freezer wrap.

9. To serve, slice at least ⅜ in. (0.9 cm) thick. Panfry in hot oil or bacon fat, turning several times, to desired crispness.

Goose Liver Sausage

Serve this sausage, which may be smoked to taste, with thin onion slices and crackers or hearty bread.

Yield: 10 pounds (4.5 kg)

U.S.		Ingredients	Metric		Preparation
5	lb	fresh goose liver	2.2	kg	trimmed
2	lb	lamb liver	900	g	trimmed
		cold milk			to cover
2	gal	game stock	7.5	l	or chicken stock
3	lb	fresh ham (pork leg)	1.3	kg	trimmed
1½	oz	fine salt	43	g	
½	oz	white pepper	14	g	freshly ground
½	oz	onion powder	14	g	
1	t	fresh sage	2	g	finely minced
1	t	fresh marjoram	2	g	finely minced
½	oz	Prague powder #1	14	g	measured accurately
2	oz	powdered dextrose	57	g	
5–6	oz	soy protein powder	142–170	g	
2–3½	in.	fibrous casings	5–9	cm	

1. Wash the goose liver and lamb liver well. Slice about ¾ in. (2 cm) thick and place in a basin. Cover with the cold milk and refrigerate for at least 1 hour. Drain the liver slices and discard the milk.

2. Place the liver into gently boiling game stock and poach until off-pink. Remove the liver and place into running cold water to cool. Reserve the stock for poaching the sausages later.

3. Cube the liver and fresh ham. Grind using a ⅛ in. (0.3 cm) plate. Grind again with a ¹⁄₁₆ in. (0.15 cm) plate.

(Continued)

4. Working in a large mixing tub, add the dry ingredients (except the soy protein powder) and mix well by hand. Add the soy protein powder to obtain the desired consistency.

5. Stuff the prepared casings. Clip and tie each end securely. Allow a bit of space for the sausages to expand as they poach.

6. Heat the reserved stock to 130°F (54°C). Add the sausages and bring the bath slowly to 165°F (74°C) and check for an internal temperature of 165°F (74°C). Allow the sausages to cool to 100°F (38°C) in the stock.

7. Refrigerate for 24 hours to mature and develop the flavor before serving.

Gravlax

This Scandinavian salt-cured salmon is appreciated around the world as an appetizer, in a smorgasbord, and on open-face sandwiches. It is often garnished with lemon slices and served with dark rye and dill mustard sauce. Use the freshest salmon for the best color, flavor, and texture.

Yield: about 1 pound (450 g)

U.S.		Ingredients	Metric		Preparation
1½	lb	fresh salmon	680	g	in one piece
2	oz	coarse (kosher) salt	57	g	
¼	oz	white pepper	7	g	freshly ground
1	oz	granulated sugar	28	g	
1	oz	ground coriander	28	g	
2	bunches	fresh dill	2	bunches	washed and dried
2	oz	100 proof vodka	59	ml	

1. Remove the backbone of the salmon and carefully separate into halves. Leave the skin on each piece.

2. Make a dry rub by combining the salt, pepper, sugar, and coriander.

3. Working on a clean flat surface, rub the dry cure into each piece of salmon very thoroughly.

4. Select a dish of glass or other nonreactive material. Place a single spray of dill in the dish and cover it with one piece of fish, flesh side up. Sprinkle with half of the vodka and spread a generous layer of dill on top of the fish. Place the second piece of fish on top of the first, skin side up, in the style of a sandwich. Sprinkle with the remaining vodka.

5. Cover the dish with plastic film. Place a flat plate on top of the "sandwich." Place a 1-lb (450 g) weight on the plate. Transfer to a convenient shelf in the cooler and baste the salmon every 12 hours for the next 3 days.

6. Remove and discard the dill. Wipe the gravlax dry and touch up as necessary. To slice, place the fish skin side down on a cutting board. Cut paper-thin skinless slices on the diagonal across the grain.

Dry-Cured Ham

This is a basic cure for making hams in the style of prosciutto. We offer several good variations. Do not store this ham in plastic, which will promote mold; a net bag will allow it to breathe.

Yield: Serves 40 or more

U.S.		Ingredients	Metric		Preparation
10	lb	pork leg, skin on	4.5	kg	
12	oz	kosher salt	340	g	
1	oz	black pepper	28	g	finely ground
7	oz	ground allspice	198	g	
1	t	ground nutmeg	2	g	
1	t	ground mustard	2	g	
5	oz	powdered dextrose	142	g	
4	oz	Prague powder #2	113	g	

1. Bone the pork leg leaving the knuckle bone in. Chill to 34°F (1°C).
2. Thoroughly mix the remaining dry ingredients.
3. Carefully rub all sides and pack the internal cavity of the leg with the dry cure. Close and form the ham to its original shape.
4. Place a layer of dry rub into a flat-bottom meat lug. Lay the ham skin side down. Sprinkle the remaining rub over the leg.
5. Place a sturdy flat board on top of the ham. Add a 40-lb (18 kg) weight such as a 40-lb lard box.
6. Refrigerate with a loose protective cover for 10 days.
7. Remove the ham and soak in tap water for 16 hours. Change the water every 4 hours.
8. Trim the ham and tie it securely to a smoking stick.

SMOKING

1. Hang the ham in a preheated smoker at 130°F (54°C). Allow to dry for 50 hours with the damper set one-half open.

(Continued)

2. Raise the temperature to 140°F (60°C). Hold for 2 more hours to finish drying.

3. Reduce the temperature to 120°F (49°C) and hold for 10 hours.

4. Remove the ham and rub by hand all over with coarsely ground black pepper.

5. Hang the ham in a dry room at 75°F (24°C) for 30 days or hang in a cooler for 50 days.

VARIATIONS

French Peasant: Before smoking, soak the ham in white wine 4–6 hours.

Parma: Rub garlic juice generously into the ham before rubbing in the cure. Add chopped fresh basil to the dry cure.

Smithfield: The pork leg must come from a peanut-fed hog. The full shank is left on. Smoke the ham with hickory wood at a cold-smoke temperature of 120°F (49°C).

Westphalian: For a reasonable facsimile, inject the ham with rum before smoking.

Roscrea Ham

This is known as the King of Irish Hams.

Yield: Serves 40

U.S.		Ingredients	Metric		Preparation
10	lb	pork leg, skin on	4.5	kg	
6	oz	pickling salt	170	g	
6	oz	Prague powder #1	170	g	
3	gal	ice water	11.3	l	
1	oz	ground cloves	28	g	
3	t	ground bay leaves	3	g	
3	oz	light brown sugar	85	g	
3	oz	white pepper	85	g	
2	oz	powdered gelatin	57	g	

1. Make the pork leg semi-boneless by removing the pelvic aitchbone and the thigh bone.

2. To make the brine, dissolve the salt and Prague powder #1 in the ice water. Add the cloves, bay leaves, brown sugar, and pepper.

3. Place the ham in a nonreactive container and cover with the brine. Turn once a day for 10 days. Be sure that the ham remains fully submerged.

4. Remove the ham and dry for 2 hours on a rack. Sprinkle the gelatin into the bone cavity. Place in a net ham bag and tie a secure hanging loop.

SMOKING

1. Place in a preheated smoker at 130°F (54°C) with the dampers set one-half open. Apply a light smoke. (Smoke for a longer period of time with a heavier smoke if desired.)
2. When the ham reaches an internal temperature of 130°F (54°C), remove and store in the cooler.

To bake: Soak the ham in cold water for 24 hours to remove the salt. Remove the skin and bake at 325°F (163°C). Glaze with molasses or brown sugar when ham is about 20 minutes from a finished internal temperature of 150°F (65°C).

To boil: Soak the ham overnight in cold water to remove the salt. Simmer the ham until tender, about 20 minutes per pound plus 20 minutes for each piece.

VARIATIONS

Cajun Ham: Omit the cloves and white pepper. Add 3 oz Cajun seasoning and 1 oz (30 ml) garlic juice to the brine. For even more flavor, use more Cajun seasoning and garlic in the bone cavity when adding the gelatin.

Schinkenspeck Ham: Use whole juniper berries instead of cloves.

Scottish Ham: Add 1 oz (28 g) ground nutmeg.

Ham and Pork Sausage

Yield: 10 pounds (4.5 kg)

U.S.		Ingredients	Metric		Preparation
5	lb	pork butt	2.3	kg	
3	lb	pork leg (fresh ham)	1.4	kg	
2	lb	smoked bacon	1	kg	
2¼	oz	salt	71	g	
1	T	ground white pepper	6	g	
1	t	ground cloves	2.5	g	
1	T	ground nutmeg	7.5	g	
¾	oz	granulated onion	21	g	
2	t	Prague powder #1	10	g	
		beef middles			
		or			
5	in.	fibrous casing	13	cm	

1. Grind the pork butt and leg through a 1 in. (2.5 cm) plate.

(Continued)

2. Cut the smoked bacon into ¼–½ in. (0.6–1.3 cm) cubes. Add it to the ground pork and mix well.

3. Combine the salt, pepper, cloves, nutmeg, onion, and Prague powder #1. Sprinkle over the meat and mix well.

4. Stuff the prepared casings. Dry the sausages for 4 hours in the cooler.

SMOKING

1. Place the sausages in the smoker for further drying at 120°F (49°C).

2. When the casings are dry, increase the temperature to 160–165°F (71–74°C). Hold until the internal temperature is 155°F (68°C).*

3. Remove from the smoker and shower with cold water until the internal temperature is 110°F (43°C).

4. Refrigerate for use.

---

*If you have used the 5-in. casings, it may take 10–12 hours to reach 155°F (68°C). To speed the process, smoke the sausages only until they take on some color. Complete the cooking by poaching in 160°F (71°C) ham stock until the sausage reaches 155°F (68°C).

Salt Herring

Salt herring is very versatile and keeps indefinitely. Use it in any herring recipe. Allow extra time to presoak and rinse the herring before using it in recipes.

U.S.	Ingredients	Metric	Preparation
	fresh or frozen herring cleaned, with heads removed		
	coarse (kosher) salt		
	tap water as required to make brine to cover		

1. Weigh the cleaned herring. For each 2½ lb (1.2 kg) of fish, measure and set aside 1½ c (335 g) of coarse salt.

2. Split the fish up the belly, lay out flat, and remove the backbone. Small bones may be removed later. Rinse under running water.

3. Make a solution of salt water: ½ c (112 g) of salt to each gallon. Soak the herrings in the solution 30–35 minutes.

4. Drain the fish. Rinse and drain again.

5. Select a brining tub that will hold the fish with some room to spare. Sprinkle a layer of the measured salt on the bottom of the tub. Add an even layer of fish, skin side down, and cover with more salt. Add another layer of fish at a right angle to the preceding one. Layer the remaining fish in this fashion. Place the last fish layer skin side up and finish with a final layer of salt.

6. Cover the container with plastic wrap and foil. Refrigerate. The fish will shrink and develop a brine. Gently swirl and rearrange the fish from time to time. Keep them completely immersed in the brine. After a minimum of 2 days (for frozen fish) and 10 days (for fresh fish), the salt herring is ready for use.

Hot Water Paste

This rather heavy and durable dough is used for raised pies and for enclosing terrines and other forcemeats. It is also useful for decorative touches on charcuterie items.

Yield: 1½ pounds (680 g)

U.S.		Ingredients	Metric		Preparation
¼	pt	water	118	ml	
4	oz	lard	113	g	
1	lb	bread flour	450	g	sifted
1	t	salt	5	g	

1. Heat the water and lard. Add the sifted flour and salt. Stir to make a dough ball.

2. Knead until dough is smooth. Cover and allow to rest for 1 hour.

3. Use at once or refrigerate for future use. Keep well-covered.

Hot Creole Sausage

In Louisiana, where these sausages are fiery hot, they are known as Chaurice. This recipe is moderately seasoned; use more or less hot pepper to your taste. We recommend chopping the meat rather coarsely by hand. It can be ground with a machine, but the authentic texture will be lost.

Creole sausage is an ingredient in jambalaya, the New Orleans version of Spanish paella. It should complement, not dominate, the other ingredients. These versatile sausages can be used in many other ways. Broil, fry, or deep-fry them for breakfast and serve with steaming grits. They can be cooked with cabbage or slowly baked with beans. Add them discreetly to various salads.

Yield: 6 pounds (2.7 kg)

U.S.		Ingredients	Metric		Preparation
4	lb	trimmed lean pork	1.8	kg	diced
2	lb	pork belly	900	g	diced
2		large Spanish onions	2		finely diced
4–6		garlic cloves	4–6		minced
2	T	ground black pepper	12	g	
2	t	kosher or canning salt	9	g	
2	t	ground sweet paprika	2	g	
2	t	hot red pepper flakes	2	g	
		or			
1	t	cayenne pepper	1	g	
6		fresh parsley sprigs	6		minced
4		fresh sage leaves	4		
2		fresh thyme sprigs	2		minced
2		small bay leaves	2		crumbled
⅛	t	ground allspice	1	g	
⅛	t	ground mace	1	g	
		ice water or dry red wine			as needed
6	yd	lamb casings	5.4	m	

1. Combine the meats and all the seasonings. Mix very well. Add some ice water or dry red wine as necessary to blend.

2. Stuff the prepared casings. Tie into links of desired length; shorter sausages are good for table use, longer are useful for adding to other dishes.

3. Wrap well and refrigerate. Let the sausages mellow for 8–12 hours before use.

This sausage will remain fresh for 3–4 days. Although it is always better to use sausages fresh, this sausage will keep up to 1 month in the freezer if necessary.

Hungarian Beef Sausage

This is a fresh sausage to grill or panfry.

Yield: 5 pounds (2.2 kg)

U.S.		Ingredients	Metric		Preparation
4	lb	lean beef	1.8	kg	
1	lb	suet	450	g	
1½	T	fine salt	22	g	
4	T	paprika	12	g	
½	t	cayenne pepper	0.5	g	
1	T	chopped garlic	6	g	
1	oz	fresh sage	28	g	chopped
8	oz	ice water	237	ml	
		hog casings	35	mm	

1. Grind the beef and suet separately through a ³⁄₁₆ in. (0.45 cm) plate.
2. Mix in the seasonings and ice water.
3. Stuff the prepared casings. Tie into 4 in. (10 cm) links.
4. Rest for 12 hours in the cooler to develop flavors before use.

Indian-Style Sausage

This is an intriguing hot sausage. Poach the links in a strong chicken stock and serve sliced with basmati rice and a mild Madras curry sauce.

Yield: 10 pounds (4.5 kg)

U.S.		Ingredients	Metric		Preparation
8	lb	poultry meat	3.6	kg	
1	lb	chicken skins	450	g	
10	oz	red bell peppers	284	g	diced
6	oz	shallots	170	g	finely chopped
10	oz	fresh papaya	284	g	diced
		butter			as needed
2	oz	fresh ginger	57	g	finely grated
3	oz	Madras curry powder	85	g	
3	oz	salt	85	g	
2	oz	ground white pepper	57	g	
6		eggs	6		beaten
16	oz	yogurt	473	ml	
		lamb casings	30	mm	

1. Grind the meat and skins using a ¹⁄₁₆ in. (0.15 cm) plate. Return to the cooler.
2. Briefly sauté the red peppers, shallots, and papaya in a little butter.
3. Add the ginger, curry powder, salt, and pepper. Cool.
4. Mix the seasonings into the ground meats very well. Add the eggs and yogurt.
5. Stuff the prepared casings. Tie into 4 in. (10 cm) links.
6. Wrap and refrigerate for use.

Irish Breakfast Sausage I

Hafners of Dublin was famous for this sausage.

Yield: 8 pounds (3.6 kg)

U.S.		Ingredients	Metric		Preparation
8	lb	pork shoulder	3.6	kg	
2	c	ice water	475	ml	
3	t	fine salt	15	g	
3	t	ground black pepper	6	g	
3	t	dried thyme	3	g	
3	t	dried sage	3	g	
1	t	dried chopped onion	1	g	
8	oz	dried bread crumbs	227	g	
		casings	36	mm	

1. Grind the pork using a ½ in. (1.3 cm) plate. Grind again using a ³⁄₁₆ in. (0.45 cm) plate.
2. Put the water in a container and stir in the salt, pepper, thyme, sage, and onion. Add the solution to the meat and mix evenly.
3. Add the bread crumbs and mix thoroughly. Pack down, cover, and chill for 3 hours.
4. Stuff the prepared casings. Tie into 3 in. (8 cm) links.
5. Refrigerate the links for 24 hours before use to develop the flavor.

Irish Breakfast Sausage II

This sausage has long been a favorite of Chef Kinsella for home use. We have found it to be a real treat for the Sunday breakfast.

Yield: 10 pounds (4.5 kg)

U.S.		Ingredients	Metric		Preparation
8	lb	pork shoulder	3.6	kg	
2	lb	pork butt	900	g	
16	oz	ice water	475	ml	
1	oz	salt	28	g	
½	oz	black pepper	14	g	
2	t	fresh sage	2	g	
1	t	mace	1	g	
8	oz	fresh bread crumbs	227	g	
		hog casings	28–32	mm	

1. Grind the meats together. Refrigerate for 1 hour.
2. Put the water in a container and stir in the salt, pepper, sage, mace, and bread crumbs. Pack the forcemeat into tubs and refrigerate overnight to develop flavor.
3. Stuff the prepared casings. Tie into 4 in. (10 cm) links.
4. Refrigerate for use. Grill and serve.

Irish Soft Brine

Use this subtle brine for curing about 2 pounds of meat. Use for English bacon and for brining York hams, Roscrea hams, and bacon.

Yield: 1 gallon (3.8 l)

U.S.		Ingredients	Metric		Preparation
1	gal	soft water	3.8	l	
1	lb	salt	450	g	
1	lb	brown sugar	450	g	
1	oz	juniper berries	28	g	
2		bay leaves	2		
2	oz	black peppercorns	57	g	
1		sachet bag	1		parsley, thyme, rosemary
3	oz	Prague powder #1	85	g	

1. Bring the water, salt, and sugar to a boil and stir to dissolve thoroughly. Remove from heat.
2. Add the juniper berries, bay leaves, peppercorns, and sachet bag. Cool.
3. When the mixture is cooled, add the Prague powder #1 and stir to dissolve.

Irish Venison Sausage

Hafners of Dublin were famous for this sausage, which is sometimes called Nob's Sausage. It is the only game sausage from Ireland. Grill and serve.

Yield: 10 pounds (4.5 kg)

U.S.		Ingredients	Metric		Preparation
8	lb	venison	3.6	kg	
1	c	dry red wine	237	ml	Burgundy style
2	lb	fatback	900	g	
2	c	ice water	475	ml	
3	t	salt	15	g	
3	t	black pepper	6	g	coarsely ground
3	t	fresh thyme	3	g	
3	t	fresh sage	3	g	
1	oz	shallots	28	g	chopped medium
8	oz	dried bread crumbs	227	g	
3	tsp	fresh fennel	6	g	chopped medium
		casings	36	mm	

1. Marinate the venison, refrigerated, in the wine for 1 full day. Drain the venison and reserve the marinade.

2. Grind the meat and fatback using a ½ in. (1.3 cm) plate. Grind again using a ³⁄₁₆ in. (0.45 cm) plate.

3. Combine the salt, pepper, thyme, and sage. Put the ice water and marinade wine in a container and stir in the seasonings. Pour the solution over the ground meat and mix well.

4. Add the shallots, bread crumbs, and fennel and mix well.

5. Stuff the prepared casings. Tie in loops of 4 in. (10 cm) links.

6. Refrigerate for 24 hours to develop flavor.

Irish White Pudding

Grill or sauté these sausages to serve hot.

Yield: 10 pounds (4.5 kg)

U.S.		Ingredients	Metric		Preparation
3	lb	white chicken meat	1.4	kg	
3	lb	lean pork meat	1.4	kg	
1	lb	fatback	450	g	diced
1	T	salt	12	g	
½	oz	ground pepper	14	g	equal parts black and white
1½	lb	onions	680	g	grated
½	oz	sage, thyme, parsley	14	g	equal parts, chopped
2	lb	dried bread crumbs	900	g	
2	pt	milk	946	ml	
8		eggs	8		beaten
		hog casings	32	mm	
		milk for poaching			

1. Grind the chicken and pork through a ³⁄₁₆ in. (0.5 cm) plate. Add the salt, pepper, onions, and herbs.
2. Soak the bread crumbs in the milk.
3. Sauté one fourth of the fatback. Cool, then mix well into the forcemeat.
4. Add the bread crumbs and eggs and mix.
5. Purée the mixture in a food processor.
6. Fold in the remaining diced fatback.
7. Stuff the prepared casings. Tie into rings.
8. Gently poach in simmering milk until the pudding reaches an internal temperature of 155°F (68°C).
9. Remove from the liquid and cool. Refrigerate for 24 hours to develop flavor.

Italian Cheese Sausage

Grill or bake this sausage. Use it within 24 hours of production.

Yield: 10 pounds (4.5 kg)

U.S.		Ingredients	Metric		Preparation
7	lb	pork	3.2	kg	
3	lb	veal or turkey trimmings	1.4	kg	
10	oz	white wine or water	296	ml	
2	oz	salt	57	g	
½	t	ground white pepper	1	g	
2	t	whole fennel seeds	2	g	cracked
1½	t	Italian red pepper	1.5	g	
1	oz	white corn syrup	30	ml	
3	oz	grated Parmesan cheese	85	g	or grated Cheddar
		casings	28–32	mm	

1. Grind the pork and veal/turkey through a ⅜ in. (0.9 cm) plate.
2. Put the wine in a container. Combine the salt, pepper, fennel seeds, red pepper, and corn syrup and stir them into the wine. Add the solution to the ground meat and mix well.
3. Fold in the grated cheese.
4. Stuff the prepared casings and tie into 4 in. (10 cm) links.
5. Refrigerate for use.

Italian Pepperoni I

This is a dry-cured pepperoni. Do not use casings whose diameter is larger than 36 mm. This formula is only for casings of that size or smaller.

Yield: 10 pounds (4.5 kg)

U.S.		Ingredients	Metric		Preparation
4	lb	boned beef	1.8	kg	
1	lb	pork	450	g	
5	lb	pork butt	2.26	kg	lean
1	T	cayenne pepper	6	g	
4½	oz	salt	127.5	g	
5	t	ground anise seed	5	g	
2	oz	corn syrup solids	57	g	
1	t	ground allspice	1	g	
2	t	Prague powder #2	10	g	measured accurately
1	oz	powdered dextrose	28	g	
		lamb casings	24–36	mm	

1. Grind the chilled meats through a ³⁄₁₆ in. (0.45 cm) plate. Add the remaining ingredients and mix thoroughly in an electric mixer.

2. Grind the mixture again using a ⅛ in. (0.31 cm) plate. It is essential to have the force-meat well-chilled to avoid smearing. Chill at 32–34°F (0–1°C) prior to stuffing.

3. Stuff the prepared casings. Tie into loops and hang on sticks.

4. Hold the pepperoni for at least 2 days at 70°F (21°C) at 75% relative humidity.

5. After drying, hold the sausages in the cooler for 20 days, counting from the start of production. The pepperoni is then ready for consumption.

Italian Dry-Cured Sausage Pepperoni II—
The "Original" Italian Pepperoni

This sausage has its roots in the kitchens of the Italian chefs. It was created for use in various pasta dishes, by the chefs who desired a dry-cured sausage. It is full of old country character.

You will enjoy the use of this versatile sausage in your fine Italian dishes. When served speared with gaily colored or fancy toothpicks, accompanied with fruits and well-presented raw vegetables, a balanced, tasty and most handsome appetizer is at once at hand.

Yield: 10 pounds (4.5 kg)

U.S.		Ingredients	Metric		Preparation
10	lb	pork butt	4.5	kg	trimmed and cubed
3	oz	salt	85	g	
1	T	ground coriander	3	g	
1	T	fennel	3	g	finely cracked
1	t	pure garlic powder	1	g	
1–2	T	red pepper flakes	3–6	g	
2	t	Prague powder #2	10	g	measured accurately
1	oz	powdered dextrose	28	g	
2	oz	corn syrup solids	57	g	powdered
		casings	38	mm	

1. Grind the pork through a ½ in. (1.3 cm) plate.
2. Combine the remaining ingredients and mix into the ground meat.
3. Press the forcemeat into tubs, removing air pockets. Cover and keep at 34°F (1°C) for about 36 hours.
4. Grind the mixture again through a ¼ in. (0.6 cm) plate.
5. Stuff the prepared casings, avoiding air pockets.
6. Dry in the smoker for 2 days at 60°F (16°C) at 70% relative humidity.
7. Refrigerate for 25 days. The sausage will finish curing and show a typical bloom.

Italian Garlic Hot Sausage

This is a classic Italian sausage to grill and use in many dishes such as pizza and pasta.

Yield: 10 pounds (4.5 kg)

U.S.		Ingredients	Metric		Preparation
10	lb	pork	4.5	kg	
1	oz	fine salt	28	g	
½	oz	red pepper flakes	14	g	
¼	oz	ground mace	7	g	
¼	oz	ground nutmeg	7	g	
1	t	ground cloves	1	g	
2½	t	fresh garlic	5	g	minced
1	pt	ice water	475	ml	
		sheep casings	32–35	mm	

1. Grind the pork using a ⅜ in. (0.9 cm) plate. Add the salt, red pepper, mace, nutmeg, cloves, and garlic and mix well in an electric mixer.
2. Grind again through a ⅛ in. (0.3 cm) plate while adding the water.
3. Stuff the prepared casings. Tie into 3 in. (8 cm) links.
4. Wrap and refrigerate for use.

Italian Hot Sausage

These sausages are especially attractive if they are left chain-linked for display. There are at least four sizes of hog casings available in the size range given below; any of them will work for this sausage. We recommend serving them with a marinara or other meatless sauce, accompanied by pasta and a salad. See the related Italian Sweet Sausage.

Yield: 8 pounds (3.6 kg)

U.S.		Ingredients	Metric		Preparation
6½	lb	pork butt	2.9	kg	
1½	lb	fatback	700	g	
1	pt	ice water	475	ml	
2	oz	canning or kosher salt	58	g	
½	oz	red pepper flakes	14	g	
2	oz	paprika	57	g	
1	oz	fresh thyme	28	g	
½	oz	whole fennel seed	14	g	cracked
2	oz	fresh garlic	57	g	crushed
		hog casings	32–42	mm	

1. Put the ice water in a container. Combine the salt, pepper flakes, paprika, thyme, fennel seed, and garlic and stir into the water. Chill.

2. There are two grinding options: *For a finely textured sausage,* grind the pork butt and fatback separately through a ¼ in. (0.6 cm) plate. Combine the two and grind again. *For a coarsely textured sausage,* combine the pork butt and fatback, and grind once through a ¼ in. (0.6 cm) or ⁵⁄₁₆ in. (0.8 cm) plate.

3. Pour the chilled seasoning solution over the meat. Mix well to distribute the ingredients evenly.

4. Pack evenly into shallow pans. Cover and chill for 30 minutes.

5. Stuff the prepared casings, eliminating all air pockets. Tie into 5 in. (12 cm) links and coil onto chilled clean trays.

6. Refrigerate for use.

7. To cook, separate the sausages and bake in a 325°F (163°C) oven for 20 minutes, turning every 5 minutes to cook evenly.

Italian Sweet Sausage

This sausage and the Italian Hot Sausage are valuable to use in many Italian and other dishes. Small slices make good appetizers.

Yield: 8 pounds (3.6 kg)

U.S.		Ingredients	Metric		Preparation
6½	lb	lean pork butt	2.9	kg	
1½	lb	fatback	700	g	
1	pt	ice water	475	ml	
2	oz	canning or kosher salt	57	g	
1	oz	cracked black pepper	28	g	#10 mesh
2	oz	whole fennel seeds	57	g	cracked
¼	oz	red pepper flakes	7	g	
2½	oz	powdered dextrose	71	g	
		hog casings	32–42	mm	

1. Put the ice water in a container. Combine the salt, pepper, fennel seeds, pepper flakes, and powdered dextrose and stir into the water. Chill.
2. Grind the pork butt and fatback separately using a ⅜ in. (0.9 cm) plate. Combine them and grind again to blend.
3. Combine the ground meat very thoroughly with the seasoning solution. Cover tightly and return to the cooler for 12 hours.
4. Stuff the prepared casings. Twist and tie into 3½ in. (9 cm) links.
5. Wrap and refrigerate or freeze for use.
6. To pan-broil, place the sausage in a scant ⅛ in. (0.3 cm) of water in a heavy skillet. Poach over medium-high heat. When the water is gone, reduce heat and finish browning, turning several times. The sausages may also be baked in a 325°F (163°C) oven for 10–15 minutes or until they are no longer pink. Do not overcook.

Jagwurst

Yield: 10 pounds (4.5 kg)

U.S.		Ingredients	Metric		Preparation
1½	lb	fresh ham	680	g	trimmed
4½	lb	lean pork butt	2	kg	
4	lb	fresh bacon	1.8	kg	
3½	oz	salt	99	g	
1	T	ground white pepper	2	g	
1	T	ground coriander	3	g	
1		garlic clove	1		crushed
¾	oz	powdered mustard	21	g	
1	T	ground nutmeg	3	g	
1	T	ground ginger	3	g	
2	t	Prague powder #1	10	g	
½	oz	powdered dextrose	14	g	
3½ in. × 24 in.		clear fibrous casing	8.9 cm × 60 cm		

1. Grind the fresh ham and pork butt through a ⅛ in. (0.3 cm) plate.
2. Grind the fresh bacon and the ground ham/pork mixture through a ⅜ in. (0.95 cm) plate.
3. Add the remaining ingredients and mix thoroughly.
4. Stuff the prepared casing. Allow to dry at room temperature for 30–40 minutes.

SMOKING

1. Place the sausage in a preheated smoker at 130°F (54°C) for 1 hour without smoke.
2. Increase the temperature to 165°F (74°C). Hold at this setting until the internal temperature of the sausage reaches 150°F (65°C). Apply smoke for 30 minutes or less during this time. A too-heavy smoke flavor will mask the pleasant taste of the jagwurst.
3. Remove the sausage from the smoker and spray with cold water until the internal temperature drops to 100°F (38°C) or less.
4. Refrigerate for use.

Jerky I

Use for beef, lamb brisket, turkey jerky, and game. This version requires 8 to 12 hours of marinating, then another 8 to 12 hours of smoking. Be sure to have everything ready! lesser cuts will make jerky, but remember: "The better the meat—the better the jerky!" See Jerky II. This recipe offers another very reliable brining solution and method well suited for all "domestic meat." Game meats and other meats, especially tougher and thicker cuts, will require some adjustment to formulas and times. Once established, your methods will enable consistently good results. This is not a difficult process at all, but one calling for some patience and observation.

Yield: Up to 8 pounds, depending on the fat ratio

U.S.		Ingredients	Metric		Preparation
10	lb	meat	4.5	kg	
1	c	curing salt	240	g	
4	T	black pepper	24	g	fine or coarse
½	c	brown sugar	112	g	dark
1	t	fresh garlic juice	5	ml	
2	qt	water	1.9	l	

FOR THE DRY RUB:

Choose garlic salt, onion salt, pepper, or other prepared seasoning.

1. Prepare the meat by carefully removing any fat and membrane. Cut into strips 1–1½ in. (2.5–4 cm) wide by ¼ in. (0.6 cm) thick.

2. Make the brine by combining the salt, pepper, sugar, garlic juice, and water. Place the meat in a nonreactive tub and cover with the brine. Place a board and weight on top of the meat so that it is totally immersed in the brine.

3. After brining for 8–12 hours, remove and rinse each piece of meat in clean, fresh water. Let stand or hang to air dry for about 12 hours.

4. Rub the pieces of meat with the dry seasonings of your choice.

SMOKING

1. Place the meat in a preheated smoker at 130–140°F (54–60°C) with a light-to-medium smoke. After the first hour, increase the temperature to 155°F (68°C).

2. Remove the meat from the smoker when it is like a stiff, but not brittle, piece of rope.

3. Wrap the jerky and store it in a cool, dry place.

Jerky II

Use this formula and method for up to 20 pounds of any nongame meat. It is reliable and will give consistent results.

Yield: Up to 16 pounds, depending on the fat ratio

U.S.		Ingredients	Metric		Preparation
20	lb	meat	9	kg	or less
½	gal	water	2	l	
2	c	kosher salt	6.8	kg	not table salt
1	t	ground black pepper	2	g	
1	c	dark brown sugar	224	g	or light brown
1	c	apple cider	237	ml	unrefined "natural" style
1	t	ground cloves	1	g	
1–2	t	finely minced garlic	2–4	g	

1. Put the water into a nonreactive pot. Stir in the salt, pepper, sugar, cider, cloves, and garlic. Bring the solution to a boil.

2. Trim the meat of any fat, membrane, or gristle. Cut it into pieces of uniform thickness. Determine the total weight of meat to be brined.

3. Working in batches, immerse the pieces of meat into the boiling brine for a period of 5 minutes per pound (450 g). Stir the meat to keep it evenly distributed in the hot brine.

4. Remove quickly and rinse each piece under cold running water. Pat the pieces dry with clean towels and put them on a rack to drain. Air dry for about 1 hour.

SMOKING

1. When dry, place meat into a preheated smoker at 130–140°F (54–60°C). Use a light or heavy smoke as desired. Depending on the size of the pieces, the jerky may be finished in 8–12 hours. Even more time may be needed. The jerky is ready when it bends with some resistance but is not completely brittle.

2. Store in a cool, dry place.

Jugged Hare Terrine

Yield: 5 pounds (2.3 kg)

U.S.		Ingredients	Metric		Preparation
3	lb	hare or rabbit	1.4	kg	boned
12	oz	lamb liver	340	g	cubed
12	oz	pork butt	340	g	cubed
12	oz	fatback	340	g	cubed
1	oz	muscatel wine	30	ml	
4	t	salt, black pepper, and cayenne pepper	11	g	equal parts mixture
8	oz	dry red wine	237	ml	
3	oz	onion	85	g	diced
1		garlic clove	1		crushed
1	oz	fines herbes	28	g	
1	t	marjoram	1	g	
5	lg	eggs	5	lg	beaten
1	oz	gelatin	28	g	
24	oz	lardons	680	g	

1. Cut the hare into strips.
2. Make the marinade with the muscatel, salt, black and cayenne peppers. Marinate the meat, refrigerated, for 24 hours.
3. Remove the meat from the marinade and drain. Reserve the marinade.
4. Make a fine paste of the lamb liver, pork butt, and fatback in a food processor. Stir down several times as needed.
5. Add the reserved marinade to the purée. Add the red wine, onion, garlic, fines herbes, marjoram, eggs, and gelatin. Mix lightly but thoroughly.
6. Line two 2-lb (1 kg) terrines with the lardons. Fill the mold with alternate layers of force-meat and pieces of hare.
7. Cover the molds and place in a water bath. Bake at 350°F (177°C) for 2 hours or until terrines reach an internal temperature of 155°F (68°C).
8. Place a light weight on each terrine. Refrigerate for 24 hours before serving.

Kielbasa I

This fresh, spicy Polish sausage is a fine grilling and baking variety.

Yield: 5 pounds (2.3 kg)

U.S.		Ingredients	Metric		Preparation
5	lb	pork butt	2.3	kg	
1	pt	ice water	475	ml	
1	oz	salt	28	g	
2	oz	cracked black pepper	57	g	
½	oz	garlic	14	g	chopped
2	oz	green onions	57	g	finely diced
1	oz	sugar	28	g	
1	oz	marjoram	28	g	
		sheep casings	28–35	mm	

1. Grind the pork through a ⅜ in. (0.95 cm) plate.
2. Place in an electric mixer and add all the remaining ingredients. Blend well. Chill as necessary to keep the forcemeat at 34°F (1°C).
3. Stuff the prepared casings. Tie in 4 in. (10 cm) links.
4. Refrigerate for use.

Kielbasa II

This sausage has a distinctive combined coarse and fine texture. Take special note of the dual grinding techniques.

Keep this fresh kielbasa refrigerated and use it within 6 days. As with other fresh sausages, it will keep for 4 weeks in the freezer if well-wrapped. These hearty sausages combine well with other ingredients in casseroles. You may also poach them in water in a skillet for 7 minutes on each side; pour off the water and finish by browning them lightly on all sides.

Yield: 14 pounds (6.4 kg)

U.S.		Ingredients	Metric		Preparation
6½	lb	trimmed lean pork	2.9	kg	cut in 1 in. (2.5 cm) cubes
3¼	lb	trimmed beef shin meat	1.5	kg	cut in 1 in. (2.5 cm) cubes
4½	lb	fatback	2	kg	cut in ½ in. (1.3 cm) dice
6	T	kosher salt	90	g	
3	T	coarse black pepper	18	g	freshly ground
15	T	Hungarian sweet paprika	50	g	
5	t	dried rubbed marjoram	5	g	
2½	t	dried rubbed summer savory	2.5	g	
3½	t	finely minced garlic	7	g	
2	c	ice water	475	ml	
10	yd	35–38 mm hog casings	9	m	

1. Have the meats well-chilled. In a large mixing tub, combine the pork, beef, and fatback.

2. Combine the salt, pepper, paprika, marjoram, savory, and garlic. Sprinkle the seasonings and ice water evenly over the meat. Mix well and divide in half.

3. Coarsely grind one half of the forcemeat through a ⅜ in. (0.95 cm) plate.

4. Finely grind the remaining forcemeat, in batches if necessary, through a buffalo chopper or food processor. Try to achieve a fine grind, but not a paste or purée.

5. Thoroughly mix the two grinds, scraping down the sides of the tub to achieve a very uniform mixture. Cover and chill the forcemeat for 3 hours.

6. Stuff the prepared casings. Tie into 12–30 in. (30–76 cm) lengths and loop onto hanging sticks. Alternatively, tie into 18 in. (45 cm) rings.

7. Hang on sticks in a *refrigerated* drying room until the casings are smooth, uniformly dry, and starting to crackle. This should take approximately 24 hours.

8. Refrigerate for use within 6 days.

Kielbasa III

This is our smoked version of the Polish kielbasa.

Yield: 25 pounds (11.3 kg)

U.S.		Ingredients	Metric		Preparation
25	lb	boneless pork butt	11.3	kg	trimmed
24	oz	ice water	709	ml	
7	oz	kosher or canning salt	200	g	
1	oz	ground black pepper	28	g	#34 mesh
1	oz	granulated sugar	28	g	
1	oz	fresh garlic	28	g	crushed
¼	oz	dried rubbed marjoram	7	g	
12	oz	powdered soy protein	340	g	concentrate
1	oz	Prague powder #1	28	g	measured accurately
		hog casings	38–42	mm	

1. Cut the pork into smaller pieces, separating the lean from the fatty portions. Grind the lean pieces through a ⅜ in. (0.95 cm) plate. Grind the fatty pieces through a ⅛ in. (0.3 cm) plate. Combine the two mixtures.

2. Put the ice water in a container. Combine the salt, pepper, sugar, garlic, marjoram, soy protein, and Prague powder #1 and stir into the water to dissolve. Pour this solution over the meat. Mix thoroughly by hand or with an electric mixer.

3. Stuff the prepared casings without air pockets and arrange in loops on hanging sticks.

SMOKING

1. Put the sausage to dry in a preheated smoker at 130°F (55°C) with the dampers wide open. The sausage will be dry in about 1 hour and will start to take on color.

2. When the casings are uniformly dry, adjust the dampers to one-quarter open. Gradually, in 3 steps during the next 90 minutes, increase the temperature to 165°F (74°C). Start a heavy smoke.

3. In the third hour of heavy smoke, monitor the internal temperature. When it reaches 152°F (67°C), remove the kielbasa from the smoker. Shower at once with cold water to an internal temperature of 110°F (43°C).

4. Hang for 30–60 minutes at room temperature. The sausage will dry and develop a characteristic bloom.

5. Refrigerate for use.

Kosher Salami

This is an all-beef kosher salami. The amount of salt, onion, and garlic in a salami are always considered a matter of individual preference. Bring out the best flavor by serving this and other salamis in very thin slices.

Yield: Three 3-pound salamis; serves up to 100

U.S.		Ingredients	Metric		Preparation
9	lb	very lean beef	4	kg	cubed
1	lb	kidney suet	450	g	
4	T	table salt	50	g	
2½	T	black pepper	15	g	coarsely ground
1	T	paprika	6	g	
1½	T	ground ginger	4.5	g	
3	t	ground nutmeg	3	g	
1	t	garlic powder	1	g	
1	oz	onion powder	28	g	
2	oz	corn syrup solids	57	g	
4	T	powdered dextrose	50	g	
2	t	Prague powder #1	10	g	measured accurately
16	oz	ice water	475	ml	
3½ in. × 24 in.		4 ea fibrous casings	9 cm × 60 cm		

1. Grind the beef using a 1 in. (2.5 cm) plate. Grind the suet using a ³⁄₁₆ in. (0.5 cm) plate. Combine the suet and beef in a mixing tub.

2. Mix the salt, pepper, paprika, ginger, nutmeg, garlic powder, onion powder, corn syrup solids, dextrose, and Prague powder #1 with the ice water. Be certain that the Prague powder is completely dissolved. Add this solution to the beef mixture and mix well. Cover and refrigerate for a full 8 hours to set up the forcemeat and to start the curing process.

3. Remove from the cooler and grind using a ³⁄₁₆ in. (0.5 cm) plate.

4. Tie one end of each casing with a butterfly knot and stuff the casings. Secure the open ends with twine or hog rings. Make sturdy loops for hanging. Pack this sausage very tightly with no air pockets.

SMOKING

1. Arrange the salamis on hanging sticks. Place them in a preheated smoker set at 130°F (54°C) with the dampers wide open. Allow the salamis to dry for 1–2 hours without smoke.

2. Adjust the dampers to one-quarter open, raise the temperature to 140°F (60°C), and create a heavy smoke for 1 hour.

(Continued)

3. Increase the temperature to 160°F (71°C) and maintain the smoke for 1 more hour.

4. Raise the temperature to 170°F (77°C) and shut off the smoke. Hold at this setting until the internal temperature of the salami reaches 152°F (67°C).

5. Remove the salamis from the smoker. Spray with cold water to lower the internal temperature to 110°F (43°C) or less.

6. Hang the salamis at room temperature, free from drafts, to dry until an attractive bloom appears on the surface.

7. Refrigerate the salamis overnight. The salami is now ready to use, but the flavor and texture will improve over several weeks.

Krakowska

This recipe is from Rytec Kutas' *Great Sausage Recipes and Meat Curing.*

Yield: 10 pounds (4.5 kg)

U.S.		Ingredients	Metric		Preparation
10	lb	boneless fresh hams	4.5	kg	
½	pt	ice water	236	ml	
5	T	salt*	75	g	see note
1	T	ground white pepper	6	g	
2	t	Prague powder #1	10	g	measured accurately
2	T	powdered dextrose	25	g	
2	T	garlic powder	18	g	
1	t	ground coriander	1.5	g	
2	T	ground mustard seeds	10	g	
½	t	dried marjoram	0.5	g	
2–3½ in. × 24 in.		fibrous casings	5–9 cm × 60 cm		

1. Grind the meat through a ⅜ in. (0.9 cm) plate.

2. Place the meat in an electric mixer. Add all the ingredients and mix until everything is evenly distributed. Pack the meat tightly into shallow pans or tubs 6 in. (15 cm) deep or less. Refrigerate overnight.

3. Stuff the prepared casings.

---

*The original recipe calls for 6 tablespoons of salt. Salt to your taste.

SMOKING

1. Place the sausages in a preheated smoker at 130°F (54°C) with dampers wide open for 1 hour. Apply a heavy smoke, gradually increasing the smoker temperature to 160–165°F (71–74°C) with dampers one-quarter open.

2. Leave the sausage in the smoker until it attains the desired color or until the internal temperature reaches 152°F (67°C). If you are using a steam cabinet, you may remove the krakowska from the smoker when the internal temperature is 130°F (54°C).

3. Shower the sausage with cool water until the internal temperature drops to 110°F (43°C). Leave at room temperature for 45 minutes or until desired bloom is attained.

4. Refrigerate overnight.

Landjäger

This is a traditional Swiss sausage. It is delicious lightly grilled and served hot or sliced cold as an appetizer.

Yield: 10 pounds (4.5 kg)

U.S.		Ingredients	Metric		Preparation
9	lb	beef	4.1	kg	cubed
1	lb	fatback	450	g	diced ¼ in. (0.6 cm), frozen
12	oz	kirsch	355	ml	or sweet sherry
2	oz	fine salt	57	g	
1	oz	ground black pepper	28	g	
1	t	minced garlic	2	g	
1	t	caraway seed	1	g	bruised
3	t	ground cardamom	6	g	
1	t	ground coriander	2	g	
1	t	ground nutmeg	2	g	
1	oz	corn syrup solids	28	g	
1	oz	powdered dextrose	28	g	
1	oz	Prague powder #2	28	g	
		hog casings	35	mm	

1. Grind the beef using a ³⁄₁₆ in. (0.5 cm) plate. Place in a mixing tub and chill.

2. Put the kirsch in a container. Combine the salt, pepper, garlic, caraway, cardamom, coriander, nutmeg, corn syrup solids, dextrose, and Prague powder #2. Mix them into the kirsch and add to the beef. Mix well.

(Continued)

3. Fold in the frozen fatback lightly but thoroughly by hand. Work quickly to avoid smearing.

4. Stuff the prepared casings. Tie into 4 in. (10 cm) links. Keep the sausage links chained together for easy hanging.

5. Hang at 40°F (4°C) for 24 hours.

SMOKING

1. Transfer to a preheated smoker set at 135°F (57°C). Raise the temperature every 30 minutes until the smoker reaches 165°F (74°C). Maintain this temperature until the internal temperature of the sausage is 155°F (68°C).

2. Remove from the smoker and shower at once with a cold water spray. Hang to dry at room temperature.

3. Refrigerate for use.

Lebraska

This is a Lithuanian sausage.

Yield: 10 pounds (4.5 kg)

U.S.		Ingredients	Metric		Preparation
2	lb	pork livers	900	g	
4	lb	beef stew meat	1.8	kg	
4	lb	pork butt	1.8	kg	
3	oz	shallots	85	g	chopped
1	oz	butter	28	g	
1	oz	salt	28	g	
3	t	ground black pepper	6	g	
1	t	powdered ginger	1	g	
1	t	dried marjoram	1	g	
3	t	ground nutmeg	3	g	
4	oz	powdered soy protein	113	g	concentrate
½	oz	powdered dextrose	14	g	
3	t	Prague powder #1	15	g	
2	c	apple cider	475	ml	
3	ft	collagen casings	0.9	m	
4	pt	stock	2	l	

1. Blanch the liver. When cool, grind once, using a ³⁄₁₆ in. (0.5 cm) plate.

2. Grind the beef through a ¼ in. (0.63 cm) plate.

3. Grind the pork using a ³⁄₁₆ in. (0.5 cm) plate.

4. Sauté the shallots until they are translucent; cool.

5. Add the salt, pepper, ginger, marjoram, nutmeg, soy protein, dextrose, Prague powder #1, and the sautéed shallots to the cider.

6. Mix the liver, beef, and pork together in an electric mixer on low speed. Add the seasoning solution and blend well.

7. Stuff the prepared casings. Tie one end of each sausage with a butterfly knot and secure the other end with a hog clip.

8. Immerse the sausage in stock and poach until the internal temperature is 155°F (68°C).

9. Cool with a cold water shower to 100°F (38°C).

10. Refrigerate at least 12 hours before use.

Lenten Fish Sausage

Yield: 10 pounds (4.5 kg)

U.S.		Ingredients	Metric		Preparation
7	lb	mild white fish	3.2	kg	skinless filet
3	lb	salmon	1.4	kg	skinless filet
1	pt	heavy cream	475	ml	
12	oz	bread	340	g	
4	oz	vegetable oil	118	ml	
1	oz	salt	28	g	
1	T	sugar	12	g	
1	T	ground black pepper	6	g	
1	oz	fresh chives	28	g	chopped
1	T	fresh garlic	6	g	minced
		sheep casings	22–24	mm	
		fish stock			or court bouillon

1. Make a fine paste of the white fish in a food processor.

2. Cut the salmon into small dice. Fold the salmon dice into the white fish purée. Chill to at least 35°F (1°C).

3. Combine the heavy cream and bread to make a panade.

4. Add the oil, salt, sugar, pepper, chives, and garlic to the fish and mix thoroughly. Add the panade and mix.

5. Stuff the prepared casings. Tie into 3–4 in. (8–10 cm) links.

(Continued)

6. Immerse in fish stock and poach until the internal temperature of the sausage reaches 140°F (60°C). Remove and cool in additional cold stock until the internal temperature reaches 60°F (16°C).

7. Refrigerate for use. To serve, reheat in fish stock.

Linguisa

This smoked Greek sausage has an interesting coarse texture that is created by grinding some of the meat twice.

Yield: 10 pounds (4.5 kg)

U.S.		Ingredients	Metric		Preparation
10	lb	pork butt	4.5	kg	cubed
2	oz	fine salt	57	g	
1	t	black pepper	2	g	finely ground
1	t	fresh ginger	2	g	grated
1	oz	Hungarian paprika	28	g	
3	t	ground coriander	6	g	
1	t	ground cumin	2	g	
3	t	red pepper flakes	3	g	
3	t	granulated sugar	13	g	
3	t	garlic powder	6	g	
12	oz	powdered soy protein	340	g	concentrate
12	oz	nonfat dry milk	340	g	
3	t	Prague powder #1	15	g	measured accurately
4	oz	red wine	118	ml	
2	c	ice water	475	ml	
		casings	36	mm	

1. Grind the pork using a ½ in. (1.3 cm) plate. Grind 3 lb of the pork again using a ³⁄₁₆ in. (0.5 cm) plate. Combine all of the ground pork in a mixing tub.

2. Combine the salt, pepper, ginger, paprika, coriander, cumin, pepper flakes, sugar, garlic powder, soy protein, dry milk, Prague powder #1, and wine with the water. Distribute the solution evenly over the ground meat and mix very well.

3. Stuff the prepared casings. Tie into 4 in. (10 cm) links.

SMOKING

1. Preheat the smoker to 155°F (68°C). Place the links on hanging sticks and load into the smoker. Air dry for 1 hour with the dampers wide open.
2. Raise the smoker temperature by 5°F (3°C). After another hour, increase the temperature by the same amount again. The final temperature will be 165°F (74°C).
3. Remove the sausage from the smoker when the internal product temperature reaches 155°F (68°C). Shower at once with cold water.
4. Refrigerate for use.

Liver Bologna

Yield: 10 pounds (4.5 kg)

U.S.		Ingredients	Metric		Preparation
5	lb	veal liver	2.3	kg	
5	lb	pork trimmings	2.3	kg	
8	oz	onions	227	g	finely chopped
6	oz	powdered soy protein	170	g	concentrate
1	oz	powdered dextrose	28	g	
½	oz	ground white pepper	14	g	
1	t	ground marjoram	2	g	
1	t	ground cloves	2	g	
1	t	ground ginger	2	g	
2	t	ground nutmeg	4	g	
1	oz	salt	28	g	
1	pt	cream	475	ml	
2 in. or 3½ in. × 24 in.		synthetic fibrous casings	5 cm or 9 cm × 60 cm		

1. Cut the veal livers into slices and cook them in boiling water. Cool the liver in cold water and grind it through a ⅟₁₆ in. (0.16 cm) plate.
2. Grind the pork through a ⅛ in. (0.3 cm) plate. Add the remaining ingredients and mix until everything is evenly distributed.
3. Stuff the prepared casings. Have ready 3 casings.
4. Place the sausage in 170°F (77°C) water and cook to an internal temperature of 160°F (71°C).
5. Refrigerate for 1 day to develop flavor.

Liver Sausage I

Compare this precooked sausage with Liver Sausage II.

Yield: 10 pounds (4.5 kg)

U.S.		Ingredients	Metric		Preparation
10	lb	pork liver	4.5	kg	
1	oz	salt	28	g	
½	oz	ground white pepper	14	g	
⅛	oz	cayenne pepper	3.5	g	
½	oz	ground ginger	14	g	
1	t	paprika	2	g	
1	pt	ice water	475	ml	
		sheep casings	32–35	mm	

1. Grind the meat using a ⅜ in. (0.95 cm) plate.
2. Add the salt, pepper, cayenne pepper, ginger, and paprika and mix thoroughly.
3. Grind the mixture again through a ¹⁄₁₆ in. (0.15 cm) plate while adding the ice water. Chill the mixture before stuffing.
4. Stuff the prepared casings. Tie into 4 in. (10 cm) links.
5. Poach the sausages to an internal temperature of 165°F (74°C). Hang briefly to dry, then wrap and label.
6. Refrigerate for use.

Liver Sausage II

This is a fine sausage to grill. Compare it with Liver Sausage I.

Yield: 10 pounds (4.5 kg)

U.S.		Ingredients	Metric		Preparation
10	lb	pork liver	4.5	kg	
2	oz	fine salt	57	g	
½	oz	ground white pepper	14	g	
¼	oz	ground allspice	7	g	
½–1	t	cayenne pepper	.75–1.5	g	to taste
¼	oz	fresh garlic	7	g	bruised
1	pt	ice water	473	ml	
		sheep casings	32–35	mm	

1. Grind the liver using a ⅜ in. (0.95 cm) plate.
2. Add the salt, pepper, allspice, cayenne pepper, and garlic to the liver and mix well.
3. Grind the mixture again through a ⅛ in. (0.3 cm) plate while adding the water.
4. Stuff the prepared casings and tie into 5 in. (13 cm) links.
5. Wrap, label, and refrigerate for use.

Louisiana Turkey Pepper Links

This colorful grilling sausage makes a nice change from pork sausages. For the best flavor and texture, we do not recommend freezing this sausage.

Yield: 10 pounds (4.5 kg)

U.S.		Ingredients	Metric		Preparation
8	lb	roast turkey meat	3.6	kg	mixed white and dark
12	oz	turkey fat	340	g	from the roasted bird
4	oz	heavy cream	118	ml	
10	oz	whole milk	296	ml	
2½	oz	kosher or canning salt	71	g	
1	T	ground white pepper	6	g	
½	oz	Cajun spices	14	g	Chef Paul's Magic blend
12	oz	white bread crumbs	340	g	fresh
1	oz	Prague powder #1	28	g	measured accurately
10	oz	rich turkey stock	296	ml	
12	oz	mixed yellow, red, and green bell peppers	340	g	in ⅛ in. (0.32 cm) dice, sautéed, and cooled
		hog casings	29–32	mm	

1. Have the meat, fat, cream, and milk chilled to near the freezing point, 32°F (0°C).
2. Grind the turkey meat and fat through a ³⁄₁₆ in. (0.5 cm) plate.
3. Add the salt, pepper, Cajun spices, bread crumbs, and Prague powder #1 to the forcemeat and mix lightly by hand.
4. Using a vertical cutting machine, mix and finely cut the forcemeat for 4 minutes. Alternatively, process by batches in a food processor. Turn the forcemeat into a tub or mixing machine.
5. Mix in the milk, cream, and stock. Fold in the diced bell peppers and mix until the ingredients are uniformly blended.
6. Pack into shallow pans, cover, and refrigerate for at least 1½ hours.
7. Stuff the prepared casings but not too tightly. Tie into 4 in. (10 cm) links.

SMOKING

1. Preheat the smoker to 110°F (43°C). Hang the sausages on sticks to dry in the smoker with the dampers wide open for 1 hour.
2. When the sausages are uniformly dry, increase the temperature every 15 minutes until it reaches 160°F (71°C).

3. Twenty minutes after the last temperature increase, check the internal temperature of the sausage. Remove the links when it reaches 155°F (68°C).

4. Spray the sausages with cold water. Wrap and refrigerate for use.

Loukanika

This fresh Greek sausage is best used fresh within three days of production. If necessary, wrap well and freeze uncooked; the quality should hold for up to one month.

Yield: 12 pounds (5.4 kg)

U.S.		Ingredients	Metric		Preparation
6	lb	trimmed lean pork	2.7	kg	cubed
3	lb	pork rind	1.4	kg	simmer 2 hours; drain, chill well, cube
3	lb	fatback	1.4	kg	cubed
2	c	Greek red wine	475	ml	
2	T	extra fine pure salt	30	g	
1	T	black pepper	6	g	freshly ground
2	T	fresh orange zest	12	g	finely minced
2	T	marjoram OR thyme	6	g	rubbed
6	med	Turkish bay leaves			ground
2	T	ground allspice	6	g	
		or			
1	T ea	coriander and allspice	6	g	
10		fresh garlic cloves	10		crushed
12	yd	30 mm hog casing	11	m	

1. Grind the pork, cooled pork rind, and fatback together through a ⅜ in. (0.9 cm) plate. Grind again through a ¼ in. (0.6 cm) plate.

2. Pour the wine and all the seasonings over the ground meats and mix very well.

3. Stuff the prepared casings but not too tightly. Tie into 4 in. (10 cm) links.

4. Wrap well and keep uncooked links refrigerated at 33°F (1°C).

5. To cook, poach gently for 20–30 minutes in water. Pour off the water and allow to brown lightly. Turn frequently. Drain on absorbent paper and serve at once.

Marinade for Venison

Yield: 2½ quarts (2.5 l)

U.S.		Ingredients	Metric		Preparation
2	bottles	red wine	750	ml	
2	c	wine vinegar	475	ml	
6		whole cloves	6		
2	t	black peppercorns	2	g	coarsely crushed
3	T	pickling salt	36	g	
3	medium	onions	3	medium	thinly sliced
6	medium	carrots	6	medium	thinly sliced
6		fresh garlic cloves	6		crushed
4		whole bay leaves	4		crushed
2		fresh thyme sprigs	2		
2	c	virgin olive oil	475	ml	
10	lb	venison	4.5	kg	

1. Combine the ingredients and pour over the meat in a nonreactive container.

2. Marinate 2–3 days in the refrigerator, turning meat every 8–12 hours.

This marinade can be used to tenderize and to flavor cuts of meat such as the saddle, loin, tenderloin, leg, steaks, and chops from an older or a wild animal. (These same cuts from a younger animal should not need tenderizing if the carcass hangs for the proper length of time.) It is best to grind or stew tougher cuts such as the shoulder, shank, and breast.

The minimum time for any marination is several hours. It is often preferable to continue the process for a full two days or more. Always keep the marinating meat at 38–42°F (3–5°C). Turn all pieces at least twice every 24 hours, and keep the meat completely immersed in the solution at all times. Always make a fresh marinade for each batch; do not reuse a marinade. Read the sections on marinades and carbonnades.

Because the new domesticated venison such as Cervena brand does not need to be tenderized like wild venison, these meats can be marinated for shorter times. Flavor is the main reason to marinate these meats.

Melton Mowbray Sausage

This is a mild grilling sausage that was inspired by a pie of the same name.

Yield: 10 pounds (4.5 kg)

U.S.		Ingredients	Metric		Preparation
10	lb	fatty veal and pork	4.5	kg	
2	oz	fine salt	57	g	
2	oz	ground white pepper	57	g	
1	t	ground cloves	2.5	g	
1½	t	ground nutmeg	3.8	g	
1	t	cayenne pepper	1.5	g	
1	pt	ice water	473	ml	
		sheep casings	32–35	mm	

1. Grind the meat using a ⅜ in. (0.9 cm) plate.
2. Place the ground meat in a mixer, and add the salt, pepper, cloves, nutmeg, and cayenne pepper. Mix well.
3. Grind the seasoned mixture through a ⅛ in. (0.3 cm) plate while adding the water.
4. Stuff the prepared casings. Tie into 3 in. (8 cm) links.
5. Wrap and refrigerate at 34°F (1°C) for use.

Minnesota Fresh Bratwurst

I first tasted this sausage in the backyard of a Chicago friend. This is the best fresh sausage I have ever tasted! My friend had secured this recipe from a retired Master Sausagemaker. I salute his talent and I am pleased to pass the formula on to you. —Chef Kinsella.

Yield: 10 pounds (4.5 kg)

U.S.		Ingredients	Metric		Preparation
5	lb	trimmed pork butt	2.3	kg	cubed
5	lb	select veal trimmings	2.3	kg	
1	pt	whole milk	475	ml	
1	oz	fine salt	28	g	
1	T	black pepper	6	g	freshly ground
1	T	powdered dextrose	3	g	
1	t	ground mace	3	g	
1	t	ground coriander	3	g	
1	t	ground nutmeg	2	g	
		hog casings	35	mm	

1. Grind the pork and veal through a ⅜ in. (0.9 cm) plate. Chill the grind in shallow pans for 1 hour.

2. Put the milk in a container and stir in all of the seasoning ingredients. Mix thoroughly by stirring from the bottom so no solids remain behind.

3. Distribute this solution over the meat and blend thoroughly. Always rechill any mix that has warmed up over 39°F (4°C).

4. Stuff the prepared casings. Tie into 4-oz (120 g) links, which will be approximately 4 in. (10 cm) long.

5. Refrigerate the sausages overnight to develop flavor.

6. These bratwurst are particularly well-suited to the outdoor grill. Gently preheat by immersing them in hot water for 10–30 minutes prior to grilling. This promotes uniform browning during the grilling process.

Mortadella

Mortadella is distinguished by the inclusion of diced fat. It must remain separate and not smear into the sausage mix. This recipe gives special consideration to making an authentic mortadella.

Yield: 10 pounds (4.5 kg)

U.S.		Ingredients	Metric		Preparation
9½	lb	lean pork butt	4.3	kg	
½	lb	pork snouts	230	g	or fatback
8	oz	Italian red wine	237	ml	
1	T	ground mace	5	g	
1	T	ground coriander	5	g	
½	t	ground cinnamon	1	g	
2	T	granulated gelatin	9	g	
½	oz	Prague powder #1	14	g	
1	pt	ice water	475	ml	
5	T	salt	75	g	
4½	oz	nonfat dry milk	128	g	
8	T	corn syrup solids	24	g	
2		large garlic cloves	2		finely minced
1	T	ground white pepper	6	g	
2	T	whole black pepper	18	g	Tellicherry
		hog stomachs			Kutas catalogue #11020
		or			
		collagen flat casings	90	mm	

1. Trim enough fat from the pork butts to obtain about 1½ lb (700 g) of firm fat. Cut this fat into uniform ⅜ in. (0.9 cm) dice. Return the fat to the cooler.
2. Grind the pork snouts and lean meat through a ½ in. (1.3 cm) plate.
3. Bring the wine to a simmer in a covered pot. Add the mace, coriander, and cinnamon. Simmer gently for 20 minutes and set aside to cool.
4. Stir the gelatin and Prague powder #1 into the ice water. Mix well to dissolve the Prague powder.
5. Place the meat in a mixing tub and sprinkle with the salt, dry milk, and corn syrup solids. Mix lightly.
6. Add the cooled wine mixture, gelatin mixture, garlic, white pepper, and peppercorns. Mix very well to evenly distribute the ingredients.
7. Grind through a ⅛ in. (0.3 cm) plate.
8. Distribute the diced fat over the forcemeat. Incorporate it uniformly, using care to avoid breaking up the dice. Keep the fat cubes and the forcemeat near 34°F (1°C) for best results.

(Continued)

9. Pack into shallow pans, avoiding any air pockets. Cover and chill for 6 hours.

10. Stuff the prepared casings.

SMOKING

1. Place the sausage into a preheated smoker at 120°F (49°C). Maintain a heavy smoke during the first hour. Gradually raise the temperature to 170°F (77°C). Hold this temperature until the mortadella reaches an internal temperature of 150°F (65°C).

2. If necessary, spray the sausage quickly with hot water to remove any grease, then shower with cool water to reduce the internal temperature to 120–125°F (49–52°C).

3. Place the mortadella in a 40–45°F (4–7°C) cooler. Age for at least 12 hours before use. Store well-wrapped for longer periods at 34°F (1°C).

Old Berliner Sausage

You may vary the degree of smoking for this classic sausage.

Yield: 10 pounds (4.5 kg)

U.S.		Ingredients	Metric		Preparation
5	lb	pork shoulder	2.3	kg	
4	lb	ground shin beef	1.8	kg	
1	lb	veal shank meat	450	g	
5	oz	fatback	142	g	
1	oz	salt	28	g	
1	T	ground white pepper	6	g	
1	T	dried onion	3	g	
1		garlic clove	1		crushed
½	oz	Prague powder #1	14	g	
2	oz	powdered dextrose	57	g	
12	oz	powdered soy protein	340	g	concentrate
1	pt	ice water	475	ml	
6	in.	fibrous casings			

1. Grind the pork, beef, veal, and fatback through a ³⁄₁₆ in. (0.5 cm) or ¼ in. (0.6 cm) plate. Chill for 2 hours.

2. Mix the remaining ingredients into the ground meats very well.

3. Stuff the prepared casings. Refrigerate for 24 hours.

4. Remove the sausage from the cooler and air dry until the internal temperature is at least 70°F (21°C).

SMOKING

1. Load the sausage into a preheated smoker at 130°F (54°C). For the first 2 hours, apply smoke while increasing the temperature by 10°F (6°C) every 30 minutes until the smoker temperature reaches 170°F (77°C). A total of 4 hours of smoke should give a desirable finish.

2. Hold at this temperature until the internal temperature of the sausage is 152°F (67°C). The sausage may be removed at this point, or it may remain in the smoker to attain a darker color if desired.

3. After removing the sausage from the smoker, shower at once with cold water to lower the internal temperature to 65°F (18°C).

4. Refrigerate for use.

Pastrami

Cut pastrami in thin slices for cold sandwiches. Cut it in thicker slices to serve hot. A typical hot presentation for pastrami would include a mustard sauce, spaetzle, and kosher dills.

Yield: 6 pounds (2.7 kg)

U.S.		Ingredients	Metric		Preparation
5–6	lb	beef silverside (in 1 piece)	2.6	kg	grade Good or better
4	oz	salt	113	g	canning or kosher
1	oz	cracked black pepper	28	g	#6 mesh
2	oz	brown sugar	57	g	light or dark
1	oz	fresh ginger	28	g	peeled and minced
1	oz	fresh garlic	28	g	crushed
1	oz	ground coriander	28	g	
		cracked black pepper			#6 mesh
		white beef stock			

1. Trim the beef.

2. Combine the salt, pepper, sugar, ginger, garlic, and coriander.

3. Working on a clean, nonporous surface, rub the seasoning mixture into all surfaces of the beef.

(Continued)

4. Place the beef with all the seasonings into a heavy-duty sealable plastic bag. Expel the excess air, and carefully tie and seal the bag.

5. Put the bag in the cooler. Rotate and lightly massage the sealed bag at least once a day for 12 days.

SMOKING

1. Preheat the smoker to 65°F (18°C). Adjust the dampers to wide open.

2. Remove the beef from the plastic bag. Using a trussing needle and strong cord, provide a secure loop to hang the meat on a smoke stick. Place into the smoker. Allow to air dry with no smoke for a full 24 hours.

3. Remove the meat from the smoker and cover loosely. Set the temperature at 130°F (54°C) with the dampers wide open. Return the meat to the smoker and hold at this setting for 2 hours.

4. Adjust the dampers to one-half open. Monitor the temperature and raise the temperature gradually over the next several hours.

5. Remove the pastrami when its internal temperature reaches 120°F (49°C). Do not shower with cold water.

6. Apply a finishing rub of cracked pepper.

7. Cool quickly and wrap tightly. Refrigerate for 2 days before using.

8. To cook, unwrap the chilled pastrami and place in a large quantity of white beef stock. Bring quickly to a full boil, reduce the heat, and simmer for 2 or more hours until tender.

9. Store the pastrami tightly wrapped and well-chilled at all times.

Pâté and Terrine Spices

Make this useful seasoning mix in quantities to suit your needs. Keep some on hand, but avoid storing herbs and spices too long. Vary the formula to your taste. We prefer to measure by volume rather than weight, especially when mixing larger quantities.

 We find Chef Paul Prudhomme's Magic Seasoning Blends very useful to fine tune our basic mixture. With seven blends available, it provides wonderful versatility.

Yield: 5½ teaspoons (9.75 g)

U.S.		Ingredients	Metric		Preparation
1	t	fine black pepper	2	g	freshly ground
1	t	ground coriander	1.5	g	
1	t	ground thyme	1	g	
1	t	ground bay leaf	2	g	
½	t	ground mace	1	g	
½	t	ground marjoram	1	g	
½	t	spice blend	1.25	g	such as Chef Paul's

1. Mix all the ingredients well and place them in an airtight container for storage. Store away from heat and light.

Pâté Maison

This is Chef Kinsella's famous Chicken Liver Pâté. Serve with melba toast or crackers.

Yield: 5 pounds (2.25 kg)

U.S.		Ingredients	Metric		Preparation
4	lb	chicken livers	1.8	kg	strictly fresh
8	oz	unsalted butter	226	g	
2	oz	onion	57	g	finely diced
1	t	fine salt	5	g	
1	t	white pepper	2	g	finely ground
3	oz	brandy	89	ml	
8	oz	heavy cream	237	ml	
8	oz	sliced bacon	226	g	optional, for lining mold

1. Using a large skillet, sweat the livers in 4 oz of the butter.
2. After 3 minutes, add the onion, salt, and pepper. Cook until the livers are just off-pink. Set aside and hold warm.
3. Line a 2½-quart mold with a single layer of the bacon slices. Chill the mold.
4. Purée the liver and onion mixture in a food processor.
5. Gently warm the remaining butter. Add to the livers with the brandy and cream. Mix again to assure uniformity.
6. Pour into the well-chilled mold. Place the mold in a water bath that reaches to 1 in. (2.5 cm) from the top of the mold. Bake 45–60 minutes at 325°F (163°C) until the pâté sets. Shake the pan gently to observe the texture. A metal cake tester should come out clean. The time will vary depending on the thickness of the mold. Record the time for future reference.
7. Remove from the oven and water bath. Cover and chill for a minimum of 12 hours.
8. Unmold, plate, and garnish for presentation.

Pickled Herring

This herring is perishable and should be consumed within 3 weeks. Label the container clearly with the production date and a "use by" date. Store in the refrigerator.

Yield: 3 quarts (3 l)

U.S.		Ingredients	Metric		Preparation
5–6	lb	salt herring	2.25–2.75	kg	
20	oz	water	600	ml	
20	oz	white wine vinegar	600	ml	5–6% acidity
7	oz	white sugar	200	g	
2	T	mixed pickling spice	7	g	
3	lg	red onions, peeled	3	lg	cut in rings
1	qt	sour cream	950	ml	optional

1. Soak the salt herring, refrigerated, in a large tub of water for 18–24 hours. Change the water twice.

2. Make the pickling solution near the end of the soaking period. Using only nonreactive utensils, put the water, vinegar, sugar, and pickling spice into a pan and bring to a boil. Reduce the heat and simmer 5 minutes. Remove from heat and allow to cool. Refrigerate and chill to 45°F (7°C).

3. To make filets, cut each herring in half lengthwise. Remove the backbone and as many smaller bones as possible with needlenose pliers. Cut the filets crosswise into 1 in. (2.5 cm) chunks.

4. Make alternate layers of fish and onion rings in a tub or large pan. Arrange the pieces rather snugly to ensure thorough coverage by the pickling solution. The herring may also be packed into wide-mouth glass jars if desired.

5. If using the optional sour cream, add it to the pickling solution. Pour the solution over the fish. Work carefully, gently prodding with a wooden spoon to eliminate any air pockets. Cover with plastic wrap. Cover all with heavy plastic sheeting or other material to protect the herring well.

6. Leave undisturbed in the cooler for 6 days (144 hours) before using. Consume within 3 weeks.

Polish Ham Sausage

Yield: 10 pounds (4.5 kg)

U.S.		Ingredients	Metric		Preparation
10	lb	very lean pork	4.5	kg	or smoked ham
1	pt	fresh ham stock	475	ml	cool, defatted
3	oz	fine salt	85	g	
1	T	black pepper	6	g	freshly ground, medium
1	T	ground coriander	3	g	
1	T	ground nutmeg	7.5	g	or to taste
2	t	Prague powder #1	10	g	
1	oz	powdered dextrose	28	g	or more to taste
3½ in. × 24 in.		fibrous casing	9 cm × 60 cm		

1. Cube the pork. Grind through a 1 in. (2.5 cm) plate. Grind any fatty meat separately using a ⅛ in. (0.3 cm) plate.

2. Put the ham stock into a container and stir in the salt, pepper, coriander, nutmeg, Prague powder #1, and dextrose.

3. Pour the seasoned stock over the meat in a mixing tub. Mix lightly but thoroughly. Chill.

4. Tie a butterfly knot in one end of the casing. Stuff the prepared casing; tie or clip to close. Make a secure hanging loop.

SMOKING

1. Hang to dry at room temperature for 2 hours. Preheat the smoker to 150°F (65°C). Load the sausage into the smoker and apply a heavy smoke at once. After 30 minutes, increase the temperature to 165°F (74°C) and continue the heavy smoke.

2. When the internal temperature of the sausage reaches 152°F (67°C), reduce the temperature to 150°F (65°C). Smoke for 2–3 hours. You may prefer a lighter or heavier smoke.

3. Remove the sausage and cool. Refrigerate for 24 hours before serving.

Polska Kiszka Watrobiana

Our thanks to Rytec Kutas for this Polish blood sausage with liver. You may choose to lightly smoke this sausage after it has been poached and dried.

Yield: 10 pounds (4.5 kg)

U.S.		Ingredients	Metric		Preparation
4	lb	pig's feet, snouts	1.8	kg	or other meat
3	lb	pork or beef liver	1.4	kg	
3	lb	unsmoked bacon	1.4	kg	
3½	oz	salt	99	g	
1	T	black pepper	6	g	table grind
3½	oz	onion	99	g	finely chopped
1	T	dried marjoram	6	g	
2	t	Prague powder #1	10	g	measured accurately
1	pt	*pork or beef blood	473	ml	fresh, well-chilled
		hog casings	35–38	mm	

1. Cook the pig's feet (and snouts or other pork) in water until tender. Save the broth. Cool and remove any bones.
2. Grind the pork, liver, and bacon through a ⅛ in. or ³⁄₁₆ in. (0.3 or 0.5 cm) plate.
3. Add the salt, pepper, onion, marjoram, and Prague powder #1 and mix until all the ingredients are evenly distributed.
4. Add the blood and mix thoroughly.
5. Stuff the prepared casings about 15 in. (38 cm) long, leaving 3–4 inches of empty casing on each end. Tie the sausage into a ring.
6. Place the sausage in 170°F (77°C) water. Cook until the internal temperature is 160°F (71°C).

SMOKING (OPTIONAL)

1. Dry the sausage at room temperature for 1–2 hours.
2. Put the sausage in a preheated smoker at 160°F (71°C) with a light smoke for 2 hours.
3. Remove from the smoker and shower with cold water until the internal temperature drops to 60–70°F (16–21°C).
4. Place the product into refrigerated storage.

---

*You may substitute a good meat broth for the blood in this recipe. Always keep blood well chilled.

Raised Pork Pie and Variations

As the several variations indicate, each city has its own version of a raised pie. Make a pie with your own preferred seasonings. The pie can be eaten hot or cold. You can make several at a time and freeze them.

Yield: Two 2-pound (two 0.9 kg) pies

U.S.		Ingredients	Metric		Preparation
1	lb	Hot Water Paste	450	g	see separate recipe (p. 153)
2	lb	lean pork	900	g	diced fine-to-medium
4	oz	smoked bacon	113	g	diced fine-to-medium
4	oz	Spanish onion	113	g	chopped
1	t	table salt	5	g	
1	t	black pepper	6	g	freshly ground
1	t	fresh parsley	2	g	finely chopped
1	t	dried sage	2	g	rubbed fine
1	t	ground allspice	1	g	or to taste
1	oz	plain gelatin	28	g	granulated
½	c	water	118	ml	
2	c	brown veal stock	473	ml	clarified
1	lg	whole egg	1	lg	beaten

1. Have ready a greased 1-quart pâté mold. Roll out one-half of the pastry to ¹⁄₁₆ in. thick (0.15 cm). Use it to line the mold and trim the excess. Set aside in a warm spot. Reserve the remaining pastry for the top crust.

2. Pack each lined mold neatly with the pork, bacon, and onions, adding the seasonings evenly as you go.

3. Soften the gelatin in water and add it to the stock. Pour it over the pies to fill generously. Reserve remaining stock to fill the cooled pie after it has baked.

4. Roll out the remaining pastry. Moisten the edges and cover the pie, sealing it with an attractive crimp. Cut steam vents and insert funnels. Decorate with leaves or other designs cut from the pastry scraps. Brush with the beaten egg.

5. Bake in a 400°F (204°C) oven for 15 minutes. Reduce to 300°F (149°C). Bake for 1–1½ hours until the pie is 165°F (74°C) at the center and it is lightly browned. Use a foil tent or other device to retard browning as necessary.

6. Remove the pie from the oven and cool to about 80°F (27°C). Warm the reserved stock and fill the pie through a funnel. Serve the pie hot or allow it to cool and set.

REGIONAL VARIATIONS

Dublin Style: Add chopped scallions and considerably more sage. Dubliners use additions to taste of reduced meat glaze instead of the clarified veal stock.

Liverpool Style I: Add ¼ t (0.4 g) cayenne pepper and omit the black pepper.

Liverpool Style II: Substitute dried ginger for the allspice.

Manchester Style: Add ¼–½ t (0.25 to 0.5 g) of dried coriander and omit the allspice. Some cooks also use nutmeg and cayenne pepper to taste.

Nottingham Style: Add 1 t (2.5 g) of mace and omit the allspice.

Yorkshire Style: Add ½ t (0.5 g) of ground thyme.

Potted Ham

Tart or sweet pickles and relishes go very well with this spread. It is excellent for finger sandwiches and hors d'oeuvre. Present it in an iced serving container.

Yield: 5 pounds (2.3 kg)

U.S.		Ingredients	Metric		Preparation
5	lb	cooked smoked ham	2.3	kg	cubed
2	oz	granulated gelatin	57	g	
4	oz	ham stock	118	ml	cold
1	oz	fine salt	28	g	adjust for salt in ham
¾	oz	white pepper	21	g	freshly ground
½	t	ground mace	1.3	g	
½	t	cayenne pepper	2.3	g	
2	oz	ice water			as needed

1. Grind the ham using a ⅜ in. (0.9 cm) plate.
2. Soften the gelatin in the ham stock. Warm the stock to 120°F (49°C), stirring to dissolve the gelatin. Cool to 80°F (27°C) and add to the ground ham.
3. Add the salt, pepper, mace, and cayenne pepper; mix thoroughly.
4. Grind this mixture using a ⅛ in. (0.3 cm) plate. Add ice water to adjust the ham to a spreading consistency.
5. Pack the product, avoiding air pockets, into serving molds or bulk containers.
6. Cover well and chill to firm for service. The flavor will mature after 1 full day in the cooler. A short period at room temperature before service will soften the spread if it is too firm.

Potted Ham and Tongue

This spread can provide a welcome flavor change. Always keep it well-chilled on ice during service. The recipe starts with cooked tongue; plan well ahead because cooking the tongue takes several hours.

Yield: 6 pounds (2.7 kg)

U.S.		Ingredients	Metric		Preparation
3	lb	cooked tongue	1.4	kg	beef, veal, lamb, or pork
3	lb	smoked ham	1.4	kg	
2	oz	gelatin	57	g	
4	oz	ham stock	118	ml	cold
1	T	fine salt	15	g	adjust for salt in ham
¾	oz	white pepper	21	g	finely ground
½	t	cayenne pepper	0.75	g	or to taste
		ice water			as needed

1. Trim and cube the cooked tongue.
2. Grind the tongue and ham together using a ⅜ in. (0.9 cm) plate.
3. Soften the gelatin in the ham stock. Warm the stock to 120°F (49°C), stirring to dissolve the gelatin. Cool to 80°F (27°C).
4. Put the ground meats in a mixing tub and add the dissolved gelatin, salt, and pepper.
5. Grind the meat again using a ³⁄₁₆ in. (0.5 cm) plate. Add ice water to adjust the meat to a spreading consistency.
6. Mix well to assure uniformity. Pack into serving molds or bulk pack.
7. Chill at once. Store tightly covered in the refrigerator for 1 full day to set the gelatin and to develop flavor.

Potted Salmon and Shrimp

Serve this savory and delicate spread for hors d'oeuvre. For best results, keep the shrimp and salmon well-chilled and work with chilled tubs, paddles, and utensils throughout preparation.

Yield: 6 pounds (2.7 kg)

U.S.		Ingredients	Metric		Preparation
3	lb	shrimp	2.7	kg	cooked in shrimp boil
3	lb	salmon	2.7	kg	cooked
2	oz	gelatin	57	g	
4	oz	cold water	118	ml	
2½	t	fine salt	71	g	
2–3	oz	white pepper	57–85	g	to taste
½	t	ground mace	1	g	
¼	t	cayenne pepper	0.7	g	
		ice water			as needed

1. Peel and devein the cooked shrimp.
2. Carefully remove the bones, skin, and dark oily flesh from the cooked salmon.
3. Combine the shrimp and salmon and grind them using a ⅜ in. (0.9 cm) plate.
4. Soften the gelatin in the water. Warm the water to 120°F (49°C), stirring to dissolve the gelatin. Cool to 80°F (27°C).
5. In a tub or an electric mixer, add the dissolved gelatin, salt, pepper, mace, and cayenne pepper. Mix well.
6. Grind again using a ⅛ in. (0.3 cm) plate, adding water as needed to obtain a spreading consistency.
7. Pack into serving molds or bulk containers. Cover and chill very well. The mixture will firm with chilling. The flavor will improve after 1 full day in the cooler.

Potted Turkey

Serve well-chilled in a handsome mold for hors d'oeuvre.

Yield: 6 pounds (2.7 kg)

U.S.		Ingredients	Metric		Preparation
6	lb	cooked turkey	2.7	kg	dark and/or light meat
½	oz	fine salt	14	g	or to taste
¾	oz	white pepper	21	g	finely ground
¼	t	cayenne pepper	0.4	g	or to taste
1	qt	aspic	946	ml	see separate recipe (p. 83)

1. Carefully pick over the cooked turkey meat to remove all bone particles and gristle. You may choose to add some turkey skin to enhance the flavor.

2. Grind the turkey using a ⅜ in. (0.9 cm) plate. Put the turkey in a mixing bowl or tub and add the salt, pepper, and cayenne pepper. Mix well.

3. Grind the mixture again, adding the aspic to adjust to a spreading consistency. The mixture should resemble mashed potatoes.

4. Pack into serving molds or bulk containers. Cover and chill well for service. The flavor will improve after 1 full day in the cooler.

Pressed Corned Beef

Serve this handsome loaf with cold German potato salad and cole slaw. This product is usually impossible to find in many areas of our country. It tastes delicious both with heavier, dark bread or with a soft white bread and is wonderful with lettuce and mayonnaise. This item is highly addictive, often unknown, and usually expensive to buy. It may easily become a welcome, signature addition to anyone's line of quality products. Yes, it's worth your making a good aspic jelly, just to enhance the scrumptious flavor!

This recipes uses the aspic on page 83, and the Pâté and Terrine Spices on page 193.

Yield: One 7-pound (3.2 kg) loaf

U.S.		Ingredients	Metric		Preparation
7	lb	cooked corned beef	3.2	kg	chilled
1	qt	aspic	946	ml	cool, but pourable see separate recipe (p. 83)
1	oz	Pâté/Terrine Spices	28	g	see separate recipe (p. 193)

1. For the most attractive loaf, cut the corned beef into ¾ in. (2 cm) batons. Arrange these strips neatly in a rectangular Pullman mold. (You may lightly spray the mold with a release agent or plan to dip the pan quickly into hot water to unmold.) Alternatively, the beef may be crumbled.

2. Pour in the aspic and arrange a maximum weight of 10 lb (4.5 kg) on top of the meat. Refrigerate for 48 hours.

3. Remove the weight and carefully unmold the loaf. Wrap and refrigerate for use.

4. To serve, slice ⅛ in. (0.3 cm) or thicker. If sliced in this manner and held well-chilled, the loaf will keep its shape and high quality.

Pressed Lamb or Mutton

This recipe was especially created to use less tender cuts of lamb and mutton. Choose one of the two seasoning mixtures below or season to your taste. Keep notes for future reference. Serve chilled in sandwiches or on a buffet with mint sauce, mustard, or other condiment.

Yield: One 7-pound (3.2 kg) loaf

U.S.		Ingredients	Metric		Preparation
7	lb	lamb/mutton shoulder	3.2	kg	trimmed
		lamb/mutton stock			to cover
1½	T	fine salt	30	g	or to taste
1	oz	seasoning mixture	28	g	choose one below
1	pt	aspic	475	ml	melted

LAMB SEASONING MIXTURES:

#1: equal parts rosemary and juniper berries, crushed
#2: equal parts white pepper, ground ginger, and marjoram

1. Cook the lamb or mutton slowly in the lamb or mutton stock. Remove the meat, drain, and cool. Cut the meat into large dice.
2. Add the salt and seasoning mixture #1 or #2. Mix lightly, but very well.
3. Place the seasoned lamb in a nonreactive mold or loaf pan. (Round molds are easy to work with and they are acceptable for presentation.)
4. Pour in the aspic. Arrange a board and a 15-lb (6.8 kg) weight on top of each mold.
5. Refrigerate for 48 hours. The flavor will mature, and the mold will set and stabilize.
6. Release the lamb by dipping the pan quickly in hot water or surrounding it with heated towels; unmold onto a serving platter. Garnish for service.

Pressed Tongue

Garnish with panache, on a suitable platter. Carve this specialty to order. Richly delicious, this extraordinary delight will soon become an oft-requested item in your line.

Select very fresh, small beef tongues [3 pounds (1.4 kg) or less]. You may also use this recipe for calf, lamb, or pork tongues. We include two recipes for tongue seasoning mix; choose one to use when you make this Pressed Tongue. To use in other tongue recipes, use 1 ounce for each 1 pound of trimmed meat. Store in a tight container in a cool place.

Yield: 12 pounds [2 6-pound (2.7 kg) loaves]

U.S.		Ingredients	Metric		Preparation
12	lb	beef tongue	5.4	kg	4 pieces, very fresh
5	qt	rich beef stock	4.7	l	
16	oz	heavy aspic jelly	475	ml	
5½	oz	tongue seasoning	156	g	choose #1 or #2 below

TONGUE SEASONING #1

2	lb	pure pickling salt	900	g	
1	lb	white pepper	450	g	finely ground
½	oz	ground ginger	14	g	
¼	oz	ground cloves	7	g	
¼	oz	ground coriander	7	g	

TONGUE SEASONING #2

4	lb	pure pickling salt	1.8	kg	
1¼	lb	white pepper	560	g	finely ground
½	lb	black pepper #10 mesh	220	g	coarsely ground
½	oz	ground nutmeg	14	g	
1	oz	ground mace	28	g	
½	oz	ground ginger	14	g	
¾	oz	cayenne pepper	21	g	

1. Scrub the tongues well. Blanch them in boiling water for 10 minutes and drain. Put them in a pot, cover with beef stock, and bring to a simmer. Cook until tender, about 10 minutes per pound (450 g). Leave in the stock until they are cool enough to handle. Peel carefully without tearing. Remove the roots, small bones, and gristle. Strain the cooking broth into a clean pot. Reduce quickly to one half of the original volume.

2. Select two nonreactive molds or loaf pans with enough space for the aspic to cover and surround the tongues. Arrange each tongue in a gentle curve with the point of the tongue at the center. Use a skewer to hold the shape.

(Continued)

3. Add the aspic to the hot reduced stock. Strain through a tammy cloth into another vessel, making sure the liquid is very clear. Add the Tongue Seasoning of your choice. Mix very well and stir frequently to keep the seasonings evenly distributed. Cover each coiled tongue with aspic. Prod the tongue and jostle the pan to eliminate air bubbles. Several very small tongues may be arranged neatly in one mold.

4. Arrange a plate and a weight on top; the pressing weight should be about half the weight of the tongues. Chill for 36 hours.

5. Carefully unmold the tongue after dipping the pans quickly in hot water or surrounding them with heated towels to release. Dress the pieces and garnish for service.

Dry-Cured Prosciutto

It's easy to understand why good prosciutto is so expensive when you see how long and involved the process is. It require time, attention, and space. Plan carefully so that prosciutto production does not conflict with daily operations. If you choose to undertake this interesting ham, you will be richly rewarded.

Select unbruised hams within the weight ranges given; having 4 hams of the same size is fine but not absolutely necessary. The ideal thickness for the outside fat is 1.5 in. (4 cm). Note that 50 pounds of ham will require the full 6 ounces of Prague powder #2.

Yield: 4 hams

U.S.		Ingredients	Metric		Preparation
4	ea		4	ea	
10–15	lb	fresh hams, skin on	4.5–7	kg	boned
8	oz	white pepper	227	g	finely ground
2	oz	black pepper	57	g	#10 mesh or finer
14	oz	ground allspice	397	g	
10	T	ground nutmeg	75	g	
2	T	powdered mustard	10	g	
6	T	ground coriander	27	g	
5	oz	powdered dextrose	142	g	
2½	lb	kosher salt	1.1	kg	
6	oz	Prague powder #2	170	g	measured accurately
		white pepper			for final rubbing
		black pepper			for final rubbing

1. Weigh and mix together the white and black peppers, allspice, nutmeg, mustard, coriander, and dextrose.

2. Weigh the salt and the Prague powder #2 individually and keep them separate.

3. To make the **rubbing** compound: Weigh all of the hams to obtain their total weight. For each 50 lb of ham, mix 3½ oz (99 g) of the spice mixture, 2 lb (900 g) of the salt, and 2 oz (57 g) of the Prague powder #2.

4. Rub all the surfaces of each ham very thoroughly with this rubbing mixture. Arrange the hams in a single layer in brining tubs. Leave a 2 in. (5 cm) space between the hams to allow for flattening.

5. To make the **packing** compound: Combine the remaining spice mixture, salt, and Prague powder #2.

6. Fill the empty spaces between the hams with the packing compound. Ensure that the packing compound is in contact with every surface of the hams. Cover the tubs tightly; use plastic wrap followed by canvas or a similar material. Arrange boards on top of the hams and add enough weights to keep the hams firmly compressed. (The weights should be approximately double the weight of the hams.) The hams will flatten to 5 in. (13 cm) or less. Press the hams for 10–12 days at a constant temperature of 36–38°F (2–3°C). Do not disturb the pack until the end of the time period.

7. Remove the hams from the tubs. Brush them off and soak them for 8 hours in a generous amount of cool water. Rinse the hams and tubs and soak them in fresh water for another 8 hours. Remove any adhering cure from each ham with a soft brush. With stout cord and a larding needle, form a hanging loop at the hock end of each ham.

SMOKING

1. Preheat the smoker to 130°F (54°C). Arrange the hams in the smoker so they do not touch each other. Set the dampers one-quarter open. Dry the hams at this setting for 48 hours.

2. After 48 hours, raise the temperature to 140°F (60°C). Over the next 2 hours, raise the temperature 10°F (5–6°C) every 30 minutes to a final setting of 180°F (82°C). Hold this setting for 2 hours.

3. Lower the temperature gradually over the next 6–8 hours to 120°F (49°C). Hold this setting for 10 hours.

4. Turn off the heat and hold the hams in the smoker until the internal temperature reaches 100°F (38°C).

5. Remove the hams from the smoker and hang at room temperature for 10 hours.

6. Make a rubbing mixture of equal parts of #6–10 mesh black pepper and ground white pepper. Generously rub the peppers into all surfaces of each ham.

7. Hang the hams in the smoker to dry at a temperature of 75°F (24°C) with 65–75% relative humidity. Hold the hams under these conditions for 30 days.

8. The hams are now ready for storage. Wrapped in stockinette bags, they will keep for at least 1 year. The optimum temperature for storage is 38–45°F (3–7°C). Avoid excessive humidity.

Rabbit Sausage—Smoked

We recommend serving this variety with a Fish Kedgeree, and Waldorf or Mango Salad. A good lager alongside is a natural.

Use sheep or hog casings for this sausage. The smaller sheep casings are excellent. The less tender hog casings are an acceptable substitute.

Yield: 10 pounds (4.5 kg)

U.S.		Ingredients	Metric		Preparation
7	lb	rabbit meat	3.2	kg	
3	lb	pork pieces	1.4	kg	not too lean
2	pt	ice water	0.9	l	
1	T	salt	15	g	
1	T	coarse black pepper	5	g	#10 mesh
1	t	garlic powder	1.5	g	
1½	t	curry powder	2.5	g	medium-to-hot
4	oz	mango chutney	113	g	commercial, puréed
2	c	powdered soy protein	240	g	
3	T	powdered dextrose	45	g	
2	t	Prague powder #1	10	g	measured accurately
		sheep casings	22–24	mm	
		or			
		hog casings	29–32	mm	

1. Grind together the rabbit and pork using a ³⁄₁₆ in. (0.5 cm) plate. Chill for at least 30 minutes.
2. Put the ice water in a container. Combine the salt, pepper, garlic powder, curry powder, chutney, soy protein, dextrose, and Prague powder #1 and stir into the water.
3. Sprinkle the solution over the meats in a tub; mix very well by hand. Chill to rest the mixture for 15 minutes.
4. Stuff the prepared casings, avoiding air pockets. Tie into 5 in. (13 cm) links.
5. Hang the chain-linked sausages on sticks to air dry at 70°F (21°C) for 1 full hour.

SMOKING

1. Preheat the smoker to 130°F (54°C) with the dampers wide open. Load the sausages and hold for 1 hour.
2. Increase the temperature in several increments over the next 2–3 hours to 145°F (63°C). Adjust the dampers to one-quarter open after the first hour.

3. Monitor the internal temperature near the end of the processing time and remove the sausage when it reaches 140°F (60°C). Shower at once with cold water and hang briefly to drain.

4. Wrap, label, and refrigerate for use.

Ring Bologna

Make this old favorite with or without the optional garlic.

Yield: 10 pounds (4.5 kg)

U.S.		Ingredients	Metric		Preparation
5	lb	beef silverside	2.3	kg	
5	lb	pork butt	2.3	kg	
1	pt	ice water	475	ml	
2	T	fine salt	30	g	or to taste
1	T	white pepper	6	g	finely ground
2	T	sweet paprika	12	g	
1	T	ground nutmeg	7.5	g	
1	T	ground allspice	6	g	
1	t	onion powder	2	g	
2	oz	fresh garlic, minced	57	g	optional
2	c	nonfat dry milk	192	g	or soy protein powder
2	t	Prague powder #1	10	g	measured accurately
		large cellulose casings, beef bungs, or mahogany casings			

1. Grind the beef and pork through a ³⁄₁₆ in. (0.5 cm) plate. Use a vertical cutting machine or a food processor to purée the meats.

2. Put the ice water in a container. Combine the salt, pepper, paprika, nutmeg, allspice, onion powder, optional garlic, dry milk, and Prague powder #1 and stir into the water.

3. Add this solution to the meat and mix well. Stir down the sides of the bowl several times.

4. Stuff the prepared casings and tie into rings. Rinse the bologna and hang securely on smokehouse sticks.

(Continued)

SMOKING

1. Place the bologna in a preheated smoker at 135°F (57°C). Adjust the dampers to three-quarters open. Hold at this setting for 30 minutes, then raise the temperature in 10°F (5–6°C) increments over 1–3 hours to a maximum setting of 165°F (74°C). Total time will depend upon which casings were used. It is essential that the temperature not be raised too rapidly.

2. Remove the bologna when the internal temperature reaches 160°F (71°C). Cool quickly.

3. Refrigerate for use.

Sausage Espagnole

This is a fully cooked dry-cured sausage that keeps especially well, for at least 60 days. Keep it on hand for soup, paella, and Chicken El Cid.

Yield: 10 pounds (4.5 kg)

U.S.		Ingredients	Metric		Preparation
5	lb	lean pork butt	2.3	kg	diced
5	lb	fatback	2.3	kg	coarsely diced
1	lb	raisins	450	g	
2	c	muscatel wine	475	ml	
5	T	fine salt	75	g	
½	oz	cayenne pepper	14	g	
5	med	sweet red peppers	5	med	finely diced
2		garlic cloves	2		finely minced
2	t	Prague powder #2	10	g	measured accurately
10	yd	42 mm natural casings	9	m	

1. Marinate the raisins in the wine for several hours.

2. Combine the pork and the fatback. Grind them through a ⅜ in. (0.9 cm) plate. This is a coarse sausage; do not over-grind.

3. Mix the salt, cayenne pepper, red peppers, garlic, and Prague powder #2 into the ground meat. Add the raisins and the marinade; thoroughly mix the forcemeat.

4. Stuff the prepared casings, but not too tightly. Tie into 5 in. (13 cm) links. Arrange the links on smoking sticks.

SMOKING

1. Preheat the smoker to 130°F (54°C). Set the dampers one-third open. Gradually increase the temperature to 170°F (77°C).

2. When the internal temperature of the sausage reaches 170°F (77°C), reduce the smoker setting to 70°F (21°C). Air dry the sausages in the smoker for 12 full hours.

3. Wrap well and refrigerate for use.

Sausage Stew

Recipe by Chef Harvey. It's a family favorite and a good way to enjoy your own sausages. *Vary your choice of the first item.* Home-baked bread and a good wine make the meal. Leftovers taste fine with proper handling. Use fresh herbs when possible.

Yield: Serves 10–12

U.S.		Ingredients	Metric		Preparation
1½	lb	veal or pork sausages	700	g	or others as desired
¾	lb	Italian sausages	340	g	sweet or hot
		vegetable or olive oil			as needed
4		medium onions	4		sliced
2		medium green peppers	2		chopped
6		garlic cloves	6		finely chopped
1	c	dry white wine	237	ml	
1	lb	waxy potatoes, skin on	450	g	cooked and cubed
1	16-oz	can stewed tomatoes	473	ml	undrained
1	14½-oz	can chicken broth	429	ml	or homemade
4	oz	canned tomato paste	118	ml	
1	lb	fresh green beans	450	g	trimmed and cut
1	t	dried oregano	1	g	
1	t	dried basil	1	g	
1	t	dried marjoram	1	g	
		salt			to taste
		ground black pepper			to taste
¼	lb	mozzarella cheese	110	g	shredded
¼	c	Parmigiano-Reggiano cheese	43	g	freshly grated

1. Heat a heavy 5-quart saucepan, add a very little oil, and sauté the sausages. Brown them lightly, but avoid overcooking. Transfer the sausages to a cutting board and cool them slightly, allowing the juices to set. Slice crosswise into 1 in. (2.5 cm) pieces. Set aside.

2. Remove the excess fat from the pan and add the onions, peppers, and garlic. Sweat the vegetables; do not overcook. Deglaze the pan with white wine. Add the potatoes, tomatoes, chicken broth, tomato paste, and the sausage. Simmer gently for 20 minutes.

3. Stir in the green beans, oregano, basil, and marjoram. Cover and cook 20–25 minutes or until the beans are just done.

4. Let stand for 1 hour, holding the stew at 140°F (60°C).

5. Carefully reheat for service. Correct seasoning and add the mozzarella. Sprinkle with Parmigiano-Reggiano cheese just before serving.

Sausage Stuffing

This recipe is ideal for large and small banquets, owing to its firm nature. In England, it is served with game, turkey, and pork. It is excellent with Beef Olives and faggots.

Yield: Serves 10

U.S.		Ingredients	Metric		Preparation
1	lb	fresh sausage meat	450	g	pork or beef
8	oz	bread crumbs	227	g	2-day-old bread
2		large eggs	2		beaten
3	oz	dry onion	85	g	finely chopped
2	oz	butter	57	g	
1	t	fresh thyme	2	g	finely chopped
		salt			to taste
		freshly ground black pepper			to taste

1. Chop the sausage quite finely. Fold in the crumbs and eggs
2. Sweat the onions in the butter until soft; add the thyme. Remove from the heat and cool.
3. Add the onions to the meat and mix very well. Season with salt and black pepper; remember that the sausage is already seasoned. Fry a small patty; taste and adjust the seasoning if necessary.
4. Wet your hands and form the stuffing into a roll or brick. Wrap in plastic and foil.
5. Refrigerate for service.
6. Use as an ingredient in various recipes or bake the unwrapped sausage stuffing in a 325°F (163°C) oven until it reaches 160°F (71°C). Garnish and serve.

Sausage with Cumin

This fine, tasty sausage is for the cumin lover. It possesses a haunting, good taste and provides variation from more usual fare. It is intended to be "hot and spicy."

Yield: 10 pounds (4.5 kg)

U.S.		Ingredients	Metric		Preparation
8	lb	trimmed shin beef	3.6	kg	
2	lb	fatty pork	900	g	trimmings
2	oz	fine salt	57	g	
¼–½	oz	black pepper	7–14	g	freshly ground
⅛	oz	cayenne pepper	3.5	g	
3	oz	ground cumin	85	g	
2	oz	fresh garlic	57	g	finely minced
2	t	Prague powder #1	10	g	measured accurately
12	oz	ice water	355	ml	
		hog casings	35–38	mm	or collagen casings

1. Combine the beef and the pork and grind using a ¼ in. (0.6 cm) plate. Grind again using a ⅛ in. (0.3 cm) plate. Chill.

2. Combine the salt, pepper, cayenne pepper, cumin, garlic, and Prague powder #1. Sprinkle over the meat and mix well by hand.

3. Add the ice water to the forcemeat while puréeing in a vertical cutting machine or a food processor. Stir down as necessary and check for a very fine texture.

4. Pack into shallow pans, cover well, and chill for at least 1 hour.

5. Stuff the prepared casings, avoiding air pockets. Allow some room for expansion during smoking. Twist-tie or string-tie into 5–7 in. (13–18 cm) links.

6. Arrange on smoker sticks and hang for 1–2 hours in a cooler to air dry fully.

SMOKING

1. While sausages are drying, preheat smoker to 125°F (52°C). Set damper to one-quarter open. Prepare a smoker pan of chips or dust to provide a medium-heavy smoke.

2. Load the smoker with the dried links. Ignite the smoker pan and smoke for 2 hours. Gradually increase the temperature during this time to a maximum of 165°F (74°C). Monitor the internal temperature and remove the sausages when it reaches 155°F (68°C). Spray with a cold shower at once.

3. Hang to dry for 20 minutes. Wrap and refrigerate for use.

Shrimp Kedgeree

During the height of the British Empire, this dish was served as a breakfast item. Smoked salmon or haddock was then the fish of choice. A lesser fish may be substituted for the shrimp. Chef Kinsella suggests the use of smoked catfish. To provide an American taste with an Indian flair, serve with basmati rice. All this serves well to make this old standard most unique.

Yield: Serves 8 as a main dish

U.S.		Ingredients	Metric		Preparation
2	T	vegetable oil	30	ml	
2	oz	Spanish onion	57	g	chopped
2	oz	bell peppers	57	g	various colors, chopped
1	t	crushed garlic	2	g	
8	oz	rice	227	g	white or brown
1	t	ground turmeric	1	g	
		salt			to taste
		freshly ground black pepper			to taste
2	pt	shrimp stock	946	ml	
2	lb	shrimp	900	g	
		marinade or light brine			
1	qt	curry sauce	946	ml	hot for service (recipe follows)

1. Heat the oil in a large sauteuse and add the onion, pepper, and garlic. Briefly sweat the vegetables. Lower the heat, add the rice, and stir for 2 minutes. Add the turmeric, salt, and pepper.

2. Add the shrimp stock and braise over medium heat, stirring occasionally, until the rice has absorbed all the liquid. Set aside and keep warm for service.

3. Brine the shrimp in a light fish brine or marinade.

SMOKING

1. Place the shrimp on a rack in a pan smoker or a mesh rack in a standard smoker. Lightly smoke the shrimp until it is cooked to an internal temperature of 155°F (68°C). Avoid overcooking the shrimp.

2. Arrange the shrimp on top of the rice or toss lightly. Serve the prepared curry sauce on the side. Garnish with chopped parsley.

Curry Sauce

This is a Madras-style sauce, one of many formulas for this versatile sauce.

Yield: 1 quart (1 l)

U.S.		Ingredients	Metric		Preparation
8	oz	onions	225	g	diced
1	ea	whole clove	1	ea	finely chopped
2	oz	oil	60	ml	
2	oz	flour	57	g	
1½	oz	curry powder	42	g	
2	pt	stock	946	ml	chicken, beef, etc.
2	oz	tomato purée	60	ml	
4	oz	apples	113	g	diced
1	oz	fresh ginger	28	g	finely grated
4	oz	coconut milk	118	ml	

1. Sweat the onions and clove for 3 minutes in the oil.
2. Add the flour and curry powder to the onions. Stir to make a light roux.
3. Add the stock slowly to the roux. Cook for about 3 minutes over low heat to develop the flavor of the curry powder.
4. Add the tomato purée and apples; cook for another 2 minutes.
5. Add the ginger and coconut milk. Whisk to keep sauce smooth. Cook at slow simmer for 1½ hours, stirring from time to time, until sauce has a sweet taste and velvety consistency.

Smoked Hungarian Sausage

This is a delicious, basic variety that is very popular for cookouts. Bake with sauerkraut and serve with mashed potatoes. Also try the Fresh Salami variation.

Yield: 10 pounds (4.5 kg)

U.S.		Ingredients	Metric		Preparation
10	lb	pork butt	4.5	kg	trimmed
1	pt	ice water	475	ml	
3½	oz	fine salt	99	g	
1	T	ground black pepper	6	g	#10 mesh or finer
1		large garlic clove	1		finely minced
1½	oz	Hungarian paprika	43	g	sweet or hot
1	oz	powdered dextrose	28	g	
2	t	Prague powder #1	10	g	measured accurately
		hog casings	35–38	mm	

1. Trim the excess fat from the pork butt; grind about 2 lb of this fat through a ⅛ in. (0.3 cm) plate. Grind the leaner meat using a ⅜ in. (0.9 cm) plate. Mix the ground fat and lean portions together.
2. Put the ice water in a container and stir in the salt, pepper, garlic, paprika, dextrose, and Prague powder #1. Stir to dissolve.
3. Distribute the solution over the meat in a mixing tub. Mix thoroughly by hand.
4. Stuff the prepared casings. Tie into 3–5 in. (8–13 cm) links. Hang on smoker sticks and air dry for about 1 hour at room temperature.

SMOKING

1. Place into a preheated smoker at 130°F (54°C) with the dampers wide open. Observe the color of the sausage. When it begins to brown, adjust the dampers to one-quarter open and increase the temperature by 10°F (5–6°C) each hour to 160°F (71°C). Hold at this setting until the internal temperature of the sausage is 155°F (68°C).
2. Remove the sausage and spray at once with cold water until the internal temperature drops to 90°F (32°C). The sausage should be a deep red-brown color.
3. Wrap the links or place them in well-covered bulk pans. Refrigerate for use.

VARIATION

Fresh Salami: Instead of stuffing hog casings, use salami-size Flat Collagen Casing (Kutas Catalogue #10141, 10142, or 10143). Increase the smoking/cooking time according to the size of the casing (1–2 hours longer). This is excellent for sandwiches.

Smoked Pork Loin I

This item may be enjoyed without further cooking. It may also be boiled in a rich ham stock, or served with red beans and rice.

Yield: 10 pounds (4.5 kg)

U.S.		Ingredients	Metric		Preparation
10	lb	center cut pork loin	4.5	kg	in one piece if possible
8	oz	Pork & Veal blend	227	g	Paul Prudhomme's Magic
3	gal	Irish soft brine	11.4	l	see separate recipe (p. 159)

1. Rub the seasoning into all surfaces of the pork loin. Cover and refrigerate for 48 hours.

2. Make the soft-water brine according to the recipe. Place the loin in a nonreactive tub and cover with the brine. Do not brush off the seasoning. Hold in the brine for 4 hours.

3. Remove the pork from the brine and hang in the cooler for 24 hours.

SMOKING

1. Place in a preheated smoker at 130°F (54°C) with the damper set at one-half open. Smoke at this setting for a full 24 hours.

2. Increase the smoker temperature to 155°F (68°C) and adjust the damper to one-quarter open. Hold at this temperature for an hour or more to reach an internal temperature of no less than 150°F (65°C).

3. Remove the pork loin from the smoker. Wrap and refrigerate for use.

Smoked Pork Loin II

This is a very succulent product. Serve it with pride, thinly sliced and fanned on the platter. Serve it alongside Smoked Pork Loin I for a fine contrast. Red beans and rice go equally well with both. Sandwiches, luncheons—all are elevated to new dimensions with this excellent product. Keep plenty on hand, for it will be very useful for many delights. Herbally delicious!

Yield: 50 pounds (22.7 kg)

U.S.		Ingredients	Metric		Preparation
50	lb	pork loin	22.7	kg	center cuts
2½	gal	water	9.5	l	warm or cold
1	lb	kosher or canning salt	450	g	
12	oz	powdered dextrose	340	g	
2	oz	Prague powder #1	57	g	measured accurately
8	oz	Pork & Veal blend	227	g	Paul Prudhomme's Magic
3	oz	fresh sage	85	g	finely chopped
1	oz	fresh rosemary	28	g	finely chopped
1	oz	fresh marjoram	28	g	finely chopped

1. Make the brine by putting the water into a container and stirring in the salt, dextrose, and Prague powder #1; stir well to dissolve. Chill the brine to 38–40°F (3–4°C).

2. Pump each loin with brine up to 10% of its weight and cure for 6–8 days in the remaining brine. Alternatively, cure the loins in the brine for 10 days without pumping. Cure in a cooler at 38–40°F (3–4°C). Keep the loins fully submerged; agitate and turn every 24 hours.

3. At end of the brining period, rinse the loins with a generous shower of cold water. Place them on racks over trays and drain well.

4. Blend the Pork & Veal seasoning, sage, rosemary, and marjoram. When the loins are dry, generously rub all surfaces with the spice mixture.

SMOKING

1. Place each piece into a stockinette bag. Hang them securely on smoke sticks. Place into a preheated smoker at 130°F (54°C) with the dampers wide open. Hold at this setting for 3–4 hours.

2. Increase the temperature to 150°F (65°C) and adjust the dampers to one-quarter open. Apply a light smoke. Hold at this setting for 2½ hours.

3. Increase the temperature to 160–165°F (71–74°C). Maintain the same smoke and damper settings. Check the internal temperature and remove the loins when it reaches 140°F (60°C).

(Continued)

4. Hang at room temperature until the internal temperature is 110°F (43°C). Refrigerate for 12 hours at 45°F (7°C). The pork loins are now ready for use.

Smoked Andouille

This Cajun specialty is traditional for Jambalaya and Gumbo. It has spicy goodness and usually a heavy smoke. Serve it cold as hors d'oeuvre. You will have constant repeat orders for this one.

Yield: 25 pounds (11.3 kg)

U.S.		Ingredients	Metric		Preparation
24	lb	trimmed pork butt	10.9	kg	cubed
1	lb	fatback	450	g	diced ¼ in. (0.6 cm), chilled
24	oz	ice water	709	ml	
6	oz	fine salt	170	g	
2	oz	black pepper	57	g	freshly ground
5	T	dried thyme	15	g	well-bruised
8	oz	fresh garlic	227	g	minced
3½	oz	ground cayenne pepper	99	g	
2	oz	granulated sugar	57	g	
12	oz	soy protein powder	340	g	
1	oz	Prague powder #2	28	g	measured accurately
		hog casings	38	mm	

1. Grind the diced pork using a ⅛ in. (0.3 cm) plate.

2. Put the water in a container and stir in the salt, pepper, thyme, garlic, cayenne pepper, sugar, soy protein, and Prague powder #2.

3. Add the solution to the ground meat and mix very well. Use an electric mixer if desired.

4. Add the diced fatback and fold in with care; it must be evenly distributed, but not smeared.

5. Stuff the prepared casings. Tie into 9–12 in. (23–31 cm) loops. Hang on smoker sticks so that the loops do not touch.

SMOKING

1. Place in a preheated smoker at 130°F (54°C) with the dampers wide open. Air dry at this setting for about 1½ hours.

2. When the andouille is fully dried, increase the temperature to 165°F (74°C) in several increments. Adjust the dampers to one-quarter open and maintain a heavy smoke.

3. Remove the andouille when the internal temperature reaches 155°F (68°C). Spray at once with cold water. After the sausage has cooled to 110°F (43°C) or less, hang to dry at room temperature for 30 minutes. A desirable bloom will develop and should remain on the sausage.

4. Refrigerate overnight before use.

Smoked (Kippered) Herring

Kippers are a cold-smoked fish; the smoker should never be hotter than 90°F (32°C). Kippers are traditional breakfast fare in the British Isles. They are very good at any meal. Serve poached, broiled, or fried lightly. A mustard sauce will complement rich flavorsome kippers.

Yield: 10 pounds (4.5 kg)

U.S.		Ingredients	Metric		Preparation
10	lb	cleaned 8-oz herring	227	g	soaked and flattened
2½	gal	tap water	9.5	l	
5	oz	kosher or canning salt	142	g	
½	oz	black pepper	14	g	freshly ground
1	oz	mixed pickling spice	28	g	
½	oz	Prague powder #1	14	g	measured accurately

1. Prepare the brine by combining the water, salt, pepper, and pickling spice in a nonreactive pan. Bring to the boil and simmer for 5 minutes. Stir to dissolve the ingredients. Remove from the heat and cool for 10 minutes. Add the Prague powder #1 and mix very well. Chill.

2. Place the chilled brine in a nonreactive tub. Put the prepared herring into the brine and let soak for 1 full hour. Remove the herring from the brine and arrange them on racks placed over drip trays. Dry until a skin, or pellicle, forms. This drying period is mandatory.

SMOKING

1. Hang the herring (or place them on lightly oiled mesh racks) in a preheated smoker at 90°F (32°C) with a light smoke and the dampers wide open. (The herring are easier to handle on the mesh racks and are less likely to drop.)

(Continued)

2. After one hour, provide a heavy smoke and maintain the 90°F (32°C) setting. Adjust the dampers to one-half open. Allow 3 hours for the herring to reach the desired color. (Longer smoking will give better flavor and keeping quality. With some experience, you will know the timing and smoked finish that you prefer.)

3. When the kippers are smoked as desired, remove them from the smoker and cool. Enhance their appearance by oiling them lightly with a neutral vegetable oil. Wrap them individually in parchment paper or plastic wrap. Store them in the cooler for the longest shelf life.

Smoked Herring Pâté

Serve from the chilled mold. This is excellent with Melba toast or fancy crackers, and lemon should also be close at hand.

Yield: 3 pounds (1.3 kg)

U.S.		Ingredients	Metric		Preparation
2	lb	Smoked Herring	900	g	see separate recipe (p. 221)
1	lb	clarified butter	450	g	melted and cooled
1	t	ground nutmeg	2.5	g	or to taste
1	t	cayenne pepper	1.5	g	or to taste
		salt			to taste
		freshly ground pepper			to taste
		wine or lemon juice			to taste

1. Soak the fish in very hot water for 5 minutes. Remove and cool. Remove the skin.

2. Purée the fish in a food processor or similar device. Stir down the sides of the bowl several times. The mixture must be uniformly smooth and fine-grained.

3. With the food processor running, add the butter.

4. Add the nutmeg and cayenne pepper. Adjust the seasoning with salt and pepper. Add some wine or lemon juice if desired.

5. Pack the pâté into one or more molds. Cover and chill for several hours to develop flavor.

Smoked Salmon I

Wet Method Preparation

This superb product forms a pièce de resistance on any table. Serve on a well-garnished platter. Accompany with lemon, chopped capers, cream cheese. Slice paper thin, on the diagonal, across the grain. Transfer each rosy slice with a measure of aplomb to the guest's plate. *Also study Smoked Salmon II. This details The Dry Box Cure Method. It is the authors' method of preference.*

Cure and smoke any trimmings along with the salmon filets; use them to make an excellent pâté.

Yield: 6 pounds (2.7 kg)

U.S.		Ingredients	Metric		Preparation
6	lb	salmon filets	2.7	kg	do not skin or scale
		salmon trimmings, if any			
3	qt	tap water	2.8	l	
5	oz	very fine pure salt	142	g	
1	bag	crab boil	1	bag	commercial mixture

1. Put the water in a nonreactive container and add the salt and crab boil. Stir to dissolve thoroughly, then chill.

2. Immerse the salmon and trimmings in the chilled brine. Cover with a board and weight. Cure 1–1½ hours depending on the size of the filets. Try the longer time first; experience will indicate the optimum time.

3. Remove the fish and rinse it lightly but well. Use your hands or a soft brush on the skin side to remove any brine particles. Avoid damaging the fish.

4. Dry the fish on oiled mesh racks in the cooler for a full 24 hours. A thin pellicle, which is essential for success, will form.

SMOKING

1. Preheat the smoker to 90°F (32°C) with the dampers wide open. Hang the fish securely on hooks or lay them on lightly oiled racks (the more secure method). Place the fish in the smoker and run a light smoke for 6 hours.

2. Adjust the dampers to one-half open. Over the next hour, raise the temperature to 100°F (38°C). Do not exceed this temperature. Adjust to a heavy smoke and hold for 36–48 hours.

(Continued)

3. When a satisfactory color is attained, remove the salmon and cool completely. Rub all surfaces with a neutral vegetable oil to impart a handsome sheen. Turn the fish over with care; it should release easily if the grids were oiled.

4. Wrap, label, and refrigerate for use.

Smoked Salmon II

Dry Box Cure Preparation

You will find this dry box curing method very simple and very effective. Please refer to the comments given with Smoked Salmon I. The qualities and wonderful presentation possibilities are equal for each method. The authors do prefer this Dry Box Cure Method for sheer ease of preparation.

Yield: 12 pounds (5.4 kg)

U.S.		Ingredients	Metric		Preparation
12	lb	salmon filets	5.4	kg	do not skin or scale
(4 3-lb pieces)			(4 1.4-kg pieces)		
2	lb	kosher/canning salt	900	g	
1	t	pure garlic powder	3	g	
1	oz	light brown sugar	28	g	
3	oz	Old Bay Seasoning	85	g	commercial blend
1	oz	Prague powder #2	28	g	measured accurately

1. Combine the salt, garlic powder, brown sugar, Old Bay Seasoning, and Prague powder #2.

2. Lay the salmon on a clean work surface and rub the dry mixture into both sides of the fish. Cover all surfaces well, but avoid damaging the fish.

3. Place the two filets skin side down in a clean meat lug; place the remaining filets skin side up on the first pair. These "sandwiches" will be flesh-to-flesh with the skin sides out.

4. Cover and refrigerate for a full 8 hours.

5. Using your hands and cold running water, gently but thoroughly wash each piece. If required, use a very soft brush to remove any remaining particles from the brine. Handle with care.

SMOKING

1. Preheat the smoker to 90°F (32°C) with the dampers wide open. Arrange the filets on an oiled mesh rack. Place them in the smoker and run a light smoke for 6 hours.

2. Adjust the dampers to one-half open. Over the next hour, raise the temperature to 100°F (38°C). Do not exceed this temperature. Adjust to a heavy smoke and hold for 36–48 hours.

3. When a satisfactory color is attained, remove the salmon and cool completely. Rub all surfaces with a neutral vegetable oil to impart a handsome sheen. Turn the fish over with care; it should release easily if the grids were oiled.

4. Wrap, label, and refrigerate for use. **Do not use clear wrap.** It promotes molding.

Smoked Beef Tongue

Smoked tongue is a fine delicacy. It is particularly useful on the appetizer tray. Serve it neatly slice, then fanned on a platter. Include it in shapes, and in terrines of all sorts. Tongue is excellent when made into pates or other spreads. Sauces Creole, chaud-froid work, and treatments in aspic are all impressive ways to utilize a tongue. Mustards, horseradish, and sauce Gribiche will enhance this wonderful smoked tongue.

This recipe calls for making two batches of brine and curing the tongues in two stages.

Yield: 10 pounds (4.5 kg)

U.S.		Ingredients	Metric		Preparation
10	lb	very fresh beef tongues	4.5	kg	gristle and roots trimmed

FOR EACH BRINE SOLUTION:

2½	gal	tap water	9.5	l	
1	lb	kosher or canning salt	450	g	
8	oz	Prague powder #1	227	g	measured accurately
		stockinette bags			1 for each tongue

1. Wash and scrub the tongues to remove any surface impurities. Do not skin the tongue at this time.

2. Make the first batch of brine by combining the water, salt, and Prague powder #1.

3. Pump each tongue with brine to 105% of its original weight. Put the tongues into the remaining solution in a brining tub. Refrigerate for 4 days at 38–40°F (3–4°C). Turn each

(Continued)

piece every day and agitate the solution from the bottom. This brings fresh solution in contact with the tongues.

4. At the end of the fourth day, discard the brine. Rinse the tongues and the tub. Make a fresh batch of the brine. Place the rinsed tongues into the new brining solution. Refrigerate for another 4 days, repeating the daily turns and agitation.

5. After the last 4 days of curing, discard the brine. Wash the tongues and place each one in a stockinette bag. Hang to dry at room temperature for about 4 hours.

SMOKING

1. Preheat the smoker to 140°F (60°C) with the dampers wide open. Load the smoker and hold this setting for a few hours to finish drying the tongues.

2. Raise the temperature to 160°F (71°C) with the dampers set at three-quarters open. Hold for 2–4 hours until the tongues reach 152°F (67°C).

3. Remove from the smoker and cool to 110°F (43°C) or less. Refrigerate for 12 hours before use. Skin the tongues as necessary when you use them.

Smoked Game Fowl

Smoked whole fowl are elegant and have a place on most any table. Not so commonly found today, these smoked domestic or game fowl lend a touch of distinction. Include this treat more often on luncheon or dinner menus. It may be presented hot or cold, and is great when sliced and arranged with other meats of contrast. Appetizer uses are limitless.

This item has long been available, but only as a costly, premium-priced commodity. You can now easily enjoy economy and versatility that is available only "to those who know how to smoke their own!" Be very sure to experiment with seasonings and various combinations. *But never experiment with the curing agent in your personal brines.* Here is an outstanding opportunity to exercise personal creativity. *This is a perishable product.* Plan to utilize it promptly. It should never be wasted. The flesh may be taken off the carcass, used at once in numerous ways. Also, the de-boned flesh may be well wrapped and freezer stored for brief periods.

Yield: 8½ pounds (3.8 kg)

U.S.		Ingredients	Metric		Preparation
10	lb	dressed game fowl	4.5	kg	or turkey or others
5	qt	tap water	4.7	l	
8	oz	kosher or canning salt	227	g	
2	oz	dried sage	57	g	rubbed well
1½	oz	ground cloves	42	g	
2	oz	Turkish bay leaves	57	g	finely crushed
3½	oz	Prague powder #1	99	g	measured accurately

1. Put two quarts of the water in a nonreactive pot. Stir in the salt, sage, cloves, and bay leaves. Simmer for 40 minutes and add the remaining 3 quarts of water. Cool slightly, then add the Prague powder #1.

2. Use a single-needle hand syringe to pump brine into the large sections (breasts and thighs) of big birds such as ostriches and turkeys; pump up to 110% of the original weight. Place the birds in the brine; follow with a board and weight to fully immerse the birds. Refrigerate for 1½–4 days. Use the shorter time for small fowl like Cornish game hens or quail and the longer time for large birds. Turn the bird and agitate the brine from the bottom of the tub every 24 hours.

3. Remove the birds from the brine and rinse inside and out with abundant cold water. Truss and hang the birds securely; use cord loops, skewers, hooks, or poultry bags. Trussing the fowl prior to smoking will greatly enhance the presentation.

SMOKING

1. Preheat the smoker to 135°F (57°C) with the dampers wide open. Load the smoker with the small birds toward the outside; they will be cooked first and it will be easy to remove

(Continued)

them without disturbing the larger ones. Do not allow the birds to touch each other or to become misshapen.

2. After 1½ hours (1 hour for small fowl), raise the temperature to 150°F (65°C).

3. After 1½ hours raise the temperature to 170°F (77°C), adjust the dampers to one-half open, and start a moderate smoke. Continue until the internal temperature of the large sections of meat reaches 155°F (68°C).

4. Remove the finished birds and shower them with cold water. Hang them to dry briefly at room temperature.

5. Place them promptly into the coldest zone of a cooler.

Smoked Turkey Kielbasa

This sausage, like most other varieties, is really best if consumed without having been frozen. Freeze only if absolutely necessary. Turkey is increasingly popular today. It is viewed as a "healthy" alternative meat. It is easily substituted, at least in part, for other meats in many established formulas.

Yield: 10 pounds (4.5 kg)

U.S.		Ingredients	Metric		Preparation
10	lb	turkey meat	4.5	kg	light and dark
1	pt	ice water	475	ml	
4	T	fine salt	60	g	
1	T	white pepper	6	g	
2	T	dark brown sugar	29	g	
1	T	fresh garlic	6	g	crushed
2	t	dried marjoram	1	g	rubbed well
1	lb	powdered soy protein	450	g	concentrate
		hog casings	38	mm	

1. Grind the turkey using a ⅛ in. (0.3 cm) plate. Transfer to a mixing lug. Chill if the turkey is over 40°F (4°C).

2. Put the ice water in a container and stir in the salt, pepper, brown sugar, garlic, marjoram, and soy protein; mix very well. Distribute the solution evenly over the ground turkey and mix thoroughly. Chill if necessary.

3. Stuff the prepared casings. Tie into 10–12 in. (25–30 cm) loops. Hang the loops securely on smoker sticks.

SMOKING

1. Place the loops in a preheated smoker at 130°F (55°C) with the dampers wide open. Hang for 1 hour or until the casings are uniformly dry.

2. Adjust the dampers to one-quarter open and start a medium-heavy smoke. Gradually raise the temperature to 165°F (74°C) over the next 2 hours while maintaining the smoke.

3. Monitor the internal temperature during the last hour. When it reaches 155°F (68°C), remove the sausage and spray at once with cold water. Cool to 110°F (43°C) or lower. Dry at room temperature away from drafts for at least 1 hour.

4. Wrap in suitable packages and label. Refrigerate for use.

Southwestern Sausage

This recipe is of Mexican origin. It has traveled and been modified over many years. You will recognize it as a departure from the commonplace. *It has considerable authority.* It is an exceptionally tasty variety useful in casseroles, to spike up dry beans, and to serve with pasta combinations. Use it in salads, with omelets, add it to cornbread. Chopped or sliced, a very small quantity will contribute much flavor. Add to appetizer mixtures, or slice very thinly for canapés of all sorts. Here is a variety you will want to keep on hand at all times. It is essential to use the best beef suet for distinct flavor.

Yield: 10 pounds (4.5 kg)

U.S.		Ingredients	Metric		Preparation
7½	lb	lean pork	3.4	kg	
2½	lb	beef kidney suet	1.1	kg	chopped
1	T	fine salt	15	g	
1	T	black pepper	6	g	freshly ground
16		garlic cloves	16		finely minced
1½	c	Spanish onion	144	g	finely chopped
12–18		fresh chili peppers	12–18		finely chopped
1	c	chili powder	136	g	Murray's brand
1½	c	cider vinegar	355	ml	
1	T	ground coriander	4.5	g	
4½	t	ground cumin	9	g	
1½	t	Tabasco	8	ml	
1	c	good brandy	237	ml	
2	t	Prague powder #2	10	g	measured accurately
20	oz	ice water	592	ml	
		casings	32–38	mm	

1. Coarsely chop the pork by hand. (The pork may be ground, but hand chopping is preferable.) Mix it with the chopped suet.

2. Combine the pork, suet, salt, pepper, garlic, onion, chili peppers, chili powder, vinegar, coriander, cumin, Tabasco, brandy, Prague powder #2, and ice water in a mixing lug. Mix very well. Hand mixing is preferred.

3. Stuff the prepared casings rather firmly. Tie into 4 in. (10 cm) links. Alternatively, form 12 in. (30 cm) ring sausages. Leave a generous amount of casing or extra cord for hanging and linking sausages. Eliminate any air pockets, pricking if necessary.

4. Hang in a cooler no lower than 45°F (7°C) to air dry and cure for a full 25 days. Do not allow the sausages to touch each other.

5. After 25 days the sausages are ready to use. They may be kept at 32–34°F (1°C) for at least 1 week.

Swedish Potato Sausage

This popular Scandinavian variety is so satisfying for breakfast, lunch, or brunch. Add fresh dill or chives for variety.

Yield: 10 pounds (4.5 kg)

U.S.		Ingredients	Metric		Preparation
3	lb	lean pork	1.4	kg	well trimmed
2	lb	lean beef	0.9	kg	well trimmed
5	lb	waxy potatoes	2.2	kg	wash, peel, grate
8	oz	onions	227	g	peel, grate
1	oz	salt	28	g	
1	oz	ground coriander	28	g	
4	qt	Irish soft brine	3.8	l	prepared ahead
		hog casings	28–32	mm	prepared

1. Trim and cube pork and beef for grinding. Grind the meats together using a ⅜ in. (0.9 cm) plate.

2. Grind a second time through a ¼ in. (0.6 cm) plate for finer texture. Leave ⅜ in. (0.9 cm) plate in place for coarser texture if desired. Chill ground meat one hour before proceeding.

3. Coarsely grate the peeled potatoes. Place immediately into ice water to cover. Hold potatoes in the cooler.

4. Prepare onions by peeling, then grate. Keep the onions well chilled until assembly.

5. After the meat has chilled for the required time, place potatoes into a colander to drain very well. Be sure to press down as necessary, to assure removal of nearly all the soaking water. The potatoes should be quite dry.

6. Combine the chilled ground meat, onions, and seasonings. Fold in the well-drained grated potatoes. Mix completely, but maintain the fairly coarse texture of the ingredients.

7. Stuff, but not too tightly, into prepared casings. Twist link about 4 in. (10 cm) long. Place sausages, as they are linked, into chilled Irish brine. Keep the finished product in the brine, well chilled, until cooked for service.

8. Poach (about 20 min.) on demand, to reach an internal temperature above 150°F to fully cook. For best appearance, follow poaching with a quick sauté, or turn (to mark them) on the grill. As with most cooked link sausage, larger quantities may be quickly finished on sheet trays in a moderate 350°F (177°C) oven. Serve this sausage at once for best presentation.

Tasso—Spicy Delight

Tasso is wet-cured, cold-smoked pork shoulder. It is distinctive, and is often used in the manner of other hams. Many Cajun dishes require Tasso, but it is rather difficult to find outside Louisiana. It is a gourmet food shop item. *Nothing replaces it for flavor. With eggs, pasta, and beans, it's spicy hot and habit forming!*

Yield: 10 pounds (4.5 kg)

U.S.		Ingredients	Metric		Preparation
10	lb	pork butt	4.5	kg	
1	lb	pure canning salt	450	g	
10	oz	sugar	284	g	
1	T	cayenne pepper	4.5	g	
2	oz	Prague powder #1	56.7	g	measured accurately
4	qt	water	3.8	l	

TASSO SEASONING:

8	oz	Cajun pork seasoning*	227	g	
2	T	dried sage	6	g	well-rubbed
2	T	dried thyme	6	g	
1	T	hot paprika	7	g	

1. Prepare the brine by combining the salt, sugar, cayenne pepper, Prague powder #1, and water. Mix well and chill.
2. Place the pork into the solution and refrigerate, well-covered, for 7 days. Turn the pieces and agitate the brine daily.
3. Dry the pieces of pork on a rack for about 8 hours. Rub each piece generously with your choice of tasso seasoning.

SMOKING

1. Hang to cold smoke at a maximum setting of 120°F (49°C) with the dampers one-quarter open. Process the pork for 24 hours.
2. Wrap tightly, label, and refrigerate for up to 1 week. Use the tasso fresh if possible; avoid freezing as the flavor will be altered.

---

*Or use Chef Paul Prudhomme's Magic Seasoning Blends. We suggest the Blackened Steak or Pork & Veal Blend.

Basic Terrine

As the name implies, this is a very good starting point in the grand adventure of terrine production. You will have a very tasty item at hand when you finish. Try this recipe using various seasoning mixtures. We have left open the choice of critical seasoning to you.

Yield: One 2½-pound (1.1 kg) terrine

U.S.		Ingredients	Metric		Preparation
1	lb	boneless pork	450	g	diced
1	lb	boned veal, lamb, or beef	450	g	diced
2		large eggs	2		beaten
1	T	dry onion	6	g	very finely chopped
2	T	lard	12	g	melted
10	oz	dry white wine	296	ml	
8	oz	jellied meat stock	237	ml	well-flavored
		salt			to taste
		pepper			to taste
		selected seasonings*			to taste

1. Finely grind all the meats. Turn them into a lug and mix together.
2. Add the remaining ingredients and mix well. Fry a small patty of the forcemeat; taste and correct the seasoning.
3. Pack the forcemeat into a buttered 5-cup (1.25 l) terrine mold. Cook the terrine in a preheated oven at 300°F (149°C) for 2 hours or until the terrine has shrunk away from the sides of the mold.
4. Cool, then chill thoroughly.
5. Turn out onto a platter and decorate as desired. Hold the terrine under refrigeration at all times.

---

*Be certain to record the choice of seasonings used.

Duck Terrine

Today, we may either choose to use commercial aspic or to make our own in the classical tradition. Our decision is generally influenced by questions of time and labor available. We hope that all students will become fully familiar with the classical method through actual practice. Reserve the carcass and remaining giblets for production of the savory aspic for this terrine.

Yield: One 5-pound (2.3 kg) terrine

U.S.		Ingredients	Metric		Preparation
4	lb	duck meat	1.8	kg	
1		duck liver	1		very finely chopped
½	lb	pork	227	g	finely chopped
½	lb	fatback	227	g	sliced
1	oz	truffle	28	g	finely diced
4	oz	brandy	118	ml	
4	oz	muscatel wine	118	ml	
		salt			to taste
		ground black pepper			to taste
1	t	fresh thyme	2	g	minced
1	pt	aspic	475	ml	see separate recipe (p. 83)

1. Marinate the duck, pork, fatback, and truffle in the brandy and wine for 24 hours.
2. Remove the duck meat and thinly slice it; set aside.
3. Thinly slice the fatback and use it to line the sides and bottom of the terrine.
4. Combine the pork, truffle, duck liver, salt, pepper, and thyme. *Note textures.*
5. Cook a small patty of the forcemeat; taste and adjust the seasoning.
6. Make several alternating layers of forcemeat and sliced duck meat. Finish with a layer of fatback. Fill the mold to within ¼ in. (0.6 cm) of the top.
7. Preheat the oven to 325°F (163°C). Arrange a hot water bath reaching halfway up the sides of the mold. Bake for 2 hours; add more hot water if necessary to maintain the level of the water bath.
8. Arrange a weight on top of the terrine while it cools. Let it stand in a catch pan while the terrine is compressed and excess fat is forced from the mold.
9. The following day, slowly fill the terrine with aspic. Eliminate any air by tapping and jiggling. Chill for 24 hours before slicing and serving.

English Pork Terrine

Production of terrines provides an excellent opportunity to apply your individual culinary and artistic style. From start to presentation, each one should reflect your best ability.

Yield: One 3-pound (1.4 kg) terrine

U.S.		Ingredients	Metric		Preparation
2½	lb	fresh pork belly	1.1	kg	ground
½	lb	trimmed pork liver	200	g	ground
1		medium onion	1		finely chopped
2		garlic cloves	2		finely chopped
2	t	fresh rosemary	2	g	finely chopped
1		egg	1		beaten
1½	oz	brandy	44	ml	
		salt			to taste
		freshly ground pepper			to taste
1		whole pig's foot	1		split
1		branch fresh rosemary	1		whole

1. Mix the ground pork belly and liver with the onion, garlic, and rosemary. (If you are using dried rosemary, crumble it fine and add it to the meats.)

2. Beat the egg with the brandy and add it to the forcemeat with plenty of salt and pepper. Blend all ingredients well. Fry a small patty; taste and adjust the seasoning.

3. Spoon the forcemeat into a greased 6-cup (1.5 l) ovenproof terrine. Press the pig's foot and rosemary branch into the center of the forcemeat.

4. Place the terrine in a water bath and put it in a preheated 375°F (190°C) oven.

5. After 15 minutes, reduce the heat to 325°F (163°C). Cook another 1–1½ hours, checking the water level occasionally. Remove when the internal temperature of the terrine is 150°F (65°C). (The terrine will shrink from the sides of the mold and the juices will run clear from the center.)

6. Remove and discard the pig's foot and the branch of rosemary. Smooth over the top of the terrine. Place a weight on top and let it cool.

7. Wrap well (to avoid other flavors in the cooler) and refrigerate for at least 1 day before serving.

Farmhouse Terrine

This terrine is thoroughly satisfying, remarkably mellow, and inexpensive to make. Serve it cold.

Yield: 6 pounds (2.7 kg)

U.S.		Ingredients	Metric		Preparation
2	lb	pork butt	900	g	
1	lb	veal trimmings	450	g	
1	lb	pork liver	450	g	
1	t	salt	5	g	
1	t	black pepper	2	g	finely ground
2	t	Pâté and Terrine Spices	4	g	see separate recipe (p. 193)
2	t	mixed fresh herbs	4	g	
4	oz	onions	113	g	chopped and sautéed
2	t	fresh garlic	4	g	minced
14	oz	fresh bread crumbs	397	g	
6		whole eggs	6		beaten
8	oz	brandy	237	ml	
2	t	fresh parsley	4	g	chopped
4	oz	caul fat	113	g	
5	oz	smoked fatback	142	g	uniformly sliced

1. Grind the pork butt, veal, and liver very fine.
2. Add all of the seasoning ingredients and mix very well.
3. Line the terrine with the caul fat. Let the excess membrane extend over the sides; it will be drawn up to enclose the terrine later.
4. Line the bottom and sides of the mold by spreading the sliced fatback evenly on top of the caul fat.
5. Fill the lined terrine with the seasoned forcemeat and level off the top. Fold over the caul fat.
6. Use more fatback slices to make a decorative lattice pattern on the top.
7. Bake in a 325°F (163°C) oven for 2 hours until the internal temperature reaches at least 150°F (65°C).
8. Place a weight on top of the terrine and chill overnight.
9. Carefully unmold the terrine and slice for service.

French Peasant Terrine

This savory terrine is well worth the effort. It will become a favorite in your repertoire.

Yield: Two 2-pound (900-g) terrines

U.S.		Ingredients	Metric		Preparation
2	lb	fresh pork fat	900	g	cubed
1½	lb	boned ham	680	g	cubed
2	lb	boned veal	900	g	cubed
1	qt	water	1	l	
2		medium onions	2		1 whole, 1 grated
1		medium parsnip	1		scrubbed and split
4	oz	celeriac	113	g	scrubbed and halved
15	oz	medium red bell peppers	427	g	halved and seeded
20		black peppercorns	20		crushed
1	lg	bay leaf	1	lg	
3		medium hard rolls	3		dry-old, crumbled
1½	lb	pork liver	680	g	trimmed and cubed
1	c	water	250	ml	
2	oz	dried mushrooms	57	g	soaked 30 mins., drained
2½	t	nutmeg	2.5	g	freshly grated
5		whole eggs	5		
4	oz	butter	113	g	melted
		salt			to taste
		freshly ground pepper			to taste
		lard and dry bread crumbs for the baking dishes			

1. Render the cubes of pork fat in a large saucepan until they are light brown. Add the ham, veal, and water; add the water carefully to avoid splattering. Cover tightly and simmer for 1½ hours. Be careful not to burn the meats. Maintain at least 1 quart of liquid in the pan while cooking.

2. Add the whole onion, parsnip, celeriac, red peppers, peppercorns, and bay leaf. Cook about 30 minutes until the stew ingredients are very soft.

3. Remove and discard the onion and celeriac. Add the hard roll crumbs, liver, and 1 cup of water. Cook for another 30 minutes. Remove from the heat and cool.

4. Grind the mixture 3 times. Add the mushrooms, nutmeg, eggs, melted butter, grated onion, salt, and pepper. Mix well.

5. Grind the forcemeat once more. The texture should be moist and uniformly fine.

6. Fry a small patty; taste and adjust the seasoning.

7. Generously grease two 2-quart (2-l) baking dishes with lard and coat with dry bread crumbs. Fill the dishes with the forcemeat, packing it very well. Allow some room at the

(Continued)

top for expansion. Cover tightly and bake in a preheated 375°F (190°C) oven for 1 hour. Remove from the oven, place a weight on top of the meat, and cool.

8. Refrigerate, weighted, for 24 hours to mellow the flavors. Serve directly from the terrine or unmold onto a platter, slice, and garnish.

Southwestern Hare Terrine

This terrine is adapted from a "Southwestern sausage" recipe, using wild game. Enjoy it.

Yield: Serves 25–30 on a buffet

U.S.		Ingredients	Metric		Preparation
6	lb	young hare	2.8	kg	finely diced
¾	lb	veal	300	g	finely diced
¾	lb	pork butt	300	g	trimmed and finely diced
¼	lb	smoked ham	113	g	finely diced
16		gelatin sheets	28	g	
8	oz	double veal consommé	237	ml	
16		bacon slices	16		
7	oz	fine white wine	207	ml	medium-dry
1	T	Mesquite Seasoning	15	g	commercial brand

1. Soften the gelatin in the consommé; heat and stir to dissolve. Hold it warm and ready for pouring.
2. Line a terrine with the sliced bacon. Leave the excess at the top to fold over later.
3. Make alternating layers of the hare, veal, and pork. Sprinkle the Mesquite Seasoning over each layer.
4. Add the wine to the consommé. Without disturbing the layers, pour it gently over the meats.
5. Cover by folding the ends of the bacon slices over the top. If necessary, use wooden picks to secure the entire arrangement.
6. Place in a hot water bath. Bake in a preheated 275°F (135°C) oven for about 1½ hours.
7. Remove from the oven with care and let it cool completely.
8. Refrigerate for at least 1 day to mellow the flavor. Slice with a sharp knife dipped in hot water and serve, or make garnished mirror/tray presentations.

Hungarian Veal Terrine

This product is simple enough, yet makes a large addition to any summer buffet. The delicately flavored veal mixture benefits from a careful adjustment of the seasoning with salt and white pepper. Remember: Always *cook* your sample when tasting! Simply fry off a tiny patty in a quick skillet.

Yield: One 2-pound (900 g) terrine

U.S.		Ingredients	Metric		Preparation
2	lb	veal shoulder	900	g	finely diced
4	oz	shallots	113	g	diced
2	oz	best butter	57	g	
1	oz	fresh chervil	28	g	finely chopped
1	oz	fresh basil	28	g	finely chopped
1½	oz	sweet paprika	43	g	best Hungarian
1–2	T	fine white pepper	6–12	g	freshly ground
1	oz	diced red bell pepper	28	g	or diced Italian tomatoes
4	lg	whole eggs	4	lg	
		salt			to taste

1. Sauté the shallots in the butter. Add and sweat the chervil, basil, paprika, and pepper. Deglaze with a very little water. Remove from the heat and cool.

2. Purée the veal, cooled seasonings, red pepper, eggs, and salt.

3. Fry a small patty; taste and adjust the seasonings.

4. Place the forcemeat into a suitable terrine. Cover tightly and immerse in a very high water bath. Bake in a preheated 325°F (163°C) oven until the internal temperature reaches 165°F (74°C). Remove from the oven and cool. Place a light weight on the terrine while cooling.

5. Refrigerate at least 24 hours to mellow and develop texture before serving.

Hunter's Terrine I

We have found this traditional and most delicious delight to be very time-efficient in the kitchen-classroom. It always brings favorable comments from company.

Yield: One 3-pound (1.4 kg) terrine

U.S.		Ingredients	Metric		Preparation
4	oz	salt pork	113	g	rind trimmed off
1	lb	boned ham	450	g	¼–⅜ in. (0.5–1 cm) dice
1	lb	boned lean pork	450	g	ground
1	lb	boned veal	450	g	ground
		salt			to taste
		pepper			to taste
1		garlic clove	1		finely minced
5		dried juniper berries	5		soaked and crushed
½	t	dried marjoram	0.5	g	
½	t	dried mace	0.5	g	
½	t	dried thyme	0.5	g	
4	oz	good white wine	118	ml	
2	T	good brandy	30	ml	
3		large Turkish bay leaves	3		whole
1		medium Turkish bay leaf	1		ground in a mortar

1. Blanch the salt pork for 5 minutes. Cut into uniform slices no thicker than ⅛ in. (0.3 cm) thick. Set aside.

2. In a nonreactive mixing lug, assemble the diced ham, ground pork, ground veal, salt, pepper, garlic, juniper berries, marjoram, mace, thyme, wine, and brandy. Mix very well by hand. Cover and marinate in the cooler for 2 hours.

3. While the forcemeat is marinating, prepare the terrine mold. Line the bottom of a fairly shallow 6-cup (1.5 l) terrine with the salt pork slices.

4. Fry a small patty of the forcemeat; taste and correct the seasoning.

5. Carefully pack the marinated forcemeat into the terrine. Cover the filled mold with additional slices of salt pork. Arrange the 3 whole bay leaves on top and sprinkle with the ground bay leaf.

6. Bake in a water bath in a preheated 300°F (149°C) oven for 2–3 hours. Remove from the oven when the internal temperature reaches 165°F (74°C) and the meat has pulled away from the sides of the pan. Place a weight on the terrine while cooling.

7. Refrigerate overnight to mature the flavor and texture before slicing and serving.

Hunter's Terrine II

This delicious variation may be described as a *pâté en croûte,* if encased in a crust. When left plain in the mold, it remains a terrine. Either way, it is excellent!

Yield: One 8-pound (3.6 kg) terrine or 3–4 small terrines

U.S.		Ingredients	Metric		Preparation
4	lb	boned hare meat	1.8	kg	diced
3	lb	boned pork shoulder	1.4	kg	diced
1	lb	trimmed lamb liver	450	g	or calf liver
5	lg	whole eggs	5	lg	
2	t	fresh thyme, sage, and basil	6	g	equal parts mixture
8	oz	Calvados	237	ml	apple brandy
12	oz	heavy cream butter	355	ml	

1. Purée the hare, pork, and liver in a food processor. Add the eggs one at a time, pulsing after each one. Add the herbs, brandy, and cream. Mix by pulsing to avoid overflowing. Stop several times to scrape down the sides of the bowl.

2. Butter the terrine(s). Fill with the puréed forcemeat and cover. Use no weights. Bake in a preheated oven at 375°F (190°C) for 15–20 minutes. Lower the temperature to 325°F (163°C) and bake until the internal temperature of the terrine reaches 145°F (63°C).

3. Remove from the oven and cool. Refrigerate 1 day to mature before serving.

VARIATION

This terrine may be lined with a pastry crust. Use either the Hot Water Paste or the Cold Water Paste recipe (see pp. 110 and 53, respectively). Make and decorate a top crust. Start baking at 400°F (200°C) and reduce to 350°F (177°C). Fill with a clear aspic when the pâté is cool.

Lyonnaise Terrine

This terrine has earned the title, "the authors' all-around favorite." It has a straightforward appeal, and a rich, smooth flavor, lending classic goodness to any presentation.

Yield: One 4-pound (2 kg) terrine or 3–4 small terrines

U.S.		Ingredients	Metric		Preparation
1	lb	veal silverside	450	g	small dice
1	lb	pork loin	450	g	small dice
1	lb	trimmed chicken livers	450	g	
1	lb	pork belly	450	g	
2	oz	shallots	57	g	finely chopped
½	oz	fresh garlic	14	g	minced
4	oz	dry onion	113	g	finely diced
1	pt	good cognac	475	ml	
2	T	fresh parsley	12	g	finely chopped
8	oz	heavy cream	237	ml	
3	lg	whole eggs	3	lg	beaten
		salt			to taste
2	t	ground white pepper	4	g	
¼	lb	pork caul fat	113	g	

1. Lightly sweat the shallots, garlic, and onion. Remove from heat. Carefully (to avoid flaming) add one half of the cognac. Stir in the parsley and set aside.

2. Combine the chicken livers and pork belly. Grind or purée in a food processor.

3. Put the diced veal and pork in a mixing lug. Add the liver/pork purée and the cooled shallot mixture. Mix very well by hand. Pack into a shallow pan and cover tightly. Chill for 12–24 hours.

4. Remove from the cooler and add the remaining cognac, cream, eggs, salt, and pepper. Mix well. Fry a small patty; taste and adjust the seasoning. Chill the forcemeat while preparing the mold.

5. Line the mold carefully with the caul fat. Let the excess membrane extend over the sides; it will be drawn up to enclose the terrine later.

6. Fill the lined mold with the chilled forcemeat; avoid air pockets. Fold over the caul fat.

7. Bake in a preheated 325°F (163°C) oven until the internal temperature reaches 160°F (71°C). Remove from the oven and cool briefly. Arrange a board and weight on top of the terrine (briefly) while it cools. This aids the removal of excess fat.

8. Cover loosely and refrigerate for at least 24 hours. Garnish and serve directly from the mold or unmold onto a serving platter.

Pork and Spinach Terrine

We have purposely left the seasoning of this terrine to the good judgment of the cook. Choose from the suggested list of seasonings or select others. Give full play to your tasting abilities. *Just make sure to cook each seasoned morsel before tasting.* Remember: All flavors will be altered in the cooked and mellowed terrine, yet the moment of decision is the mixing stage. Enjoy the experiments, and don't neglect to keep legible notes. In the event of a masterpiece, you may want to duplicate it!

Yield: One 2-pound (900 g) terrine

U.S.		Ingredients	Metric		Preparation
1	lb	fresh spinach	450	g	trimmed
1	lb	boned pork butt	450	g	fatty
1	T	fine salt	15	g	
½	t	fine black pepper	1	g	#64 mesh

Season the terrine to taste with any of the following:

          freshly grated nutmeg
          freshly ground allspice
          freshly ground coriander
          finely chopped thyme or rosemary or marjoram
          tomato paste
          onion, shallot, garlic
          fresh chopped basil
          ground cayenne pepper
          ground sweet or hot paprika

1. Wash the spinach very well to remove any grit. Remove any large coarse stems. Cook briefly in a covered pan with only the water adhering to the leaves. If there is any excess water in the cooked spinach, reserve it to add to the forcemeat. Cool the spinach and coarsely chop.

2. Trim the pork and grind once or twice through a small plate. Vary the texture to your preference.

3. In a mixing lug, combine the ground meat with the spinach, salt, pepper, and your chosen seasonings. Mix very well, scraping the sides of the lug from time to time. Fry a small patty; taste and adjust the seasoning. Repeat until you are satisfied.

4. Pack the forcemeat solidly into a 3-cup or slightly larger terrine. Place in a hot water bath reaching halfway up the terrine.

5. Bake in a preheated 350°F (177°C) oven until the internal temperature of the terrine reaches 150°F (65°C). The terrine will shrink away from the sides and be firm to the touch; it should not be browned. Remove from the oven and cool.

6. Chill for 24 hours before serving. Place a light weight on the terrine while chilling.

Quail Terrine

This terrine is so excellent that it is fully acceptable both with and without the truffles. Enjoy it often!

Yield: 6 pounds (2.7 kg); serves 50

U.S.		Ingredients	Metric		Preparation
12	lg	quails	12	lg	
4	oz	good brandy	60	ml	
1	lb	fatback	450	g	
4	oz	goose liver	113	g	
10	oz	lean pork	284	g	
4	oz	Pâté and Terrine spices	113	g	see separate recipe (p. 193)
2	lg	whole eggs	2	lg	
4	oz	dry vermouth	118	ml	
½	oz	truffle peelings	14	g	
1	t	salt	5	g	
1	lb	sliced bacon	450	g	

1. Carefully bone the quail. Rub the pieces with the brandy. Cover tightly and refrigerate for 12 hours.

2. Purée the fatback, goose liver, pork, Pâté Spices, eggs, and vermouth in a food processor or vertical cutting machine.

3. Mix in the truffle peelings and salt. Refrigerate the forcemeat while preparing the mold.

4. Line the mold with the bacon slices, leaving the ends hanging over the sides. They will enclose the terrine later.

5. Cut the marinated quail into strips and large pieces.

6. Spread a layer of forcemeat in the bottom of the mold. Follow with a layer of quail. Continue making alternating layers until the mold is almost full; finish with a layer of forcemeat. Fold the bacon over the top. Cover tightly. Set into a water bath reaching almost to the top of the mold.

7. Bake in a preheated 275°F (135°C) oven for 2 hours until the temperature at the center of the mold reaches 170°F (77°C). Cool.

8. Refrigerate overnight. Place a light weight on the terrine as it chills. Slice and serve fanned on a mirror or use another elegant presentation.

Salmon and Eel Terrine

We suggest serving this "gift from the sea" with a sharply flavored green salad or perhaps a new potato salad. Obtain eels of approximately the size indicated, or cut to suit. (The eel is the center object of the mold. It is kept in position by salmon paste.)

Yield: One 4-pound (1.8 kg) or two 2-pound (900 g) terrines

U.S.		Ingredients	Metric		Preparation
4	lb	smoked salmon	1.8	kg	
4	6-oz	smoked eels	680	g	skinned
1	pt	English brown ale	475	ml	
8	oz	aspic	237	ml	at pouring consistency
1	T	fresh parsley	6	g	chopped
1	T	fresh sage	6	g	chopped
1	T	fresh sorrel	6	g	chopped
1	T	fresh chives	6	g	chopped
1	T	fresh tarragon	6	g	chopped
		salt			to taste
		freshly ground black pepper			to taste

1. Grind the smoked salmon or make into a fine paste in a food processor. Mix in the ale, aspic, and herbs. Taste and adjust the seasoning with salt and pepper. The saltiness of the fish will vary, so taste each batch.

2. Cover the bottom and sides of the mold with a thick layer of the salmon paste. Place the pieces of eel end-to-end down the center of the mold. Surround the eel with the remaining salmon paste. Bang the mold down sharply on a folded towel to remove any air pockets. Scrape the excess salmon paste from the top with a palette knife.

3. Cover and refrigerate for 12 hours to set and to develop flavor.

Teal and Nut Terrine

This traditional terrine is very popular in the game lodges of England and France. The value of having ingredients ready and in place is clear when making this and other such recipes. Here, the correct sequence of assembly must be understood and followed, keeping a clear mental picture of the finished piece.

Yield: 2 pounds (900 g)

U.S.		Ingredients	Metric		Preparation
1	lb	teal leg meat	450	g	
1½	lb	teal breast meat	680	g	2 halves
¼	lb	pork butt	113	g	1 in. (2.5 cm) dice
4	oz	sherry wine	118	ml	dry or medium-dry
2	oz	good port wine	59	ml	
1	t	fresh rosemary	2	g	chopped
1	t	fresh thyme	2	g	chopped
1	t	fresh sage	2	g	chopped
6	oz	good brandy	177	ml	
14	oz	smoked bacon	397	g	sliced
		salt			to taste
		freshly ground black pepper			to taste
2	oz	nutmeats of choice	57	g	pistachios, walnuts, etc.

1. Combine the port and sherry with the herbs. Place the leg meat into this marinade. Cover tightly and refrigerate for 24 hours.

2. Gently rub the brandy over the breast meat. Cover tightly and refrigerate for the same 24-hour period. Keep separate from the leg meat.

3. While the meat is marinating, line the terrine with the bacon. Arrange the slices so they may be folded over the top of the terrine later. Cover and chill.

4. Remove the leg meat from the marinade; reserve the marinade. Cut the leg meat into medium dice and set aside.

5. Remove the breast meat and set aside. Combine any liquid with the leg marinade.

6. Combine the diced pork with the leg meat in a mixing lug. Stir the reserved marinades and pour one half into the meat. (The remaining marinade may be discarded or used in a stock that will be fully cooked.) Season the meat with salt and pepper.

7. Spread one layer of the pork/leg meat into the lined mold. Cover with 1 breast piece. Sprinkle with one half of the nuts. The mold will be about one-half full. Repeat the layering, finishing with the nuts. Fold the bacon over the top, trimming if necessary to make an attractive appearance.

8. Set the terrine into a water bath and fill almost to the top with hot water.

9. Bake in a preheated 325°F (163°C) oven for 2 hours. If necessary, cover with aluminum foil to control browning. Remove from the oven when the internal temperature reaches 160°F (71°C).

10. Fit a board and a 3–4 lb (1.4–2 kg) weight on the terrine. Refrigerate, weighted, for 24 hours before serving.

Traditional Terrine

Try this one with the traditional "Quatre-Épices" mixture. We have included one well-known classical recipe for it. Or you may well prefer, as do we, the pâté spice mixture on page 193. The pleasure of a choice is yours!

Yield: One 2½-pound (1.2 kg) terrine

U.S.		Ingredients	Metric		Preparation
1	lb	boned pork loin	450	g	or shoulder
1	lb	boned beef	450	g	or lamb or veal
2	lg	whole eggs	2	lg	beaten
1		medium dry onion	1		finely chopped
2	T	lard	28	g	
12	oz	dry white wine	355	ml	
1	t	quatre épices*	2	g	
4	oz	jellied meat stock	118	ml	clarified
		salt			to taste
		freshly ground black pepper			to taste

1. Grind the meats, once or twice depending on the preferred texture, using a ³⁄₁₆ in. (0.5 cm) plate. Work into a mixing lug.

2. Add all the remaining ingredients. Mix very well by hand. Fry a small patty; taste and adjust the seasoning.

3. Pack the forcemeat into a buttered 6-cup (1.5 l) mold. Bake in a preheated 300°F (149°C) oven for 2 hours until the temperature at the center of the terrine reaches 155°F (68°C).

(Continued)

---

*We offer this timeless formula with a touch of sentiment for a book that so many, including ourselves, still take pleasure in consulting—a link with our past and an inspiration for our future: Four Spices (Quatre Épices) from *Larousse Gastronomique* by Prosper Montagné (1961 ed. © Crown Publishers Inc.): 1⅛ c (125 g) white pepper, 1½ T (10 g) powdered cloves, 3½ T (30 g) ginger, 4 T (35 g) grated nutmeg. You may also use 1 t (2 g) of our Pâté and Terrine Spices found on page 193.

The meat will shrink away from the sides of the mold. Watch closely and avoid over-cooking.

4. Refrigerate for 24 hours to fully develop flavor. Place a top weight on the terrine while chilling. Unmold and serve as desired.

Tongue Sausage

This is a European grilling sausage that can be tied into shorter or longer links as you prefer.

Yield: About 10 pounds (4.5 kg)

U.S.		Ingredients	Metric		Preparation
10	lb	beef tongue	4.5	kg	3-lb and under pieces
1	oz	fine salt	28	g	
½	oz	white pepper	14	g	finely ground
¼	oz	ground mace	7	g	
1	t	ground nutmeg	2.5	g	
1	t	ground ginger	2	g	
1–1½	t	cayenne pepper	1.5–2.5	g	
1	pt	ice water	475	ml	
		sheep casings	28–32	mm	
		rich beef or chicken stock			

1. Cook the beef tongues. Chill well, then skin and dress them. Cut into 1 in. (2.5 cm) dice for grinding.
2. Grind the tongues using a ³⁄₁₆ in. (0.5 cm) plate. Transfer to a mixing lug.
3. Combine the salt, pepper, mace, nutmeg, ginger, and cayenne pepper. Distribute the dry mixture over the meat and mix very well.
4. Grind again through a ¹⁄₁₆ in. (0.16 cm) plate. Add the ice water and mix well.
5. Stuff the prepared casings. Tie into 2–3 in. (5–8 cm) links. If you prefer, tie these sausages into 4–5 in. (10–13 cm) links.
6. Cover the sausages with stock and poach until the internal temperature reaches 140°F (60°C). Hang the sausages briefly to dry.
7. Wrap well, label, and refrigerate for use.

Turkey Andouille

Use this sausage in gumbo, jambalaya, and other Creole dishes. We have specified the right amount of cayenne for a moderately hot sausage; vary it to your taste. It may be worthwhile to offer several levels of "heat" when producing or serving these sausages. Use a combination of light and dark turkey meat. A reasonable amount of turkey skin will add good flavor and may be included with the fat. The finished product should have a coarse, well-defined texture.

Yield: 25 pounds (11.3 kg)

U.S.		Ingredients	Metric		Preparation
22	lb	turkey meat	9.9	kg	boned and trimmed
3	lb	turkey fat	1.4	kg	
2	qt	ice water	1.9	l	
6	oz	canning salt	170	g	
1	oz	black pepper	28	g	#10 mesh
1–1½	oz	cayenne pepper	28–42.5	g	or to taste
5	T	dried thyme	15	g	well-bruised
1	c	fresh garlic	96	g	minced
2	oz	granulated sugar	57	g	
12	oz	soy protein powder	340	g	
1	oz	Prague powder #1	28.4	g	measured accurately
		hog casings	35–38	mm	

1. Grind the turkey meat and fat together through a ³⁄₁₆ in. (0.5 cm) plate.
2. Put the water in a container and stir in the salt, pepper, cayenne pepper, thyme, garlic, sugar, soy protein powder, and Prague powder #1. Pour the solution over the ground meat and mix very well by hand or with a power mixer.
3. Stuff the prepared casings. Tie into large loops or make into an "endless" sausage.

SMOKING

1. Hang the andouilles on smoking sticks and load into a preheated smoker set at 120°F (49°C). Set the dampers wide open and dry for about 1½ hours.
2. When the sausages are well-dried, adjust the dampers to one-half open. Gradually raise the smoker temperature over several hours to 165°F (74°C). After the second hour, adjust the dampers to one-quarter open and apply a medium smoke.
3. When the internal temperature of the andouilles reaches 155°F (68°C) and they have a desirable smoke finish, remove and spray them with cold water. Reduce the internal temperature to 100°F (38°C) or less.

(Continued)

4. Hang to air dry at room temperature for at least 30 minutes. A good bloom should appear.

5. Refrigerate for 12 hours to finish before using.

Turkey Bologna

Make this with or without garlic, but to the true garlic lover, it may be just *baloney* if you dare make it without plenty of fresh garlic. To reduce sodium content, try using a good salt substitute. Experiment with various brands and amounts of salt substitute to maintain an excellent flavor. Some people are fond of fried, thick-sliced bologna, others enjoy it with lettuce and pickle on a sandwich.

Yield: 10 pounds (4.5 kg)

U.S.		Ingredients	Metric		Preparation
6	lb	boned white turkey	2.7	kg	diced
4	lb	boned dark turkey	1.9	kg	diced
1	pt	ice water	475	ml	
3	T	kosher or canning salt	36	g	
2	T	ground white pepper	12	g	
1	T	ground paprika	7	g	
1	T	ground allspice	6	g	
2	t	ground nutmeg	5	g	
2	t	ground cloves	5	g	
1	T	pure onion powder	9	g	
4	t	granulated garlic	18	g	oil-packed; optional
1	lb	soy protein powder	454	g	
2¼	t	Prague powder #1	11.25	g	measured accurately
4–8	in.	synthetic fibrous casing or beef bung	10–20	cm	

1. Grind the turkey using a ⅜ in. (0.9 cm) plate. Grind again through a ⅛ in. (0.3 cm) plate. The grind should be very fine. If you prefer, purée the meat in a food processor.

2. Put the water in a container and stir in the salt, pepper, paprika, allspice, nutmeg, cloves, onion powder, optional garlic, soy protein powder, and Prague powder #1. Pour this solution over the ground turkey and mix for several minutes to combine the ingredients thoroughly.

3. Stuff the prepared casing or beef bung. Tie very well and make a strong loop.

SMOKING

1. Preheat the smoker to 130°F (54°C) with wide open dampers. Hang the bologna securely and air dry for 1 full hour.

2. Raise the temperature to 145°F (63°C) and adjust the dampers to one-quarter open. Start a heavy smoke and process for 1 hour.

3. Increase the temperature to 170°F (77°C) and adjust to a light smoke. Check the internal temperature of the sausage and remove at 155°F (68°C). Shower with cold water and hang to dry for 1 hour.

4. Refrigerate for 24 hours before use.

Turkey Sausage

This emulsified poultry sausage with pork makes an excellent meal anytime. Our thanks go to Rytec Kutas for this and all the other genuine inspirations we have gained from our travels through his *Great Sausage Recipes and Meat Curing,* Macmillan, 1987, a versatile book that has long had a special spot on each of our bookshelves. This sausage is quite simple yet a real favorite in many taste tests in our kitchens. We did take away an ounce of salt and add some white pepper. You may wish to try your own combinations, too. That can be a big part of the joy of making your own sausage.

Yield: 10 pounds (4.5 kg)

U.S.		Ingredients	Metric		Preparation
7½	lb	boned turkey meat	3.4	kg	light and dark meat
2½	lb	fatty pork butt	1.1	kg	trimmed
2½	oz	fine salt	71	g	
1	T	white pepper	6	g	optional
2	t	Prague powder #1	10	g	measured accurately
1	oz	powdered dextrose	28	g	
5	oz	soy protein powder	142	g	
2	pt	ice water	1	l	
		hog casings	32–35	mm	

1. Grind the turkey and pork through a ³⁄₁₆ in. or ¼ in. plate.

2. Add the salt, optional pepper, Prague powder #1, dextrose, and soy protein powder. Mix well to distribute the ingredients evenly.

(Continued)

3. Purée the meat in a food processor; add the ice water while the machine is running.

4. Stuff the prepared casings. Tie into 4 in. (10 cm) links. Dry the sausage at room temperature while the smoker is preheating.

SMOKING

1. Preheat the smoker to 130°F (54°C). Put the sausage in the smoker and hold for 1 hour.

2. Increase the smoker temperature to 150°F (65°C), apply smoke, and hold for 1 hour.

3. Raise the temperature to 165°F (74°C) and maintain until the internal temperature of the sausage reaches 155°F (68°C). Remove and spray with cool water for 20 minutes.

4. Refrigerate overnight before use.

Turkey and Duck Wieners

"We loved this sausage. The best of the poultry types." This was the unanimous opinion of all the students and teachers who sampled the sausage. Serve it with a Creole sauce and some "Cajun style" noodles.

Yield: 10 pounds (4.5 kg)

U.S.		Ingredients	Metric		Preparation
7	lb	boned turkey meat	3.2	kg	white and dark
3	lb	boned duck leg meat	1.4	kg	
1	oz	fine salt	28	g	
1	T	white pepper	6	g	finely ground
10	oz	durum wheat flour	284	g	
2¼	t	Prague powder #1	11.25	g	measured accurately
4	oz	nonfat dry milk	113	g	
1	t	orange extract	5	ml	
12	oz	duck stock	356	ml	well-chilled
1	pt	turkey stock	475	ml	well-chilled
		hog casings	28–32	mm	

1. Chill the meats to almost 32°F (0°C). Grind through a ¼ in. (0.6 cm) plate.

2. Add and mix in the salt, pepper, flour, Prague powder #1, dry milk, and orange extract. Scrape down the sides of the mixing lug.

3. Process in a food processor or vertical cutting machine while gradually adding the duck and turkey stocks. Scrape down the sides as necessary. Chill if the mixture has warmed to 40°F (4°C).

4. Stuff the prepared casings. Twist into 4 in. (10 cm) or longer links. You may adjust the link size to fit a bun.

SMOKING

1. Preheat the smoker to 135°F (57°C) with the dampers wide open.

2. Loop the wieners on hanging sticks and load into the smoker. Air dry for 30 minutes or more as necessary.

3. When the wieners are fully dry, gradually increase the temperature to a maximum of 170°F (77°C) and apply a medium smoke. Set the dampers to one-eighth open. (This will shorten the finishing time.)

4. When their internal temperature reaches 160°F (71°C), remove the wieners and spray them at once with cold water to lower it to 50°F (10°C).

5. Wrap and refrigerate for use.

Turkey and Pepper Sausage

Mild and flavorful, great for summer grill-outs, this sausage is ideal for those who do not eat pork.

Yield: 10 pounds (4.5 kg)

U.S.		Ingredients	Metric		Preparation
8	lb	boned turkey meat	3.6	kg	well-chilled
12	oz	turkey fat	340	g	pan fat or from carcass
2	oz	fine salt	57	g	
1	T	white pepper	6	g	finely ground
½	oz	Magic Pork & Veal blend	11	g	Chef Paul Prudhomme's
12	oz	white bread crumbs	340	g	day-old
2	t	Prague powder #1	10	g	measured accurately
10	oz	whole milk	296	ml	well-chilled
5	oz	heavy cream	118	ml	well-chilled
10	oz	rich turkey stock	296	ml	
12	oz	bell pepper	340	g	diced and sautéed
		hog casings	32–35	mm	

1. Grind the turkey and fat through a ³⁄₁₆ in. (0.5 cm) plate.

2. Add the salt, pepper, Chef Paul's spice blend, bread crumbs, and Prague powder #1. Mix well by hand.

3. Purée in a vertical cutting machine or process in batches in a food processor. With the machine running, gradually add the milk, cream, stock, and peppers. Do not rush; we usually process for a full 4 minutes.

4. Stuff the prepared casings firmly and shape as desired.

SMOKING

1. Preheat the smoker to 130°F (54°C). Loop the sausages on sticks, load them into the smoker, and air dry with the dampers wide open.

2. After 1 hour, increase the temperature every 10 minutes to a maximum of 170°F (77°C).

3. When their internal temperature reaches 160°F (71°C), remove the sausages and spray them immediately with cold water to lower the temperature to 70°F (21°C). Dry at room temperature for 1 hour.

4. Refrigerate for use.

Dry-Cured Turkey Salami

Chef Kinsella has created this new American-style sausage. It eats so very well and utilizes the dark meat of the turkey. The number of different preparation steps may discourage the new student or even the more experienced. *Do understand that all the detail given should serve to assure that your efforts will be successful the first time around* and, most important, that the product will be very safe for consumption. We heartily encourage your making this and every other variety. We could say, "Best of luck to you!" but that would not be appropriate. *We do say, "Read and follow all the recipe instructions, then enjoy the results!"*

Yield: 10 pounds (4.5 kg)

U.S.		Ingredients	Metric		Preparation
7	lb	boned dark turkey meat	3.2	kg	
2	lb	boned white turkey meat	900	g	
1	lb	turkey skin and fat	450	g	½ in. (1.3 cm) dice
2	t	fine salt	12.5	g	
1	T	whole pink peppercorns	9	g	
1	T	whole green peppercorns	9	g	
1	oz	soy protein powder	28	g	
1	oz	powdered dextrose	28	g	
2	oz	corn syrup solids	57	g	
1	T	Prague powder #2	15	g	measured accurately
4	oz	ice water	118	ml	
3½ in. × 24 in.		flat collagen casings	90	mm	

1. Spread the skin and fat on a small tray lined with plastic wrap and freeze.

2. Grind the dark turkey meat through a ⅛ in. (0.3 cm) plate. Grind the white turkey meat through a ¾ in. (1.9 cm) plate. Combine the two and chill at once.

3. Combine the salt, pink and green peppercorns, soy protein, dextrose, corn syrup solids, and Prague powder #2 with the ice water. Set aside.

4. When the skin and fat are frozen hard, mix them into the ground turkey in a chilled mixing lug. Working rapidly, add the seasoning solution. Mix quickly but very thoroughly. The dice should retain their shape and the peppercorns should remain whole.

5. Stuff the prepared casings firmly with no air pockets. Use a clip and tie closure. Make secure hanging loops.

6. Hang to cure for 58 hours at a constant temperature of 65–70°F (18–21°C), with relative humidity of 70–80%.

SMOKING

1. After curing, hang the salami to air dry at 90°F (32°C) for 2 hours with the dampers wide open.

(Continued)

2. Gradually increase the smoker temperature to 165°F (74°C) over the next 2 hours. At the start of the second hour, adjust the dampers to one-quarter open.

3. In the third hour, monitor the internal temperature of the salami. When it reaches 160°F (71°C), remove the salami and spray with cold water. Cool rapidly to less than 80°F (27°C). Hang the salami at room temperature for a final air drying.

4. Hang in the cooler to store at an optimum temperature of no less than 45°F (7°C). Do not wrap the salami too tightly as this will promote mold.

Veal and Ham Pie

Make this pie in quantity and freeze some for convenience.* Serve it cold with an English tomato salad. For dessert, serve strawberries and cream, of course! Ascot's finest.

Yield: One large pie serving 16 (or several small pies)

U.S.		Ingredients	Metric		Preparation
1½	lb	Hot Water Paste	700	g	see separate recipe (p. 153)
2¼	lb	good veal	1	kg	cut in batons
2¼	lb	mild or unsmoked ham	1	kg	cut in batons
12		thick bacon slices	12		diced
2	oz	dry onion	57	g	finely diced
5		hard-boiled eggs	5		finely chopped
12		gelatin sheets	12		
		or			
1	oz	granulated gelatin	27	g	
8	oz	veal stock	237	ml	double strength
2	t	fresh thyme	4	g	finely chopped
		salt			to taste
		ground white pepper			to taste
1		whole egg	1		
		water			

1. Roll out the hot water paste and cut pieces to line and cover one traditional long pan (or several small pans). Line the pan and reserve the cover piece.

2. Lightly sauté the bacon and onion. Cool and add the hard-cooked egg. Set aside.

3. Spread the veal, ham, and bacon mixture in alternating layers in the pastry-lined pan.

---

*When freezing, do not add aspic; add it just before serving.

4. Soften the gelatin in cool stock; heat the stock to dissolve the gelatin and cool to a pouring consistency. Add the thyme. Adjust the seasoning with salt and pepper. Cover the layers in the pie mold with the stock.

5. Brush the edges of the pastry lining with a little cold water and lay on the cover. Seal attractively with a crimper or fork.

6. Cut 2 vent holes and insert two funnels made of aluminum foil or pastry tubes. This allows the contents of the pie to expand during baking without tearing the top.

7. Garnish the pie with decorative shapes (leaves, etc.) cut from the leftover pastry. Mix the whole egg and some water to make an egg wash and brush it over the pastry.

8. Bake the pie in a preheated 350°F (177°C) oven for about 1½ hours. Watch carefully and add more stock through the vent holes as needed.

9. Remove from the oven and add additional stock as the pie cools. The pie should be full when served. Chill for service.

Venison Pie

It is a good idea to make these savory pies ahead and carefully freeze them. They are excellent buffet fare and may be enjoyed hot or cold. Serve them with a marinated mushroom salad. This has been described as "the best venison pie in the world!" by our students and guests.

Yield: three 1-pound pies, serving 20 or more

U.S.		Ingredients	Metric		Preparation
1	lb	lean venison	450	g	¼ in. (0.64 cm) strips
8	oz	veal	227	g	
8	oz	lean pork	227	g	
1	lb	fatback	454	g	
2	oz	good brandy	59	ml	
3	oz	Madeira wine	89	ml	
1	oz	fresh thyme	28	g	
1	oz	fresh sage	28	g	
1	oz	fresh chervil	28	g	
1	oz	dried juniper berries	28	g	
		salt			to taste
		ground black pepper			to taste
1½	lb	Hot Water Paste	700	g	see separate recipe (p. 153)
12		unsmoked bacon slices	12		
2	lg	whole eggs	2	lg	beaten
8	oz	pâté de foie gras or purée de foie gras	227	g	cut into strips
1		egg	1		
		water			
1	pt	aspic	475	ml	wine-flavored

1. Make the marinade by combining the brandy, Madeira, thyme, sage, chervil, and juniper berries. Pour over the venison and refrigerate overnight. The following day, drain the meat; strain and reserve the marinade.

2. Finely grind together the veal, pork, and fatback. Add the marinade liquid to the force-meat. Season with salt and pepper. Fry a small patty; taste and correct the seasoning.

3. Roll out the dough and line the pans. (Reserve enough pastry to cover the pies. Cut decorative pieces from the pastry scraps and reserve.) Neatly place bacon strips on top of the pastry lining. Reserve some bacon to put on the top of the pie.

4. Fold the beaten eggs into the forcemeat. Spread a layer of forcemeat on top of the bacon slices. Make a layer of venison strips followed by a layer of pâté strips. Cover with a second layer of the forcemeat. Continue layering in this fashion until the pies are filled. Finish with a layer of forcemeat and top with the reserved bacon.

5. Roll and cut covers from the reserved pastry. Moisten the edges with water, lay the pastry covers on top of the pies, and crimp well to seal. Cut vent holes and insert small funnels; seal well around the funnels to preserve the appearance of the crusts.

6. Make an egg wash with the egg and some water. Use the egg wash to brush the top crust and to affix the decorative pieces of pastry.

7. Bake in a preheated oven at 425°F (218°C) for 10 minutes. Reduce the temperature to 350°F (177°C) and bake to an internal temperature of 160°F (71°C). Add aspic through the vent holes as needed.

8. Remove the pies from the oven and add more aspic* as the pies cool. They should be filled with aspic when served. Chill for service.

---

*When freezing the pies, do not add aspic. Add it just before serving.

Venison Salami

"The prince of game sausages," this salami has graced the tables of every royal house of Europe. All game meat must have been inspected by authorized inspection personnel. Check the meat source to verify this before making any game sausage products. This excellent product will utilize less tender cuts of the venison carcass.

Yield: Three 3-pound (1.2 kg) salamis; serves 50

U.S.		Ingredients	Metric		Preparation
8	lb	trimmed venison	3.6	kg	or other red game meat
2	lb	fatback	900	g	cubed and chilled
2	t	Prague powder #1	10	g	measured accurately
2	c	soy protein concentrate	450	g	
1	T	#10 mesh black pepper	6	g	
2	T	ground nutmeg	15	g	or to taste
1	T	pure garlic powder	9	g	or fresh equivalent
6	T	corn syrup solids	30	g	
2	T	powdered dextrose	12	g	
1	pt	ice water	475	ml	
		beef bungs or synthetic fibrous casing			

1. Cube the game meat and grind it through a 3/16 in. (0.5 cm) plate into a mixing lug. Add the fatback, all the dry ingredients, and the ice water. Mix well. Pack down to eliminate any air pockets. Cover and refrigerate for 24 hours.

(Continued)

2. Grind the forcemeat again through a ³⁄₁₆ in. (0.5 cm) plate.
3. Firmly stuff the prepared casing. Tie one end with a butterfly knot and tie or use a clip to close the other end. Prick any air pockets. Make a sturdy loop for hanging.

SMOKING

1. Place in a preheated smoker at 135°F (57°C) with the dampers wide open. Hold for 30 minutes.
2. Raise the smoker temperature to 145°F (63°C) and adjust the dampers to one-half open. Apply a medium-heavy smoke.
3. After 1 hour, raise the temperature to 165°F (74°C). When the internal temperature of the salami reaches 152°F (67°C), remove from the smoker. Shower with cold water until the temperature drops to 120°F (49°C) or lower. Hang to dry at room temperature.
4. Refrigerate unwrapped. A bloom is normal on this salami.

Vienna Smoked Sausage

This sausage must have a fine-grained, smooth texture. It has a complex, savory flavor that is enhanced by light or dark breads. Serve hot or cold. The light smoke is a flavor option. The unsmoked version, with its herbal character, is also very tasty.

Yield: 10 pounds (4.5 kg)

U.S.		Ingredients	Metric		Preparation
4	lb	lean beef	1.8	kg	
4	lb	lean veal	1.8	kg	
2	lb	pork	900	g	
1	pt	ice water	473	ml	
3	oz	fine salt	85	g	
1	T	ground nutmeg	7.5	g	
1	t	ground coriander	1.5	g	
½	t	ground cardamom	0.8	g	
½	t	ground cloves	1.3	g	
½	t	dried sage	0.5	g	
½	t	dried thyme	0.5	g	
2	oz	rye flour	57	g	
1	oz	powdered dextrose	28	g	
2	t	Prague powder #1	10	g	measured accurately
		sheep casings	22–24	mm	

1. Grind the beef, veal, and pork using a ⅜ in. (0.9 cm) plate. Transfer to a chilled mixing lug.
2. Put the ice water in a container and stir in all the remaining ingredients. Pour the solution over the ground meat and mix well, scraping the sides and corners of the lug to make sure all of the ingredients are incorporated.
3. Purée in a vertical cutting machine or process in batches in a food processor. Chill to near 34°F (1°C) if the forcemeat becomes warm during processing.
4. Stuff the prepared casings. Twist into links of preferred length.

SMOKING

1. Load the sausages onto hanging sticks and place in a preheated smoker set at 170°F (77°C), with the dampers one-half open. Hold at this temperature and smoke lightly. Watch carefully because these small sausages cook fairly quickly.
2. Remove the sausages when their internal temperature reaches 160°F (71°C). Shower immediately with cold water.
3. Hang briefly to dry. Cover and refrigerate for 1 day before use.

Walleyed Pike Sausage

Grill and serve this very delicate game fish sausage with a hot Creole sauce. Or poach it in fish stock and enjoy it with a classic Newburg sauce—absolutely delicious! These sausages should be used within 3 days of manufacturing for highest quality. For full enjoyment, we do not recommend freezing them, as the best flavor/texture may be lost.

Yield: 4 pounds (1.8 kg)

U.S.		Ingredients	Metric		Preparation
3	lb	walleyed pike	1.4	kg	skinned and boned
½	lb	smoked salmon	227	g	skinned
4	lg	whole eggs	4	lg	well-beaten
4	oz	white bread crumbs	113	g	fresh, crusts removed
1	T	fine salt	15	g	
1	T	white pepper	6	g	finely ground
2	oz	fresh chives	57	g	finely chopped
1	t	fresh sage	2	g	
½	t	red pepper flakes	0.5	g	or to taste
8	oz	half-and-half	237	ml	
2	qt	mild fish stock	1.9	l	
		sheep casings	22–24	mm	

1. Purée the pike and salmon in a food processor. Be certain to discard all traces of skin as it could give an undesirable flavor to the sausage.

2. Add the eggs and bread crumbs to the forcemeat in the food processor. Add the salt, pepper, chives, sage, and red pepper flakes. Pulse the food processor to blend well. If a coarser texture is desired, mix the seasonings into the forcemeat by hand.

3. Add the half-and-half to smooth out the forcemeat.

4. Stuff the prepared casings, avoiding air pockets. Twist into 3 in. (8 cm) links. Do not separate the links.

5. Add the links to the fish stock. Bring to a gentle simmer and poach until the sausages reach an internal temperature of 160°F (71°C). They may be served at once if desired.

6. If not required immediately, immerse the cooked links in a light brine (1 T of salt to 1 quart of water) and refrigerate.

Wiltshire Mutton Sausage

This savory "grill and serve" variety is for all who especially enjoy lamb and mutton. Not found in the marketplace, it is a delight for lamb lovers, and a wonderful use for lamb and mutton trimmings—just another good reason to be able to make your own sausages! It is best stored fresh, *not frozen,* to preserve its delicate flavor balance.

Yield: 10 pounds (4.5 kg)

U.S.		Ingredients	Metric		Preparation
10	lb	lamb/mutton trimmings	4.5	kg	not too fatty
1	pt	ice water	475	ml	
1	oz	fine salt	28	g	
½	oz	white pepper	14	g	finely ground
¼	oz	ground ginger	7	g	
½	t	dried marjoram	0.5	g	rubbed fine
½	t	dried summer savory	0.5	g	rubbed fine
1	oz	fresh mint	28	g	finely chopped
		sheep casings	32–35	mm	

1. Grind the meat through a ½ in. (1.3 cm) plate.
2. Sprinkle the ice water and all of the seasonings over the forcemeat in a mixing lug. Mix well.
3. Grind again using a ³⁄₁₆ in. (0.5 cm) plate.
4. Stuff the prepared casings. Twist or tie into 3–5 in. (8–13 cm) links.
5. Wrap, label, and refrigerate for use.

Appendixes

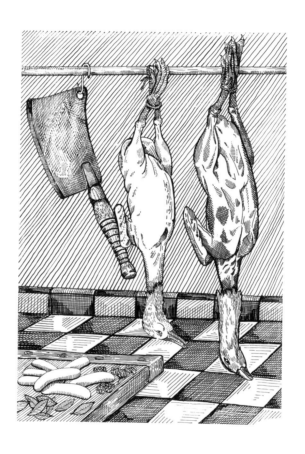

Casings Available
for Sausage Making

Compiled from *The Sausagemaker* catalogue.

For the purpose of this listing, we have grouped casings into two groups, natural and synthetic. In each group there are a number of useful and available casings.

NATURAL CASINGS

Salted casings have a very long shelf life when stored properly. When refrigerated, packed liberally in salt, they have an indefinite shelf life. If unrefrigerated, these salted casings quickly begin to give off a strong odor, even though they are not spoiled. Put them back under refrigeration, and this odor will soon subside.

Many casings are sized using the metric system of measurement. Others are sized using the avoirdupois system. Please note that 1 millimeter (mm.) is equal to 0.039 inches.

Hog Casings

Size: 29–32 mm.   Used for frankfurters, Italian and breakfast (country) sausage. Comes packed in salt. One hank makes 90 to 100 lbs.

Size: 32–35 mm.   This size is most used in making bratwurst, bockwurst, and Italian sausage. Packed in salt. One hank makes up to 115 lbs.

Size: 35–38 mm.   The diameter of this casing is larger and it is generally used for making knockwurst and Polish sausage. One bundle, in many cases, will make up to 125 lbs. of sausage. Packed in salt.

Size: 38–42 mm.   This is the largest size available, up to 1½ to 2 inches in diameter. It is very popular in making Polish sausage, summer sausage and even ring bologna or liverwurst. It is also popular in the making of pepperoni that is dry cured. Makes up to 140 lbs. of sausage.

267

Hog Middles

Medium size: This is the type of casing traditionally used to make blood sausage and sopressata. By its very nature, it has a strong odor and should be rinsed well before using. Will make between 100 and 125 lbs. of sausage.

Hog Stomachs

The principal use of this casing is for head cheese, souse, or blood sausage. Will stuff 4 to 5 lbs.

Natural Sheep Casings

Size: 22–24 mm. This casing is the size used to make pork sausage links. Sheep casings are strong, yet make extremely tender eating. The capacity of one hank is 60 to 70 lbs.

Size: 24–26 mm. This sheep casing is used when making wieners or hot dogs. The capacity of one hank is 60 to 70 lbs.

Natural Beef Casings

Size: 4 to 4½ in. One of these large casings will stuff approximately 8 to 10 lbs. Almost every sausage maker uses beef bung caps, one of the most popular items in the entire beef casing. The cap is usually gauged at the curve. Beef bungs are used for cappicola, veal sausage, large bologna, Lebanon, and cooked salami.

Beef Rounds

Two sizes: 38–40 mm. and 40–43 mm. Beef rounds are used for ring bologna, ring liver sausage, and blood sausage. They derive their name from their "ring" or "round" characteristic. Beef rounds are also used for knockwurst, mettwurst, kiska, Polish sausage, and Holsteiner sausages. Approximate capacity: 38 to 40 mm. is 70 to 80 lbs. The 40 to 43 mm. size is 75 to 85 lbs.

SYNTHETIC CASINGS

Synthetic casings are popular because they are relatively inexpensive for making the larger sausages. Use them for beef stick, salami, summer sausage, bologna and more. The fiber in these casings runs lengthwise, which makes them strong enough to stuff them tighter without breaking. They smoke just as brown as a natural casing.

Synthetic casings need not be refrigerated, simply soak them for 20 to 30 minutes in tap water before using. They are sized in inches. The dimensions specified are the stuffed diameter and length.

Fibrous Casings

Beef Stick Casings: 2 × 24 in. packed 20 to a bundle.

Deer Salami Casings: 3½ × 24 in. packed 20 to a bundle.

Cooked Salami Casings: 5 × 24 in. packed 20 to a bundle.

Bologna Casings: 8 × 24 in. packed 20 to a bundle.

Mahogany Colored Synthetic Fibrous Casings

Mahogany colored casings are very popular with the deer processors and many sausage makers. This is because they eliminate the process of smoking the salamis. Liquid smoke is simply added to the salami mixture. Stuffed into the casing, the mixture is cooked in the smokehouse, without the use of smoke. The mahogany color of the casing simulates the smoked appearance of the sausage, while the taste is provided by the liquid smoke.

Mahogany Fibrous Casing: 2 × 24 in. packed 20 to a bundle.

Mahogany Fibrous Casing: 3½ × 24 in. packed 20 to a bundle.

Clear Synthetic Protein-lined Fibrous Casings

Made for use with dry-cured sausage only. A protein coating on the inside of these casings gives them the ability to cling to the meat as it is drying. This is very important for the appearance of the finished product. Soak these casings in tap water before using.

Protein-lined Clear Casing: 2 × 24 in. packed 20 to a bundle.

Protein-lined Clear Casing: 3½ × 24 in. packed 20 to a bundle.

Casing Assortment Kit

The kit consists of the following:

5 ea. 2 × 24 in. Beef Stick Salami Casings
5 ea. 3½ × 24 in. Fibrous Deer Salami Casings
5 ea. 5 × 24 in. Fibrous Cooked Salami Casings
5 ea. 8 × 24 in. Bologna Casings
5 ea. 3½ × 24 in. Protein-lined Casings

Salami-Size Flat Collagen Casings

These casings do not require refrigeration and may be stored at normal room temperature of 50 to 80 degrees F. These casings have a wide variety of uses. Prior to stuffing, soak the casing in lukewarm water (90° F) with 1 tsp. salt added per qt. of water. Do not allow the tied end to touch the end of the stuffing tube when stuffing.

Do not overstuff! The first one-third of the casing should be stuffed gently, with normal pressure. These are available in three sizes:

60 mm. (2.3 × 24 in.):	A size most popular for beef sticks, summer sausage, and pepperoni. One 24 in. casing will hold about 2½ lbs. of raw sausage mixture.
90 mm. (3.5 × 24 in.):	Widely used for venison salami, hard and Genoa salami, also for sopressata. One casing will stuff 5 to 6 lbs. of raw finished product.
100 mm. (3.9 × 24 in.):	Can be used for semi-dry cure bologna, thuringer, cappicola, and mortadella. One casing holds 7 to 8 lbs. raw finished product.

Collagen Casings for Fresh and Smoked Sausage

There are several kinds of collagen casings manufactured today. We have collagens for fresh sausages which virtually adhere to the meat, after they are stuffed. They are so clear that one cannot tell that they are there. These thin-walled, delicate casings cannot be used for smoking, however, since the casing will not support the weight of the meat when hanging on smokehouse sticks. Collagen casings made especially for smoked sausages are available. These casings are made with a thicker wall, and will carry the weight of the meat. Sizes are listed for each type.

FRESH SAUSAGE COLLAGEN CASINGS

22 mm.	This size is very popular for making breakfast sausages. It is very easy to use. Approximate stuffing capacity per caddie is 30 lbs.

32 mm.   This size is very popular for making Italian sausage, bratwurst, bockwurst, and chorizo. Fine for making country sausage (a large diameter breakfast sausage). Approximate stuffing capacity per caddie is 40 to 43 lbs.

SMOKED SAUSAGE COLLAGEN CASINGS

19 mm.   This size is used for SLIM JIMS®. Also useful for any other dry cure or semi-dry cure sausage. Approximate stuffing capacity per caddie is 25 lbs.

32 mm.   This size is popular for making smoked sausages like bratwurst, Italian, smoked breakfast, or country sausage. Used also for dry cure pepperoni. Stuffing capacity per caddie, 40 to 43 lbs.

38 mm.   A size mainly used for large diameter sausage like Polish, knockwurst, and for dry-cure pepperoni. Approximate stuffing capacity per caddie, 60 to 70 lbs.

This information on casings is taken freely from the catalogue, *The Sausagemaker.* The authors are indebted to Rytec Kutas and others within his operation for their longstanding support and excellent communications.

Many other items, all highly useful for the sausage maker's kitchen, are listed in this catalogue, which provides much information as well as a very good overview of many specialized tools and supplies. We recommend that you send for your own copy. A well-provided workplace will greatly simplify your operation. Contact: The Sausagemaker, 26 Military Road, Buffalo, NY 14207, Phone: 1-716-876-5521; fax: 1-716-875-0302.

Suppliers of Fine Meats and Equipment

Supplier Name and Address	Main Type or Source of Supply	Secondary Type or Source of Supply
Aidells Sausage Company 1575 Minnesota Street San Francisco, CA 94107 1-415-285-6660	Sausages, tasso, hams, and a fine selection of cured products—a premium supplier.	Casings, cures, equipment, seasonings, and charcuterie condiments
The Sausage Maker 177 Military Road Buffalo, NY 14207 1-716-876-5521	All types of equipment and kits. One of the most extensive sources of equipment—a premium supplier.	All charcuterie supplies. Great starter kits and pre-mixed cures and spice blends.
Brandy Meats 112 Sidney Avenue Cincinnati, OH 45220 1-513-628-6717	A premier supplier of meats including all standard meats and game and poultry products. Cervena supplier.	All types of casings and cures.
Meco Water Smokers 1500 Industrial Road Greenville, TN 37744 1-800-251-7558	Smokers and smoker supplies.	
Cook'n Cajun Water Smokers PO Box 3736 Shreveport, LA 71133 1-318-925-6933	Smokers and smoker supplies.	

Glossary

Abats: French culinary term for offal, the edible internal organs of an animal. In the United States they are often called "variety meats." Although more perishable than muscle meats, with proper handling they are considered very usable and a special delicacy.

Abattoir: [Fr.] Slaughterhouse. A place where animals are slaughtered for human consumption.

Air drying: A method of slow drying to prepare a product for further steps in processing. Often preliminary to other necessary steps. Dry cure products are air dried for longer periods at specific temperatures. During this critical time period, curing *may* take place. Temperature specification for air drying is optional and dependent upon the application.

Amino acids: An organic compound containing both an amino group (NH_2) and a carboxylic acid group (000H). Of approximately eighty found in nature, twenty are considered necessary for human metabolism or growth. This group is further divided into *essential* and *nonessential* amino acids. Meat is a complete protein, containing all the essential groups.

Andouille: A Cajun sausage which (easily) has over 200 recipe variations in existence! It is a highly popular regional sort, with a growing, wider appeal.

Arterial pump: A large syringe used to inject saline or other solutions into the veins or arteries of the joint. Used also to inject (in wet curing) the *muscle tissue* in larger cuts and for hams, etc. Assures deep penetration of the desired solution.

Ascot pie: The nobility's answer to the common classes' "pork pie." Henry VIII, penned the aire, "Scarborough Fair" in which herbs in a traditional pork or raised pie are described as "parsley, sage, rosemary and thyme." The Smithfield market in London, to this day, uses that same recipe from Henry's time.

Aspic: A savory jelly, often clear (tomato aspic is opaque) derived from *clarified* meat, fish, and/or vegetable stocks and gelatin. Used for glazing cold dishes and presentation pieces. The binding agent for many molded dishes and products. Served cubed, as accompaniment for cold meats, fish, and fowl. (*Also see* Mousse, Gelatin.)

Ballotine (also ballottine): Strictly: "A boned, stuffed and rolled, (bundle shaped) cut of meat." Today, the term is accepted for dishes made from fish and fowl as well. The term has been misapplied frequently over many years to dishes which are in fact *galantines*. Today, the term is commonly accepted as "a kind of galantine—served hot or cold."

Banger: English term for beef or pork sausage, which while cooking tends to burst with a *bang;* hence the name. As in "bangers and mash" (sausages and mashed potato).

Bard: To tie onto or insert strips of selected fat to lean meats or fowl to prevent drying out during roasting. Effective as a method of self-basting; considered necessary for certain leaner meats. Will add flavor and moisture to the finished cut or bird, etc. When laid atop a piece, the fat is generally removed, the piece is then browned for proper appearance and served.

Barding needle: A large sewing needle used to "sew" thin strips of fat into flesh. Very useful as a practical aid in charcuterie work.

Black pudding: Blood sausage, as below. British term for blood sausage.

Block sausage: A sausage mixture made in a press and shaped into a "block shape." Dry-cured "Plockwurst" is an example.

Blood sausage: A sausage using fresh liquid blood to comprise a major proportion of the main or animal ingredient. Also known as black pudding, blood pudding.

Bloom: In culinary usage, bloom is a whitish, vegetative, powdery coating that normally appears on the casings of many sausages placed into proper storage. It is harmless, and easily removable by wiping with a damp cloth. To the practiced eye, bloom denotes sausage that has been fully processed and properly aged. Bloom is commonly observed on fresh grapes and especially on dry and semi-dry sausages. (*vt*) To bloom: as for gelatin preparation. Granular and leaf type gelatin must be first mixed or soaked into a small quantity of cool water to cause expansion of the dry granules or sheet. Blooming facilitates subsequent mixing into the main batch of liquid without lumping, which would spoil the recipe.

Botulism: A severe, sometimes fatal food poisoning caused by ingestion of food containing botulin, caused by the activity of *Clostridium botulinum*. Symptoms include: nausea, vomiting, disturbed vision, muscular weakness, and fatigue. Improper, incomplete curing of meats, canned foods, etc., is but one source of this pathogen.

Brawn: British name for "head cheese." In France—"fromage de tête." Made with bits of head of calf, pig, sheep, or cow, in a gelatinous meat broth, fully cooked, then molded. It is usually served sliced thinly; best flavor is at near room temperature.

Brine: A saline (salt) solution used to pickle, salt, and/or "cure" meats, poultry, and fish. Other ingredients are often included in the brining formula. These may be nitrates, flavor enhancers, sugars, natural or artificial seasonings and conditioning agents. Exacting formulation, with full attention to time and temperature call-outs when brining, is vital to successful food processing. In large-scale commercial production, brines are often (and properly) renewed for longer term usage. Small operations should make up fresh batches and not re-use brines.

Bulk sausage: Any sausage mixture which is not otherwise molded or stuffed into a casing. Very popular, economical method for pork and pork mixture sausages used for breakfast patties, sauces of many sorts, stuffings, pizza, and countless other uses. For some sausage aficionados, bulk sausage is never quite as tasty as that which has been properly stuffed and cooked in a casing.

Bung: Commercial term for the large intestine of a beef animal when used as casing material for the production of certain sausages. Diameters of 4 to 4½ inches, with stuffing capacity of 8 to 10 pounds, makes them ideal for large bologna, cooked salami, etc. Referred to as beef bungs in most catalogues.

Burlap bag smoking: Used in the Cajun country of Louisiana. This method has been described by Chefs Paul Prudhomme and John Folse, C.E.C., as a good method to "cold smoke over a damp wood smoking source." The bags serve to insulate the product against excessive heat. Chef Kinsella has tried this method with great success.

Butcher's block: A very heavy-duty cutting table. For many years, this was made of wood with a unique construction that enabled many years of surface renewal, when properly maintained. Today, some plastics and man-made compounds are finding their way into the making of these professional blocks.

Butcher's meat: A general term referring to meats used by sausage makers. Wholesome trimmings are well utilized for forcemeats and sausages.

Canner: A grading standard grade of beef at the lower end of the grading chart. Will generally have excellent good flavor but may lack tenderness. Quite satisfactory for many charcuterie items.

Capon: A castrated cockerel. The fowl has abundant, tender meat. Very useful for ballottines, terrines, and smoked whole fowl. Used for pâtés, etc.

Carbonnade: Culinary technique using a protracted beer or ale marinade, combined with slow cooking. Generally applied to beef and game meats. Observed by the crusaders and brought back to England. The method became very popular in the time of George I, and remained in vogue until the French influence in cooking took over in the late nineteenth century. Swedish carbonnades are used in cooking cod, haddock, and whiting. The dish will be designated as a "Carbonnade of ——." It will be characterized by rich full flavor and abundant natural sauce, which results from the method. Highly recommended by the authors.

Carcass: The torso of a butchered (slaughtered) animal, after head, hide, edible organs, and offal have been removed. It is *"the dressed animal."* An entire carcass is further "broken down" into sides and then to other recognized cuts or joints of usable meat.

Casing clip: Preformed, metal clips that may be used to seal any size of casing. Easy to apply with pliers. Applied before stuffing, the remaining end is usually secured with a hog ring or butcher twine. Provides easy, quick closures.

Caul fat: The mesentery or thin fatty membrane that lines a hog stomach. When used to wrap sausages, terrines, and some roasted meats, it will add ease of preparation, extra flavor, good conservation of juices. It serves very well to hold everything together. Unique and valuable as a "wrap" in that it requires no additional labor for its removal after the item is cooked. It simply disappears during cooking.

Chipolata: A small spicy sausage, used as a garnish or an hors d'oeuvre. A main dish (ragout) is so named when the sausages are the main ingredient. Seasoned highly with thyme, chives, sage, coriander, cloves. Hot red pepper flakes are often added to these coarse-textured pork sausages. The French use *"a la chipolata"* to describe a garnish including these little delights which accompanies roasts.

Choice: A meat grading term. The most commonly used grade of meat in the United States. High-quality meat with less marbling than prime grade.

Cincinnati: Southwestern Ohio city. Well known throughout most of the nineteenth century as a center for meat processing. Pork production was most impressive with 450,000 hogs slaughtered in 1872. The city came to be called "Porkopolis." The by-products of the animals created the largest soap manufacturers in the world, Proctor and Gamble, and Jergens soap company. Because of the large blue-collar work force, Cincinnati supported 40 local breweries prior to Prohibition. Cincinnati had the most breweries per capita in the United States during that world-famous and extended era.

Clarification: Culinary term. To make clear a liquid such as a broth, brew, vintage, or stock. Agents are added with additional regulated agitation or cooking time. The process varies widely, depending on the cloudy liquor that requires sediment to be removed. Fats, such as butter, are commonly clarified to modify their properties, when used for culinary purposes. When properly done, the clarification will determine the excellence or mediocrity of any fine cuisine in which it is required.

Cold smoking: A very useful process used to impart smoke flavor into fish or meats without cooking. Exacting temperature requirements must be carefully followed for quality products. Equipment must be capable of holding close temperature settings.

Collagen: Also *collogen*. An insoluble fibrous protein. Found abundantly in the connective tissues (skin, bones, tendons) of all vertebrates. Obtained from the slaughter of food animals and valuable in the manufacture of glue, gelatin, leather products, and casings. It swells when it comes in contact with water.

Collagen casing: Manufactured, as opposed to natural, casing material. These man-made casings utilize slaughter animal hides and other animal parts containing high quantities of collagen. This high-quality material is economically available in good variety to fully meet requirements of a large number of sausage types. Importantly, they make possible today's high production of sausages, by supplanting the limited supply of natural casings. Convenient storage, fast, easy preparation for use, economy, and uniformity are positive factors in selection of collagen type casings. (*Also see* Natural casing.)

Collar: Upper part of the shoulder or neck area. Applies to a side of meat.

Collop: In charcuterie, usage indicates a *small portion* of food, such as a slice of meat or fish, etc., as used in terrine assembly. An ingredient call, for example, might be: "collops of fish."

Court bouillon: Traditional broth with a strong flavor of herbs, a variety of savory vegetables, including onion. Vinegar, lemon juice, and/or wine provide an acid for fiber modification. Easy, quick to make, with a short 30-minute cooking time. Vegetable ingredients are left in broth as it cools. Used for poaching seafood of all kinds, and other vegetables. Especially fine for poaching large fish, such as salmon.

Crackling: Heat-rendered rind of a pig hide. Before cholesterol intake became a matter of concern, very popular snack item with broad usage in many other dishes. Used in pâtés, some English sausages. Served in northern England with roast pork.

Cross contamination: Undesirable transfer of bacteria from one food to another. Can occur when food preparation surfaces, such as cutting boards, used for any raw meat or poultry are not immediately and fully cleaned and made sterile. This extends to one's hands, kitchen tools, and any towels, etc. Avoiding cross contamination is indeed vital to any food preparation operation. It requires training and constant awareness by all personnel.

Cud: In butchery, the jowl of a pig or cow. Also in the kitchen or elsewhere, "chewing the cud" denotes "talking to oneself or others." Word derives from ruminating animals having the capability to bring up food for additional mastication from the first stomach. Goats, sheep, cows, camels, and antelope are ruminants.

Cure/Curing: Properly defined as "the treatment of foods to preserve them." Note that pickling, salt curing, corning, brining, etc., are all closely associated processes. Yet all differ to a significant degree. This difference in formulation and handling methods for different food items must be fully understood and practiced. Curing may occur during the smoking of sausages. It is very important to note, however, that curing is induced by other agents and processes preceding the actual smoking. *Proper curing (when applicable) of all charcuterie is absolutely essential to product safety for the ultimate consumer.*

Cutlet: A thin, tender cut of meat (usually from lamb, pork, or veal) cut from the rib or leg section. The cut should be quickly sautéed or grilled for best eating. Cutlets are with natural bone, or may be formed using finely chopped meat(s) and bound with heavy sauce. The formed type is often crumbed and pan-fried.

Darne: A slice of fish, a cutlet. It is cut across (perpendicular) to the backbone of a fish. A thick fish steak or wedge, cut from the middle part of larger fish such as salmon, cod, and turbot.

Devein: To remove, with a sharp knife or deveining tool, the dark dorsal vein of shrimp. Small and medium shrimp are shelled and deveined for cosmetic purposes. Larger shrimp have grit in the vein. Always remove it.

Dextrose: Available in a fine-powder form. Other names are corn sugar, grape sugar, glucose. Somewhat less sweet than table sugar (sucrose). A naturally occurring sugar, very useful in many sausage formulas as a flavor modifier.

Dry cure: Refers to specific methods for the production of sausage products that have moisture removed over a time period that may vary from 30 days to 6 months. Today, refrigeration and air conditioning play an important part in this drying process. There are dry and semi-dry sausages. All combine curing and drying to assure full safety for consumption without any additional processing or cooking.

Escalope: French term for a very thin slice of meat or fish. Usually served flattened, requiring but a few seconds sauté on both sides. In the United States it is known as a "scallop." Pork and veal are most utilized for this cut.

Faggot: 1. A mixture of finely ground pork, bread crumbs, and offal, also known as *savory ducks*. Hand shaped and wrapped in pig's caul. Typically, these small, individual portions are arranged around roasts and larger platter presentations. May include other tiny link sausages such as white or black boudin. Faggots may be slow cooked, "en casserole," or smothered in a mellow sauce. 2. As garniture (a *faggot of herbs*), the term is equivalent to today's bouquet garni.

Farce: French for "stuffing." "*Farci* denotes stuffed." A farce may be made of fine dice meat, vegetable, or fish, with a light binder, and seasoned to complement its companion.

Fermentation: A natural process which may be induced or enhanced in effect by specific ingredients in a sausage formula. Provides a unique flavor that is the hallmark for several semi-dried and dried sausages. Thuringer, summer sausage, and dry-cure pepperoni are several tangy examples of this sausage type.

Fermento: Starter culture in powdered form available for production of semi-dry sausages requiring a specific tang. Provides a controlled level of desirable bacterial activity which yields a consistently high quality product.

Forcemeat: An exceptionally smooth mixture of very finely ground meats, fish, or fowl. Carefully seasoned, often formulated with fruits, vegetables, and bread crumbs. Used by itself, to form quenelles, or as a stuffing. Widely used in sausages, pies, terrines, galantines, ballottines.

Free range (poultry): Birds are allowed to run free. They are raised in the natural state, as opposed to caged birds. Thought to provide a more desirable taste and texture owing to their "natural" diet of insects, worms, and so forth. They often command a premium price. Caged birds, in contrast, are today raised on formulated feeds and may not ever touch the ground before slaughter for market.

Galantine: Prior to 1800, "a boned, stuffed and pressed chicken, served cold in its own jelly." Later, other birds and various meat and fish varieties found a place in the galantine. Note: *The word galantine, used by itself, does imply a poultry presentation.* When any other meat or fish is used, this must be indicated, for example, "galantine of grouse." (*Also see* Ballottine, Game meats, Terrine.)

Gammon: European term for the *cured* leg of pork. The terminology serves to make distinction between bacon and *fresh* pork.

Gammon rasher: British Isles term for a thin slice of cured ham. Commonly served at breakfast.

Gelatin: A transparent, soluble protein used for glazing foods, and for molding of both simple and very grand charcuterie presentations. Used to make puddings, confections, and aspic. With sugar, flavor, and coloring, we know it as Jello™. Significantly, it may take many forms, including aspic. Skillful work with gelatin makes a very big difference in the excellence of a product.

Grade: Refers to established standards for meat inspection grades. Provides the informed purchaser with useful levels of many properties present in meats. Economy and suitability for the variety of charcuterie items may be established by correct choice of meat grades.

Gravlax: Raw salmon, cured in a salt/sugar/fresh dill mixture. It is a prized delicacy around the world. Perishable; it should be made in a quantity that will be consumed within a week. Store it tightly covered and very well chilled. Slice paper thin for service.

Green meat: Applied to insufficiently aged meats. Such meats are generally tough, since enzyme action has not been sufficient to properly tenderize and improve the taste and quality of the meat.

Grinder: A mechanical device used to process meats and other foods to a uniform particle size. Many models and sizes are manufactured. These range from small, hand-powered, table top (clamp on) models, to huge, powerful commercial models with large capacity. The grind size is regulated by changing the grinder plate. A worm feed and a spring-loaded knife rotate and force the meats through the plate. Hopper feed pans and pushers provide a measure of operator safety and efficiency. *A mainstay piece of equipment, deserving the best attention to proper use, careful cleaning, and proper maintenance.*

Grinder plates: Hardened, tool steel plates with differing hole sizes. See above. *Plates are made in several standard sizes and may not be interchangeable between machines of different manufacture.* Always keep plates in a clean, dry, lightly oiled condition. They are subject to rust and loss if handled carelessly. Proper assembly of the entire grinder mechanism is a must. Irreparable damage is instantly possible with misuse. (*See* Table of Grinder Plate Sizes, p. 6.)

Hafners: A famous sausage house in Dublin, Ireland. Their chipolatas were the toast of Dublin. Their choice seasoning for their famous bangers is still the envy of most sausage makers.

Head cheese: Sausage variety made principally with bits of meat from calf, pig, sheep, or cow head. Held together by a gelatinous broth and fully cooked in a mold. Flavor is considered best when sliced and eaten at room temperature. Known in England as brawn, in France as fromage de tête. (*Also see* Souse.)

Hock: 1. The lower part of the leg (corresponding to the ankle) of an animal. We think at once of the ham hock. Usually smoked and used to season various dishes, such as beans. 2. In England, the term is used for any Rhine wine.

Hog: Slang word for pig. Pigs are young hogs. The hog has been defined as the most productive of all animals for its complete usefulness and versatility. The phrase "use everything but the squeal" comes from the Cincinnati pork butcher's guide for apprentices when Cincinnati was known as the "Porkopolis of the World."

Hog casing: This natural, tubular membrane is the small or middle intestine obtained from the hog at slaughter. Various sizes are marketed and come packed, wet or dry, in salt. Both forms require some careful preparation, prior to stuffing with sausage mixtures. Hog middles and stomachs are used for casings as well. (*Also see* Collagen casing.)

Hog ring clippers: A plier-like hand tool (powered models are available) used to hold and secure hog rings in the closure of casings. Efficient and widely used, recommended for every charcuterie.

Hygeia: Ancient Grecian goddess of health. The word is here included to underscore this fact: An individual's understanding, constant focus, and practice of excellent personal hygiene and every related sanitation practice is paramount to acceptable operation of a charcuterie.

Hygrometer: Any of several precision measuring instruments used to measure the relative humidity (R.H.) of the atmosphere. This factor is very important and requires close control, especially for dry curing of various sausages. It has influence, along with time and temperature, on proper processing of the product.

Jowl: Commonly used to describe the boneless cheek meat of a hog, sometimes called jowl bacon. It may be smoked or fresh. An economy cut, it is useful as a seasoning and to add just a little meat to the dish.

Jugging: A method of preparation of hare and rabbits. The fresh blood is carefully reserved for later addition to the slow-cooked, well-seasoned, serving pieces of hare. The blood is incorporated into the sauce which has generated during the cooking. A classic French dish.

Lamb casings: Available in less plentiful quantity than beef or hog products at the slaughter of the animal. Short supply for today's market demands a premium price for this superior casing material. Provide a very tender but strong, natural casing. Especially recommended for all finer, delicate varieties. Also called sheep casings.

Lard: From the French verb *larder*, to insert thin strips of fat into the lean portion of a cut of meat or whole animal. Distinguished from *bard*, which is to lay fat upon or over a cut for roasting. Each culinary practice is done to add succulence to the roast. With today's dietary recommendations for fat and cholesterol, the practice has fallen into considerable disuse. Special, long hollow body needles with large eyes are available in sizes for those who still depend on larding for superb presentations.

Lardons: Also known as *lardoons*. Strips of fatty meat, usually pork fat or smoked bacon, that is used to lard the meat. These are threaded into the meat as described under lard. The French culinary term also refers to diced, blanched, and fried bacon used for garniture.

Link(s): Segments or portions formed when a continuous casing is constricted in more or less regular intervals by tying or twisting. Linking is the act of forming such individual portions and contrasts with roping or continuous stuffing of a casing. Sausages may be linked to provide accurate portion control. This is based on uniform diameter of man-made and natural casing. Skinless links may be extruded and layer packed by machinery. Other skinless sausage is produced by modern machinery which removes existing casing on a newly stuffed, cooked sausage and packages the product at great speed.

Liquid smoke: Commercially available distilled essence of hardwood smoke. Applications include use in conjunction with both wet and dry curing of meats. Full directions for this and other food applications are furnished on the container. Effective substitute for burning of wood.

Liverpool roux: A flour and water mixture first used in World War I by the British Army. The term was adopted to describe stews served in local eateries by the merchant marine owing to the observation of white floury lumps in the offerings. A slurry is an accurate descriptive for the mixture.

Loop: Sausages tied in loops are also known as ring-tied sausage. Longer link chains of sausage are often looped over smoking sticks and hung in this manner in the smoker. Looping provides economy and speed for the stuffing operation and the product has considerable eye appeal.

Marinade: Seasoned liquid mixture used to soak meat, fish, or vegetables. Purpose is to tenderize, flavor, and enhance cooking qualities of the food. Usually compounded from an acid (lemon juice, wine, or vinegar), herbs, spices, oils, and other seasonings. The acids tenderize by breaking down fibers. Keep foods well chilled and always use an inert container to marinate foods. Once used, marinades are often discarded. In some cases, with proper cooking, the marinade may be incorporated into the dish or sauce. Spoilage and bacterial contamination are factors that must be considered when using any marinade.

Mince: Cutting of food into very small pieces. A cutting action, with smaller particles than a chopped food.

Monosodium glutamate (MSG): A natural amino acid used widely in Chinese and Japanese cooking and commercially processed foods. An effective flavor enhancer which adds no flavor of its own. Will cause reactions in some individuals which include flushing, headache, and dizziness. Widely used in many processed foods. Presently, its use is highly favored by many and avoided by others.

Mousse: An airy, rich, fine-textured paste. It may be sweet or savory and eaten hot or cold. Served alone with garnish—often used in fanciful combination in "haute cuisine." Mousses and mousselines are not transparent. They are light, even frothy, due to addition of beaten egg whites or whipping cream. Gelatin is used to fortify and stabilize the mousse. (*Also see* Aspic, Gelatin.)

Mousseline: Fine-textured forcemeat lightened by addition of whipped cream or egg whites. A "*savory* mousseline" is distinguished from certain baked goods and sauces which are also mousselines. Savory mousselines are widely used in hot and cold charcuterie.

Panade: Also known as *panada*. 1. A thick paste of bread crumbs, rice flour, etc. and water, stock, milk. Butter and egg yolk optional. Used to bind forcemeats, quenelles, fish cakes, meat dumplings, etc. 2. A savory or sweet soup, thickened with bread crumbs or other starchy ingredients. The panade is usually strained and made very smooth.

Pork pie: A traditional raised pie version. After World War II, a rough puff pastry was used to top this pie in Manchester, England. It was then renamed a Manchester pie.

Quenelle: A small dumpling. Should be light and delicate. Made of seasoned minced or ground veal, fish, chicken, or game. The mixture is bound with eggs or panade. Quenelles are poached in stock and may be served with a rich sauce as a first course or as a garnish.

Raised pies: Pork (or other meat) pies. Due to their cooking method and the use of hot water paste, raised pies became standard fare for the English poor. The term alludes to the poor quality meat put into the pie and the use of aspic (thus raising the pie) at the end of the cooking process. Henry VIII penned the air "Scarborourgh Fair." Therein we hear the lyrical line of seasonings, "parsley, sage, rosemary and thyme." The Smithfield Market in London still uses recipes for Ascot and pork pie from Henry's time.

Rasher: 1. A thin slice or strip of meat such as bacon or ham. 2. A serving of one to three slices of such meat. The quantity will vary at the discretion of the establishment.

Saint Kevin: A hermit monk who lived at the lakeside of Glendalough, county Wicklow, in the seventh century. Described as a great writer of his time and is thought to be the inspiration behind "The Book of Kells." We find earliest reference to smoking of fish in these writings.

Salmonella: A strain of bacteria commonly present on many meats, eggs, poultry. Easily transferred to edible foods when proper handling procedures are not followed. The presence of dangerous contamination is not easily detected, as no off smell or taste is apparent. *Salmonellosis,* while seldom fatal, requires medical attention and is the unpleasant result of ingestion of contaminated foods. (*Also see* Cross contamination.)

Side: A butchery term. Denotes one half of the dressed animal. The side may be further divided into quarters, such as forequarter, hindquarter. Further breakdown of the quarter results in various commercial cuts of the entire carcass.

Smearing: An undesirable texture change that may occur in a sausage product that should display a visible and well-defined separation of the fatty portion and leaner portion. Certain varieties, of which mortadella is a prime example, call for a dice of fat to show distinctly. This serves to distinguish the type. Procedure to eliminate smearing is given in comprehensive recipes for all such sausages. In many other varieties, with the exclusion of *emulsified types,* the fat and lean particles also must remain quite separate. This is an important criterion for judging well-made sausages.

Sodium acetate: A chemical used to maintain essential moisture levels during the production of dry and semi-dry sausage. Necessary only in environments lacking enough natural humidity. Available in food grade quality for food production purposes. *Not a food additive,* it is placed in the curing/drying chamber, fully contained in a holding pan for effective use. Can provide ideal 75% relative humidity at room temperature or under refrigeration.

Sodium nitrate: Widely used and an approved curing agent for certain meat products. Included in Prague powder #2. Provides important time-release action, breaking down over a longer period, to effect curing of dry-cure type sausages. Must be carefully measured for any formulation of sausage products. Not for use in products requiring heat by cooking, smoking, or canning.

Sodium nitrite: Formulated with common salt (sodium chloride) to make Prague powder #1. Approved as a curing agent in controlled amounts for all meats that require cooking with heat, including that accomplished by smoking and canning. **Never interchange Prague powder #1 with Prague powder #2.** It is absolutely essential to fully understand and recognize the application of the two Prague powders for acceptable and food-safe sausage production.

Soy protein concentrate: A powdered ingredient that is useful in sausage production. Alters texture, binds fat and lean to improve juiciness and handling qualities of many sausages. Adds nutritive value, reduces shrinkage. Excessive use will detract from the flavor and high quality of any formula. (*Also see* TVP.)

Staphylococcus: *S. aureus* is the common bacterium which produces the toxins responsible for staphylococcal food intoxication. Protein foods, that is, meats, fish, and poultry, are implicated sources for the pathogen. Cleanliness and proper food handling greatly reduce the occurrence of any problems.

Streaky: British Isles term for a thin slice of bacon.

Tasso: A Cajun specialty. The "genuine article" is hard to find outside of Louisiana. Made with a lean hunk of pork or beef, first heavily seasoned, then cured and double smoked. Garlic, red pepper, and filé powder are main seasonings with much individual variation. Final result is a firm, tangy, very smoky flavored meat. Principally used as a distinctive seasoning agent in bean, egg, and regional pasta dishes. Keeps for a week, if refrigerated and well wrapped. Nothing really takes the place of a well-made tasso.

Tranche: This French word denotes a cut of meat, especially bacon. A cross-grain cut of meat or a piece. *En tranches* means in slices or sliced.

Trichinosis: Foodborne illness caused by *Trichinae spiralis.* Symptoms appear 2 to 28 days after eating of parasite (tiny larvae are encysted in the flesh) contaminated meat. Pork, bear meat, and some other game meats can carry this biological hazard. Recommended safeguard for contagion is cooking to an internal temperature of 160°F (71°C) or 10°F higher (77°C) for microwave. Freezing also eliminates the hazard by killing the larvae contained in meats. Freeze at this schedule/temperature: 5°F (−15°C) for 30 days; −10°F (−24°C) for 20 days; −30°F (−35°C) for 12 days minimum. While the incidence is greatly reduced today, precautions are still in place and should be followed. This applies to federally inspected meat as well. Avoid cross contamination and use reliable thermometers to check all temperatures.

TVP: Acronym for Textured Vegetable Protein. Can be a valuable additive in many sausage formulas. Derived from soy beans, application and effect is quite similar to the powdered form (soy protein concentrate). Depending on the market, usage amounts may be regulated by law.

Water added: This labeling statement is sometimes required on various products, such as hams. All producers must be informed and follow any applicable regulations pertaining to addition of water. The practice of adding water has long been used in meat processing. It serves to distribute additives for curing and flavoring and to favorably alter texture and processing methodology.

Index

Recipes Index

286